OXFORD ENGLISH MONOGRAPHS

Edwardian Poetry

KENNETH MILLARD

CLARENDON PRESS · OXFORD
1991

Oxford University Press, Walton Street, Oxford OX2 6DP
Oxford New York Toronto
Delhi Bombay Calcutta Madras Karachi
Petaling Jaya Singapore Hong Kong Tokyo
Nairobi Dar es Salaam Cape Town
Melbourne Auckland
and associated companies in
Berlin Ibadan

Oxford is a trade mark of Oxford University Press

Published in the United States
by Oxford University Press, New York

British Library Cataloguing in Publication Data
data available

Library of Congress Cataloging in Publication Data
Millard, Kenneth.
Edwardian poetry / Kenneth Millard.
(Oxford English monographs)
Includes bibliographical references and index.
1. English poetry—20th century—History and criticism.
2. Great Britain—History—Edward VII, 1901–1910.
I. Title. II. Series.
PR610.M48   1991   821'91209–dc20   91–19231
ISBN 0–19–812225–X

Typeset by Hope Services (Abingdon) Ltd
Printed and bound in
Great Britain by Bookcraft Ltd
Midsomer Norton, Bath

Acknowledgements

I WOULD particularly like to thank John Batchelor for his help with writing the thesis from which this book has emerged, and John Bayley and Martin Dodsworth for their comments when they examined it.

I would also like to thank Michael Rhodes for encouraging me to write the book in the first place, and Desmond Graham for some invaluable close reading in the final stages.

Thanks are also due to R. George Thomas for permission to see Edward Thomas's first notebook, and to Cathy Henderson and Ken Craven for their help at the Harry Ransom Center in Austin, Texas.

I would like to thank Lucinda Rumsey for reading and discussing the text at each stage of its production.

Finally I would like to acknowledge the encouragement and support of my parents, to whom this book is dedicated.

The old Edwardian brigade do make their brief little world look pretty tempting. All home-made cakes and croquet, bright ideas, bright uniforms. Always the same picture: high summer, the long days in the sun, slim volumes of verse, crisp linen, the smell of starch. What a romantic picture. Phoney too, of course. It must have rained sometimes.

(John Osborne, *Look Back in Anger*)

Contents

Introduction

THERE has been considerable debate about the parameters of the Edwardian period since Richard Ellmann's essay 'Two Faces of Edward', which drew attention to this decade and argued that the word 'Edwardian' is necessary because 'there is no neat phrase in English, like "the nineties", to describe the first ten years of a century'.[1] The period takes its name from its monarch Edward VII and strictly speaking is confined to 1901–10, but the word 'Edwardian' is commonly used to describe the period 1900–14; is it legitimate to extend it further? Jonathan Rose has argued that the generally accepted outline should be extended to include the years 1895–1919, a strategy which effectively doubles Edward's reign.[2] If Edwardian characteristics can be identified outside the historical period, then can they still be termed 'Edwardian', or is it more in keeping with the spirit of the age to call them, as one writer has suggested, 'Balfourian'?[3] Does 'Edwardian' exist, as an attitude, a temperament, a turn of mind, beyond the confines of the King's reign? The purpose of this book is in part to define 'Edwardian' for the study of poetry and to discover if a characteristic style can be identified: 'Modernism did not arise out of Victorianism, then, as Romanticism did out of the eighteenth century; there was an interim, and that interim we may properly call The Edwardian Period.'[4]

The present study attempts to sharpen critical awareness of the Edwardian period and to establish what is unique about it. The following chapters offer a revision of literary history and a reassessment of some of the poetry of the early twentieth century. This is a work of advocacy, for both the period and the individual poet. Of course, historical generalizations are of limited value and any writer on a period (Hynes's *The Auden Generation*, Cunningham's *British Writers of the Thirties*) must be careful not to produce uniformity by violent or arbitrary methods. The Procrustean must be avoided, by faithfulness to the individual writer. As one reviewer

Place of publication of books cited is London unless stated otherwise.
[1] R. Ellmann, *Golden Codgers: Biographical Speculations* (Oxford, 1973), 113.
[2] J. Rose, *The Edwardian Temperament, 1895–1919* (1986).
[3] J. Hunter, *Edwardian Fiction* (Cambridge, Mass., 1982), 4.
[4] S. Hynes, *Edwardian Occasions: Essays on English Writing in the Early Twentieth Century* (1972), 9.

remarked of John Batchelor's *The Edwardian Novelists*, 'the validity of the general thesis depends on the scrupulousness with which each writer is treated'.[5] 'Edwardian' here is recognized as a problematical term rather than a given one, and a good deal of what follows is evaluative because an assessment of some of the poets as poets is the most urgent requirement.

A sense of a break with Victorian cultural attitudes was certainly pervasive at the time. H. G. Wells wrote that Queen Victoria sat on England like a great paper-weight and that after her death things blew about all over the place, and Henry Newbolt felt that 'however old-fashioned was the England of 1889, it had already rejected some of the ideas and manners of the real Victorian age'.[6] Towards the end of the nineteenth century three major Victorian poets died, Arnold in 1888, Browning in 1889, and Tennyson in 1892. The death of Queen Victoria in January 1901 and the accession of the new monarch encouraged a sense of a new beginning to the twentieth century, which many writers were eager to exploit. In this respect Richard Ellmann takes issue with Virginia Woolf's famous declaration that 'on or about December 1910, human character changed' and he argues that 'If a moment must be found for human character to have changed, I should suggest that 1900 is both more convenient and more accurate than Virginia Woolf's 1910.'[7]

Frank Kermode has drawn together evidence to illustrate that as the last decade of the nineteenth century represents some kind of an ending, then the first decade of the twentieth century might reasonably be interpreted as a new beginning, however tentative.[8] Elsewhere Kermode has argued that 'The early years of Edward's reign showed a real loss of nerve . . . There was a feeling of crisis,'[9] and he has nominated 1907 as a key year when great changes were either imminent or actually under way. Another critic has isolated 1908 as a year of special importance: it was in 1908 that Pound arrived in London, Ford Madox Ford began editing The *English Review*, and T. E. Hulme joined the short-lived Poets' Club.[10] However, Levenson's disclaimer as to the value of historical generalizations (no more than a 'preliminary convenience'[11])

---

[5] H. Lee, 'A World Unfit for Heroes', *Times Literary Supplement* (26 Mar. 1982), 335.

[6] H. Newbolt, *My World as in My Time: Memoirs* (1932), 176.

[7] Ellmann, *Golden Codgers*, 115.

[8] F. Kermode, *The Sense of an Ending* (Oxford, 1967), 97.

[9] F. Kermode, *Essays on Fiction 1971–82* (1983), 34.

[10] M. H. Levenson, *A Genealogy of Modernism: A Study of English Literary Doctrine 1908–1922* (Cambridge, 1984).   [11] Ibid. p. vii.

tends to undermine his thesis that 1908 marks a literary watershed and that the period 1908–22 is amenable to study as a historical unit. Other writers have been less enigmatical in their view of the period; Bernard Bergonzi has described the first years of the twentieth century as evincing 'an impulse of limited revolt',[12] and Samuel Hynes has identified the Edwardian period's 'consciousness of its own separateness from what went before and what followed'.[13]

The difficulties of historical delineation in this transitional period are compounded by the conflicting reports of contemporary witnesses. While Virginia Woolf's statement is an expression of her decisive artistic break with the Edwardians and so turns upon the year 1910, an equally important primary source is the memoir of W. B. Yeats, who records, 'Then in 1900 everybody got down off his stilts; henceforth nobody drank absinthe with his black coffee; nobody went mad; nobody committed suicide; nobody joined the Catholic church; or if they did I have forgotten.'[14] Perhaps Yeats is thinking of the deaths of Dowson and Wilde in 1900, which had the effect of silencing two of the leading characters who had given the decade of the 1890s some of its individuality, or perhaps for Yeats the publication of Arthur Symons's *The Symbolist Movement in Literature* in 1899 had a special importance which marked for him the advent of the twentieth century.

As the momentum of Romanticism was gradually exhausted during the nineteenth century, it is perhaps more useful to consider the trial of Wilde in 1895 than his death in 1900 as some kind of turning-point in English literature. The events of 1895 led to the replacement of Beardsley as art editor of the *Yellow Book* and changed the character of one of the most important periodicals in the vanguard of development at the end of the century. The Wilde débâcle also encouraged sales of Max Nordau's *Degeneration*, a study of the *fin de siècle* temperament first published in an English translation in 1895. The prosecution of Wilde and the popularity of Nordau's attack on much that was promising in the contemporary arts contributed to the discrediting of poetry as a means of serious artistic expression. As one writer expressed his sense of an ending of the movement of the 1890s, 'that movement

[12] B. Bergonzi, *A History of Literature in the English Language*, ed. B. Bergonzi, vii (1970), 22.
[13] S. Hynes, *Edwardian Occasions*, 1.
[14] W. B. Yeats (ed.), *The Oxford Book of Modern Verse* (1936), pp. xi–xii.

was killed by the fall of Wilde, and buried by the Boer War'.[15] Edwardian social realism might be seen as a reaction against the self-indulgent art-for-art's-sake decadence of the 1890s, and the channelling of creative resources into the novel was possibly an attempt to bring to literature an element which was less ethereal than the sometimes fanciful and abstract themes of nineties' verse. Popular poetry changed too, with Kipling, Henley, and Newbolt rising to prominence partly as a consequence of the esoteric manner of their rivals the aesthetes. A number of writers have been identified as forming a recognizable 'counter-decadence' of the 1890s.[16] The Edwardians' new engagement with contemporary social and political issues is both less contrived and more accessible than some of the theatrical posturings of the 1890s. As Rose expresses it,

1895 was a watershed in several important respects. It was the year of the Oscar Wilde trials, which triggered a sharp public reaction against Decadence. Thereafter, fin de siècle pessimism began to give way to hopeful anticipation of the new century.[17]

For writers at the turn of the century the fall of Wilde was undoubtedly an event of major cultural significance and might usefully be regarded as a turning-point.

During the Edwardian period creative talent largely turned its attention to the novel. There are two studies of the prose of the period, John Batchelor's *The Edwardian Novelists* (1982) and Jefferson Hunter's *Edwardian Fiction* (1982). These critics find themselves with several good subjects to exercise their attention, among them Conrad, Wells, Forster, Bennett, and Ford Madox Ford. This is to omit a consideration of Henry James, *Sons and Lovers*, and *Dubliners* only through pressure of space. Perhaps because of the social connotations which poetry inherited by association with Wilde, it has been argued that 'In Edwardian society poetry was not considered "smart" ',[18] and this was at a time when urbanity was an important aesthetic criterion. In support of this contention the publisher Grant Richards has left on record a statement to the effect that new verse was not a profitable venture during the first years of this century: 'Commercially,

---

[15] B. Muddiman, *The Men of the Nineties* (1920), 92.

[16] The phrase is J. H. Buckley's. See his *William Ernest Henley: A Study in the 'Counter-Decadence' of the 'Nineties* (Princeton, NJ, 1945).

[17] Rose, *The Edwardian Temperament 1895–1919*, p. xiii.

[18] A. Cruse, *After The Victorians* (1938), 214.

poetry was already on the wane when *Self's The Man* appeared, and there were few exceptions to the rule.'[19]

The work to which Richards refers is a play by John Davidson, published in 1905. Further critics to comment on the poverty of Edwardian poetry include Derek Hudson ('The period was not, in general, notable for poetry'[20]), Robert Conquest ('but let us first remember the deplorable state of English poetry in the first decade of this century'[21]), and Sir Sydney Roberts, who in a presidential address to the English Association subsequently published as *Edwardian Retrospect* remarked, 'For the political and social problems of the Edwardian era are, in fact, the very core of some of the most significant literature and drama of the period. In poetry, it is true, the association is not so clearly reflected.'[22] It is easy to see how this argument can appear plausible; unlike the narratives of Bennett, Wells, and Forster, the poetry of Housman, Hardy, and Brooke can seem to be engaged wholly by personal preoccupations. In providing some sense of an Edwardian context this study tries to show the points of connection between the poets included and so provide evidence that poetry was not necessarily less responsive to the twentieth century than other art forms.

Nevertheless, at the turn of the century poetry seemed to have lost its sense of direction; the period is partly characterized by its profusion of literary coteries, each participating in an independent form of experiment. Such groups include the Symbolistes, the Rhymers' Club, Imagists, and Georgians, poets of the decadence and poets of the counter-decadence. This splintering and fragmenting of literary culture could be seen as a breaking-up of the Victorian artistic consensus, as the dilapidation of the close relationship with a large audience which poets such as Tennyson enjoyed:

The generation of the turn of the century was hypersensitive of its identity; it was inordinately fond of labeling itself. For this generation this was the 'Age of Bovril', an age of newness of all kinds, the 'yellow nineties', the 'Beardsley period', the *fin de siècle*.[23]

[19] G. Richards, *Author Hunting* (1934), 219.
[20] D. Hudson, 'Reading', in *Edwardian England 1901–14*, ed. S. Nowell-Smith (Oxford, 1964), 308.
[21] R. Conquest, 'But What Good Came of It at Last? An Inquest on Modernism', *Essays by Divers Hands*, 42 (1982), 63.
[22] S. Roberts, *Edwardian Retrospect* (Oxford, 1963), 6.
[23] J. A. Lester, *Journey Through Despair 1880–1914: Transformations in British Literary Culture* (Princeton, NJ, 1968), 3.

Each of these labels is an attempt to give the period some degree of shape or unity, to provide a metaphor by which it might be better understood. However, critics have tended to neglect those writers who do not conform to the literary fashions of the time and whose contribution to literature is not readily categorized. There are many good poets of the turn of the century who do not fall into the creative pressure groups of the time and who had no public manifesto to sustain or advertise them. Those who cannot be assimilated into a movement find themselves conspicuously isolated:

Of the five poets whom I have just been considering, four—Doughty, Hardy, Bridges, Housman—pursued rather lonely paths. They did not belong to groups, could not easily be assigned to a school, and stood somewhat apart from the stream of contemporary literature.

What then is the stream of contemporary literature without these poets, from what characteristics do they stand apart, and do they not constitute a current in their own right? Each of them spanned the Edwardian period, publishing both before and after it, and each (with the exception of Hardy) has been slow in receiving recognition. Perhaps these writers have suffered neglect because they are not comfortably absorbed into the prevailing conceptions of the literary movements of their time, or because it is felt that they were unable to respond positively to the new or modern situation of the twentieth century. They are writers who do not conform to the existing understanding of the turn of the century despite the fact that an important part of their careers belongs to it, and although Hardy, Bridges, and Housman are writers of sufficient stature to contribute to the character of their time.

Of the groups and labels belonging to the early twentieth century, that which can prove the most elusive is 'Georgian'. Strictly speaking the term denotes only those poets published in the Georgian anthologies sponsored by Edward Marsh. These anthologies were published in 1912, 1915, 1917, 1919, and 1922, covering a period of ten years and representing the work of forty different poets. Notable absentees include Edward Thomas, C. H. Sorley, Wilfred Owen and Andrew Young, Yeats, Eliot, and Pound. Marsh undertook to produce the first anthology because he felt that at the time English poetry was enjoying something of a renaissance: 'This volume is issued in the belief that English

---

[24] R. A. Scott-James, *Fifty Years of English Literature 1900–1950* (1951), 115.

poetry is now once again putting on a new strength and beauty.'[25]
Marsh believed that English verse had emerged from the un-
distinguished anonymity of the Edwardian period and he argued
that his Georgian poets were a phenomenon of the second decade
of the century, following the death of Edward VII in May 1910
and the accession of George V. With the benefit of a few years'
hindsight, however, this distinction became less clear; in the
preface to the second anthology in 1915 Marsh explained his
decision to drop three poets from the earlier volume and conceded
that they should not, properly speaking, have appeared at all
in a Georgian context: 'they belong in fact to an earlier poetic
generation, and their inclusion must be allowed to have been an
anachronism.'

The three poets in question, G. K. Chesterton, T. Sturge
Moore, and Ronald Ross, are an anachronistic choice as leaders in
the vanguard of new poetry in 1912 because their writing demonstrably belongs to the Edwardian period whose demise Marsh
celebrates. So does most of the other poetry in the first Georgian
anthology. T. Sturge Moore's first poetry is generally considered
to be *The Vinedresser and Other Poems* of 1899, but the Walpole
collection of the Bodleian Library of Oxford has a pamphlet
entitled *Two Poems* ('About Hope' and 'Mountain Shadows')
which, published in 1893, precedes even *The Vinedresser* by six
years. That is to say, Sturge Moore's first poetry appeared nineteen
years before *Georgian Poetry 1911-1912*. This poet published a
considerable body of verse during the Edwardian years: *Aphrodite
Against Artemis* (1901); *Absolom* (1903); *The Centaur's Booty* (1903);
The Rout of the Amazons (1903); *Danae* (1903); *Pan's Prophecy* (1904);
The Gazelles and Other Poems (1904); *To Leda and Other Odes* (1904);
Theseus, Medea and Lyrics (1904); *The Little School, Rhymes* (1905),
and *Correggio* (1906). By 1912 Sturge Moore was no longer new to
the poetry-reading public. Similarly, Ronald Ross published his
first work, a novel, *The Child of Ocean*, as early as 1889, his first
poetry *The Deformed Transformed* in 1890, and he continued writing
throughout the Edwardian period: *In Exile* (1906), *Fables* (1907).
G. K. Chesterton's first book of poetry *The Wild Knight* appeared in
1900, twelve years before the first Georgian anthology. Yet all
three of these poets were included in *Georgian Poetry 1911-1912* as
part of the post-Edwardian poetic revival. Georgian Poetry was
founded on a historical anachronism.

---

[25] *Georgian Poetry 1911-1912*, ed. E. Marsh (1912), Preface.

Further candidates for the Edwardian generation which Marsh implicitly distinguishes are writers such as John Davidson, Henry Newbolt, and A. E. Housman. Davidson provided his most original and valuable contribution to modern writing during the Edwardian period but died in 1909. Newbolt's first poems appeared in 1897 (*Admirals All and Other Verses*), and went through twenty-one editions. During the Edwardian period Newbolt 'had almost daily enquiries from editors who wanted poems from him'.[26] Housman's *A Shropshire Lad* was published in 1896 and continued to exercise a pervasive influence for many years (although not followed up until 1922 with *Last Poems*). The Edwardian reputation of *A Shropshire Lad* was sufficient for Housman to be approached by Marsh about inclusion in *Georgian Poetry 1911–1912*. Housman excused himself however, on the grounds that: 'I do not really belong to your "new era"; and none even of my few unpublished poems have been written within the last two years.'[27] But although *A Shropshire Lad* was published in 1896, Housman did not consider himself an integral part of the decade to which his most famous collection belongs: 'to include me in an anthology of the Nineties would be just as technically correct, and just as essentially inappropriate, as to include Lot in a book on Sodomites.'[28]

Housman continued writing during the twentieth century, publishing his *Last Poems* in 1922; *More Poems* was released from private notebooks by his brother when A. E. Housman died in 1936. But he belongs to an earlier time than that which saw the publication of Woolf's later fiction (*The Years*, 1936), and his poetry can best be elucidated by reference to the specifically English rural verse of Hardy and his turn-of-the-century contemporaries.

One critic has identified Edwardian poetry specifically, but only in terms of disparagement: 'However nostalgically one may look back on the uncomplicated Edwardian days of the bicycle and bloomers . . . surely one cannot claim that the age produced, with one or two obvious exceptions, any but mediocre verse.'[29] Few commentators would concur with the notion of 'uncomplicated Edwardian days', and this critic's 'obvious exceptions' are conspicuously absent. In fact, Ross's characterization of the turn of the century in terms of 'bicycles and bloomers' bears out Richard Ellmann's observation that 'The word "Edwardian" has taken its

---

[26] P. Howarth, *Play Up and Play the Game: The Heroes of Popular Fiction* (1973), 2.
[27] *The Letters of A. E. Housman*, ed. H. Maas (1971), 125.
[28] Ibid. 271.
[29] R. H. Ross, *The Georgian Revolt: Rise and Fall of a Poetic Ideal 1910–22* (1967), 29–30.

connotations from social rather than literary history',[30] but more disturbing than Ross's historical generalization is the discovery that many of the Georgians whose qualities he extols had published a substantial body of their verse during the Edwardian decade; they had established individual voices independently of one another long before the advent of *Georgian Poetry*. It is precisely this standing which recommended many of them as candidates for the new propagandist volume. Ross in fact is merely following the same mistake as regards chronology that Marsh made in the preface to *Georgian Poetry 1911–1912* when he wrote that 'Two years ago some of the writers represented had published nothing.' This is simply not true; of the seventeen poets on display there were only three who could be described, with any confidence, as new in 1912: John Drinkwater, whose first volume *Poems 1908–14* was published in the wake of the Anthology's success, Edmund Beale Sargant whose *Casket Songs and Other Poems* of 1911 was the only poetry he ever published, and perhaps Rupert Brooke, who conceived with Edward Marsh the original idea of the anthology and proposed to write all of the poems himself under various pseudonyms. All of the others were already known in some way to the poetry-reading public: Harold Monro had published his *Before Dawn* two years earlier in 1910; Stephens published *Insurrections* in 1909; D. H. Lawrence had had three long poems placed in the *English Review* (one of the most prestigious Edwardian periodicals) in November 1909; Abercrombie's *Interludes and Poems* came out in 1908; Flecker had published *The Bridge of Fire* in 1907; W. H. Davies, *The Soul's Destroyer and Other Poems* (1905) and *The Autobiography of a Super-Tramp* with the aid of Bernard Shaw in 1908; W. W. Gibson, *Urlyn The Harper and Other Song* (1902); Masefield, *Salt-Water Ballads* (1902); de la Mare, *Songs of Childhood* (1901); Robert Trevelyan, *Mallow and Asphodel* (1898).

Of the others this leaves Chesterton, Sturge Moore, and Ronald Ross who have already been considered as belonging to 'an earlier poetic generation', and finally Gordon Bottomley, a Georgian whose first poems *Mickle Drede and Other Verses* was published in 1896, a full sixteen years before the appearance of *Georgian Poetry 1911–1912*. Bottomley's friend Edward Thomas was not included because he had written no poetry at the time (and Marsh did not think him worthy of inclusion in subsequent anthologies), but as one of the most consistently astute of Edwardian critics, Thomas

[30] Ellmann, *Golden Codgers*, 113.

recognized the error upon which was founded the idea of a post-Edwardian renaissance: 'Not a few of these had developed their qualities under Victoria and Edward, and it cannot be said that any uncommon accession of power has very recently come to Messrs Chesterton, Davies, de la Mare, Sturge Moore and Trevelyan.'[31]

Clearly it is difficult to distinguish the poetry of the 1912 anthology simply by contrasting it favourably with the poetry of the previous twelve years. Further, the poets whose work was substantially the strength of the first volume remained in the second; it is not until much later, with the advent of 'Georgianism' and 'neo-Georgianism' that Georgians and Edwardians can easily be separated. The word 'Georgian' remains in use as an often arbitrary designation for a kind of insipid rural verse: applauding the appointment of the present Poet Laureate, Ted Hughes, the *Observer* of 23 December 1984 described him as a new kind of nature poet, 'anti-Georgian'.

Gordon Bottomley (1874–1948) appears in four of the five volumes of *Georgian Poetry*, but despite his apparent assimilation into the Georgian fold he belongs to a smaller and more definite community of poets, who established their identities in verse before the advent of the Georgians. One critic has written,

For the moment Gordon Bottomley's poetry is little read. The work of Binyon, Sturge Moore, Abercrombie and R. C. Trevelyan, all of them his friends, suffers the same neglect. The time must come when the writings of this group will be more closely regarded and more equitably valued.[32]

Each of these poets could be described as an Edwardian for whom, in the absence of an Edwardian critical context, the label 'Georgian' has acted as an inaccurate and inapposite appellation. Since the publication of *Georgian Poetry 1911–1912* many Edwardians have been obscured and disparaged by their association with an amorphous term, which once provided a sense of focus but which now has little interpretative value. 'Georgian' covers forty different poets and a ten-year period between 1912 and 1922; it must account for writers as diverse as D. H. Lawrence, Chesterton, Sassoon, Graves, de la Mare, and Victoria Sackville-West. The most unfortunate casualty of the term's misuse has been Edward Thomas, a poet whose appreciation was certainly delayed because

---

[31] *A Language not to be Betrayed: Selected Prose of Edward Thomas*, ed. E. Longley (Manchester, 1981), 112.
[32] C. C. Abbott, introduction to *Poems and Plays* by G. Bottomley (1953), 14.

of his association with the Georgians, despite the fact that he appeared in none of the Georgian anthologies. James Reeves, in his *Georgian Poetry* selected in 1962, included eight poems by Thomas, as well as verse by Housman, Sorley, and Andrew Young, none of whom ever had a poem in a book of Georgian poetry. This is evidence of the malleability of the term; it is too often used to refer to any early twentieth-century poet who wrote a rural lyric. This book tries to distinguish some of those poets and provide them with a literary context which might help to elucidate their work. Of the group named by Abbott, above, it has been observed by one commentator: 'They are, all of them, writers who came into maturity in the decade of Edward VII . . . they demand examination in common and in relation to the state of the arts in their time.'[33]

This book tries to bring a greater clarity to the period of transition from Victorian to modern literature. The publication of *Georgian Poetry 1911–1912* is a pre-war event and as such merits consideration as a contribution to the Edwardian character; and I argue that most of these early Georgians are properly 'Edwardians' in that the Edwardian period provides the appropriate context for their interpretation and evaluation.

This is not to say that the Georgians should simply be renamed Edwardians. With the exception of Brooke and Masefield these 'Georgian' Edwardians are not given space here. This book has three central contentions: that the poets included are worthy of more serious critical attention than they commonly receive; that the shaping of an Edwardian context is a necessary work of literary history; and that taken together the historical period and the individual writer represent a line of British poetry which has survived as a valuable contribution to modern writing. It is the purpose of this study in part to suggest the outline of a kind of modern British poetry which might profitably be distinguished from the more radical Modernism of the years subsequent to the Edwardian period and associated with the names of Joyce, Eliot, Pound, Lawrence, and Woolf. The tradition of British modern poetry is seen at its strongest in the work of Edward Thomas and John Davidson, both of whom anticipate the advances of Modernism in different but important ways. It is argued that the lesser Edwardian figures do not make a significant innovative contribution to the advance of poetry in their time. This might seem arbitrary,

---

[33] 'Edwardian Poets', *Times Literary Supplement* (20 Mar. 1953), 186.

but I would argue that unlike the poetry of those considered here, the verse of de la Mare, W. H. Davies, T. Sturge Moore, Wilfred Gibson, and Laurence Binyon has little intrinsic merit; neither is their poetry representative in a way which adds anything further to an understanding of the period beyond that included here.

Yvor Winters, for one, would disagree; in 1967 his *Forms of Discovery* devoted considerable attention to the poetry of T. Sturge Moore, and he has made large claims for it: quite simply 'Mr. Moore is a greater poet than Mr. Yeats'.[34] This is a remarkable lapse of judgement. Sturge Moore wrote nothing that bears comparison with Yeats's best work. Yet Douglas Bush believed that the Edwardian poet's writing was characterized by 'its fine integrity, meditative power, and technical accomplishment',[35] and Moore's biographer argued that he was 'an important poet and a unique figure in modern culture'.[36] The poetry however is very weak; it remains for another writer to argue the case for T. Sturge Moore.

Despite the omission of Moore from this book, Henry Newbolt is included as a representative of those who have been termed 'late-Victorian and Edwardian versifiers'.[37] Responses to Newbolt reveal the prevailing attitude to pre-war English poetry and he is an integral part of the Edwardian character. Similarly John Masefield is included here, as one of the 'Georgian' celebrities whose best work belongs to the Edwardian period because it attempts to come to terms with contemporary anxieties about the role of the artist in a way in which his post-war poetry does not. Rupert Brooke is also included here, as a minor poet whose poetry urgently requires fresh and sympathetic consideration within a context more meaningful than that of the numerous war poetry studies which routinely use him as a standard by which to praise Owen. On the terms of this book, neither Brooke nor Edward Thomas are war poets. Brooke's death, however, in some respects represents the zenith and the beginning of the end of the prevailing trend of Edwardian poetry prior to the London coup of Eliot and Pound. Newbolt, Masefield, and Brooke are included here not because they will ever rival Eliot (or Owen) in stature, but because they are representative of certain Edwardian characteristics and they make a contribution to the character of the period. Further, in

---

[34] Y. Winters, *Uncollected Essays and Reviews*, ed. F. Murphy (1973), 139.

[35] D. Bush, *Mythology and the Romantic Tradition in English Poetry* (Cambridge, Mass., 1937), 444.

[36] F. L. Gwynn, *Sturge Moore and the Life of Art* (1952), 1.

[37] B. Bergonzi, *Heroes' Twilight: A Study of the Literature of the Great War* (1965), 39.

writing about Edwardian poetry reference is sometimes made to the prose works of the poets on the grounds that it would be foolish to ignore them and because the Edwardians were men of letters; none of them wrote only poetry.

While this study does not include a number of those Georgians who published extensively during the Edwardian period, neither does it devote a chapter to Kipling. A recently published collection of Kipling's early poetry contains more than 300 pieces written during the years 1879–89;[38] none of the Edwardians could claim to have produced and developed so much before even the 1890s began. Moreover, the influence of Kipling on John Masefield's Edwardian writing illustrates that the former poet was sufficiently established (by his association with W. E. Henley and the *Scots Observer*) to transmit his style to the younger poets. Kipling's best poetry, such as *Barrack-Room Ballads* (1892) belongs to the nineteenth century, perhaps because he was profoundly affected by his first-hand experiences of the Boer War (1899–1902), which administered an uncomfortable blow to his political consciousness (and to the ego of Empire in general). One of Kipling's biographers describes the poet's Edwardian years as being covered by 'the chill cloud of oblivion'[39] and can only account for it in terms of 'a watershed'.[40] During the Edwardian period Kipling settled in Sussex and was engaged primarily in the composition of prose; perhaps following the Boer War of 1899–1902 there was little public interest in poetry of the services. At the turn of the century Kipling published *The Day's Work* (1898), *Stalky and Co.* (1899), *Kim* (1901), *Just So Stories* (1902), *Puck of Pook's Hill* (1906), *Rewards and Fairies* (1910). Kipling is a poet of the late nineteenth century rather than the early twentieth century, and he can most usefully be considered as a part of the 'counter-decadence' of the 1890s.

A similar case could be made for Robert Bridges (1844–1930), for although he was appointed Poet Laureate in 1911 as successor to Alfred Austin, Bridges's first edition of *Poems* appeared in 1873, he wrote eight plays between 1885 and 1894, and his *Collected Shorter Poems* of 1893 could draw on the work of the previous twenty years. Bridges's association with G. M. Hopkins (and especially their mutual enterprise in experiments with poetic metre) suggests the way for a more helpful understanding of his literary context than the Edwardian period could hope to provide.

The transitional nature of the turn of the century was responsible

---

[38] *Early Verse by Rudyard Kipling, 1879–1889*, ed. A. Rutherford (Oxford, 1986).
[39] Lord Birkenhead, *Rudyard Kipling* (1978), 216.   [40] Ibid. 228.

for some curious partnerships. The robust and sometimes aggressive John Davidson moved to London from Glasgow in 1890 and is known to have attacked Yeats and the Rhymers' Club because they lacked 'blood and guts'. But Davidson was given his start as an Edwardian reviewer by the effete Richard Le Gallienne whom the obituaries called the Golden Boy of the 1890s and who seemed to epitomize that kind of febrile affectation which Davidson ridiculed. The extensive unpublished correspondence between these writers (collected at the Harry Ransom Humanities Research Center at the University of Texas at Austin) testifies to the extent to which they relied upon one another for creative support, for mutual encouragement, and criticism. So much was this true that Le Gallienne was accused of 'log-rolling' on Davidson's behalf. Davidson wrote to Le Gallienne expressing his astonishment that the incident 'had assumed such proportions, and hurtled with such prodigious theatrical thunder about your ambrosial locks'.[41] Davidson, always an interesting letter-writer, confided his amazement at 'the pertinacity, the utter unintelligence, and bitter venom of these impotent and inept scribblers' and ends his letter by saying of his friend: 'it more than becomes me to say how much I admire him and the lonely appreciative height where he stands barked at by scavenging dogs of depreciation.'[42]

Davidson's letters address Le Gallienne as 'My Dear Dick' and in their sense of companionship they express a tenderness which mitigates against the usual portrait of Davidson as austere and severely reticent. The Scottish poet has been characterized as exhibiting a 'resentment' which was his fatal weakness, 'despite an intellectual courage in which he had few equals in his time'.[43] Davidson's letter on the death of Le Gallienne's wife in 1894 is a model of genuine condolence and sympathy. This is not the only interesting relationship to which Davidson was partner; he is known to have met (in the company of Yeats) D. H. Lawrence, Ford Madox Ford, and Ezra Pound just a month before he committed suicide in April 1909.[44]

There is in fact some form of individual personal connection between almost all of the poets included here; they were not simply contemporaries but often knew one another, even if they were not close friends. T. Sturge Moore is worth considering here briefly,

    [41] HRHRC MSS Le Gallienne, Richard/Recipient. Cf. R. Le Gallienne, *The Romantic '90s* (1926), 202.
    [42] Ibid. 203.   [43] H. Jackson, *The Eighteen Nineties* (1913), 222.
    [44] J. B. Townsend, *John Davidson: Poet of Armageddon* (New Haven, Conn., 1961), 168.

not least because he was an Edwardian whose poetry Yeats took seriously. Their lengthy exchange of letters reveals Yeats's respect for Sturge Moore,[45] and Yvor Winters believed not only that Moore was a great poet but that 'In his arguments with Yeats, in their correspondence, he is invariably the winner on points'.[46] Moore lived until 1944 and was sufficiently regarded by T. S. Eliot to be courted as a contributor to what later became the *Criterion*. The extensive collection of letters between Sturge Moore and Eliot (gathered in Texas) covering the years 1922–8, harbours such expressions as 'please be sure of the very high importance I attach to securing something from you; and I shall importune you soon again'.[47] In a letter of June 1922 Eliot wrote, 'I must express my great pleasure at hearing that my hope of support from you is so near to being realised . . . I only hope that you will have reason to be satisfied with the company in which your work will appear.'[48] When Sturge Moore's contribution materialized, Eliot wrote to him: 'I have read your essay with great pleasure and interest: it would certainly give distinction to any review in which it appeared. On the first reading I seem to find myself wholly in agreement with you. I did not know that Binyon was so good.'[49]

These letters might of course be interpreted as nothing more than fastidious and polite attempts to raise copy for a new venture, but the fact that they exist at all from such a hand as T. S. Eliot's suggests the survival of T. Sturge Moore's reputation well into the twentieth century. Furthermore, Sturge Moore's essay, 'The Story of Tristram and Isolt in Modern Poetry', was actually included in the first issue of the *Criterion*, where it was immediately followed by the entire text of *The Waste Land*. This is not the only illustrious company in which the Edwardian poet found himself; Eliot's editorial début includes the 'Plan of a Novel' by Dostoevsky, co-translated by Virginia Woolf, a critical exposition of Joyce's *Ulysses*, and a feature on contemporary German poetry by Herman Hesse. Sturge Moore tactfully expressed his reservations about the new writing in the following unpublished draft of a letter sent to Eliot:

Dear Mr Eliot, I am highly honoured to receive from you the little poem you send me [kindly sent me]. I have long felt uneasy about your [poetry] poems in which I could admire [so many things] intellectual [such

---

[45] *W. B. Yeats and T. Sturge Moore: Their Correspondence 1901–37*, ed. U. Bridge (1953).
[46] Y. Winters, *Forms of Discovery* (1967), 236.
[47] *The Letters of T. S. Eliot*, i. *1898–1922*, ed. V. Eliot (1988), 520.
[48] Ibid. 528.   [49] Ibid. 553–4.

artistry] and artistic qualities and yet [always] felt [so unmoved] quite
[so] cold to its impulse, so that I could never claim to have any authentic
appreciation of them.[50]

Despite the apparent incongruity of an artistic affinity between
these two poets, Eliot published a sequel to Sturge Moore's article
on Tristram and Isolt in the second issue of the *Criterion* in January
1923, and prose pieces by Sturge Moore appeared regularly in
Eliot's quarterly review every year until 1931. Eliot also published
Sturge Moore's poetry in the *Criterion*: 'The Vigil' was included in
April 1925. The relationship was social as well as professional; in
1928 Eliot was writing to Sturge Moore, 'Thank you very much for
your hospitable invitation. My wife has been ill with influenza
lately, so that we have not been able to make any engagements,
but I hope that we may be able to see you and Mrs Moore
sometime after Easter.'[51]

There is a network of associations which includes all the poets of
this study and serves to disrupt some of the critical and historical
preconceptions that exist about the Edwardian period. The chain
of social and epistolary links reveals that there were certain
correlations which might have been taken up privately, especially
considering the closeness of the work of some of them in its aims
and methods (a claim which it is the purpose of the following
chapters to substantiate). These poets are not included simply
because they were contemporaries, or on a random and arbitrary
basis, but because it is argued that they are the final living
embodiment of an English lyrical tradition which has been overshadowed by the innovations of the Modernists. This idea has
been argued in a highly polemical fashion by Philip Hobsbaum:

The chief heroes of English modernism died sixty years ago, in the First
World War. I am thinking particularly of Edward Thomas, Wilfred
Owen and Isaac Rosenberg. They seem to me quite distinct from the
Georgians, on the one hand, and the modernists on the other . . . Their
uncompleted work was not sufficient to prevent the tradition of which
they were the latest development from falling into misunderstanding and
neglect.[52]

Hobsbaum makes an implicit distinction between what he calls
'English modernism' and foreign 'modernists' and in doing so he
argues both that the English poets were as radically innovative as

---

[50] HRHRC MSS Moore, Thomas Sturge/Letters.
[51] HRHRC MSS Eliot, Thomas Stearns/Letters.
[52] P. Hobsbaum, *Tradition and Experiment in English Poetry* (1979), 298–9.

the Modernists, and that they represent a specifically English tradition into which the Modernists are a foreign incursion. These arguments are difficult to sustain: Edward Thomas would have regarded himself not as English but as Welsh (similarly Donald Davie advocates the importance of *Thomas Hardy and British Poetry*, but all of his poets are English and Thomas is not mentioned once). Also, the poetry of Thomas, Owen, and Rosenberg as we have it is not systematically and self-consciously preoccupied with the effort to 'make it new', and they are consequently disqualified from inclusion in the Modernist canon. Hobsbaum offers three poets as the vanguard of 'an essentially English modernity'[53] and he is at pains to attack other modern writers as alien: 'Certainly it is true to say that the influence of Eliot and Pound on English poetry has, so far, been damaging.'[54] Can this really be true of Auden, MacNeice, Empson, and Geoffrey Hill?

Hobsbaum's intuition is not entirely misplaced, and while this study does not argue for an 'English modernism' it might yet be proposed that there are ways in which the poets included here could be regarded as modern while distinguishing them from the achievements of Joyce, Eliot, Pound, Lawrence, and Woolf. One study of Modernism has argued that, 'Not only did the modernist artist see himself confronted by the infinite complexity of reality, he also saw that his medium itself might be part of the problem.'[55] It is precisely this recognition which distinguishes the work of Edward Thomas and Housman, and Hardy's *The Dynasts*, from much late nineteenth-century poetry. The writing of these three in particular reveals an acute anxiety as regards the efficacy of art and its value both to the writer and to the society in which he works. The poetry of Thomas, Housman, and *The Dynasts* is produced under the pressure of a reticence indicative of formal anxiety, and their words are chosen with a characteristic uncertainty. Much Edwardian poetry expresses a sense of apprehension at the prospect of writing; it is an awareness of formal limitations comparable to Modernist misgivings as to the vicissitudes of the verbal and linguistic medium. But what distinguishes Edwardians is largely their inability to exploit the shifting indeterminacy of language to the full; their awareness of linguistic artificiality works to inhibit rather than to liberate their creative impulse. The Modernists were less daunted by the prospect of the formal challenge they felt they had discovered, and their

---

[53] Ibid. 304.   [54] Ibid. 291.
[55] P. Faulkner, *Modernism* (1977), 14.

achievements are consequently of major stature. To put this another way, the Edwardians were conscious of a split between the poet and the man, which restricted their utterance; Modernists allowed themselves a greater indulgence with the freedoms of an artistic persona. Yet it is part of the attraction of the Edwardian poets that they are rarely knowing, over-ingenious, or obscure in their writing; they express the difficulties of a transitional stage without completely resolving them. This study tries to show how each of the poets included exhibits an awareness of emergent formal complications in a way which identifies them as modern writers, but refrains from any single prescriptive or procrustean argument which might distort an individual poet's identity. Each of the following chapters is primarily a work of advocacy for the poet and the Edwardian period, but it is hoped that their value will be shown to have survived.

In illustrating the continuing value of the poetry included here, reference is made particularly to Philip Larkin. English writers of the 1950s are in part characterized by their collusion in the revisionist impulse exemplified by Hobsbaum above; they were eager to re-establish links with a pre-Modernist tradition of poetry about English subjects and English places. When Larkin made his selections for *The Oxford Book of Twentieth-Century English Verse* (1973) he explained that,

I had in my mind a notion that there might have been what I'll call, for want of a better phrase, an English tradition coming from the nineteenth century with people like Hardy, which was interrupted partly by the Great War, when many English poets were killed off, and partly by the really tremendous impact of Yeats, whom I think of as Celtic, and Eliot, whom I think of as American.[56]

As the chapter on Henry Newbolt points out, Larkin's statement is heir to the xenophobic pronouncements of the Edwardian Poet Laureate Alfred Austin, who regretted the intrusion of French literature at the turn of the century. Yet recent studies by Barbara Everett,[57] Andrew Motion,[58] and Roger Sharrock,[59] have shown that Larkin's cultivated English persona is indebted, especially in

[56] P. Larkin, 'A Great Parade of Single Poems: Interview with Anthony Thwaite', *Listener* (12 Apr. 1973), 473.

[57] B. Everett, 'Philip Larkin: After Symbolism', *Essays In Criticism*, 30 (1980), 227–42.

[58] A. Motion, *Philip Larkin* (1982).

[59] R. Sharrock, 'Private Faces in Public Places: The Poetry of Larkin and Lowell', *English*, 36/155 (summer 1987), 113–32.

its equivocation, to the modernist advances of French symbolism. One critic has noted that, ' "Englishness" for Larkin is a means to perpetuate a form of cultural regression for which England has not always been notable. But by "Larkin" here I mean only his pronouncements and attitudinizings. The poems themselves . . . are different.'[60]

The relationship between Larkin's English subject-matter and his poetic style is not a simple one, and to return to the poets of this study (to some of whom Larkin's poetry reveals a profound debt) is to discover that the relation to England has never been simple. It is partly the purpose of the following chapters to examine the notion of a British provincial tradition, by reference to Hardy's Wessex, Housman's Shropshire, Davidson's Scotland, and the south country of Edward Thomas. The relationship of each of these poets to the environment they depict is often one of difficulty and loss. They are relationships which invariably involve displacement, deracination, and a degree of consolatory fictionalization.

One critic has written that in Larkin's poetry 'Place expresses self',[61] but Larkin's England is constantly changing, and so must the persona with which it is identified. This is one of the most important ways in which Larkin is related to the Edwardian poets of this study; each of them in his own way is seeking to preserve a vision of an England which had hardly known such rapid social change as during the Edwardian period. Edwardian poetry in many ways is an attempt to capture and retain a picture of England which was quickly disappearing. The same is true of Philip Larkin, whose England is not a static idyll but a landscape littered with post-Eliot suburban detritus. Larkin's 'Going, Going' for example (from *High Windows*) records the tide of industrial pollution which threatens to engulf the countryside, 'And that will be England gone'. The Edwardian poets created their England from a similar sense of anxiety, they were eager to retain that which they felt was being lost. The closeness of Larkin's procedure to that of the Edwardians is illustrated by his feeling that 'the impulse to preserve lies at the bottom of all art'.[62]

Blake Morrison in his book on English writing of the 1950s has,

[60] E. Neill, 'Modernism and Englishness: Reflections on Auden and Larkin', *Essays and Studies*, 36 (1983), 92–3.

[61] J. Reibetanz, 'Lyric Poetry as Self-Possession: Philip Larkin', *The University of Toronto Quarterly*, 54/3 (spring 1985), 275.

[62] *Poets of the 1950s: An Anthology of New English Verse*, ed. D. J. Enright (1955), 78.

perhaps fancifully, suggested that for Larkin's poem 'MCMXIV'
the 'long uneven lines' are not only those of enlisting soldiers but
represent the broken syntax of Eliot and Pound, 'Waiting to
replace the "Domesday lines" of Hardy, Housman, Edward Thomas
and their forefathers'.[63] Morrison argues that Larkin's anthology
choices draw these lines to favour the pre-war English poets: 'In
this way tradition is re-ordered so that the Modernists have less of
a role than that usually allotted to them.'[64] Larkin's strategy
might seem negative or parochial but his attempt to shift the
perspective of twentieth-century poetry is a venture which has
received intelligent and well-argued support from a number of
good critics. As the twentieth century advances, the impact of
Modernism is sometimes presented as a more isolated and less
central event than has hitherto been accepted. As early as 1960
Harry Levin was asking, 'What Was Modernism?' and felt sufficiently detached to look back on a cultural revolution which now
seemed rather remote: he found that 'we Americans have smoothly
rounded some sort of cultural corner'.[65] In 1966 Frank Kermode
wrote about 'Modernisms' in a way which tended to disperse the
impact of the twentieth century's central and most calculated
assault on literary and cultural decorum.[66] More recently, Robert
Conquest has conducted 'An Inquest on Modernism' and concluded
that 'it is dead, or nearly dead, as a live idea inspiring worthwhile
work',[67] and Hugh Kenner has written on the theme of 'Modernism
and What Happened To It', where, in an elegiac mood, he
described Modernism as 'a precarious moment's opportunity'.[68]
Kenner suggested that considering the polyglot nature of the
Modernist enterprise 'Philip Larkin perhaps announced the end
of it when he denied that foreign languages were of any value'.[69]

While it is not the purpose of this study to become involved in
the critical debate about the nature of Modernism and the character
of post-modernism, it is nevertheless true that the poets of this
book must benefit from any argument which places the impact of

---

[63] B. Morrison, *The Movement: English Poetry and Fiction of the 1950s* (Oxford, 1980),
202.
[64] Ibid. 204.
[65] H. Levin, *Refractions: Essays in Comparative Literature* (New York, 1966), 274.
[66] F. Kermode, 'Modernisms', in his *Continuities* (1968).
[67] Conquest, 'But What Good Came Of It At Last?' 64.
[68] H. Kenner, 'Modernism and What Happened to It', *Essays in Criticism*, 37/2 (Apr.
1987), 109.
[69] Ibid. 108.

Modernism in a broader historical perspective. It is perhaps only by first widening the context by which Modernist achievements are measured that the value of the poets here, for so long obscured, can be recognized and appreciated.

I

Henry Newbolt: 'this sceptred isle'

HENRY NEWBOLT is one of the most unfashionable poets in English. Although he enjoyed immense popularity up to and during the First World War, criticism of his work has been universally hostile since the 1920s. He is accused of popularizing 'the public school athletic-military code of honor',[1] of espousing 'an especially nasty kind of Imperialistic jingoism',[2] of 'jingo-sadomasochism',[3] and of expressing 'exalted public school verities'[4] by means of his 'nebulous aphorisms . . . ardent confusion . . . (and) simple moral rectitude'.[5] Henry Newbolt, one of 'the most sacred names of the Establishment',[6] represents 'the fag end of Victorian rhetoric and the entrenched forces of literary conservatism';[7] he is a poet whose 'high-minded obtuseness betrayed him into writing . . . rhapsodic nonsense'.[8] Newbolt's poetry of the war is not only opportunistic, but 'chauvinistic rubbish',[9] which tries to 'shroud the ghastly reality in a pious commonplace';[10] they are the kind of poems for which 'words like vicious and stupid would not seem to go too far'.[11] For one critic, an image of Newbolt's is 'the best illustration of the level to which poetry had sunk',[12] that is, to the point of 'irrelevance and absurdity'.[13] There is a book called *Play Up and Play the Game* which propounds 'the species homo newboltiensis or Newbolt Man'[14] whose author complains that 'In all Newbolt's works I have been unable to find a line which seems to me true poetry'[15] because, he argues,

---

[1] J. H. Johnston, *English Poetry of the First World War* (Princeton, NJ, 1964), 107.

[2] J. Lucas, *Modern English Poetry from Hardy to Hughes* (1986), 61.

[3] R. Jenkyns, 'Jumping the Q', *Times Literary Supplement* (26 June 1987), 680.

[4] M. van Wyk Smith, *Drummer Hodge: The Poetry of the Anglo-Boer War (1899–1902)* (1978), 42.

[5] Ibid. 55.

[6] R. H. Ross, *The Georgian Revolt: Rise and Fall of a Poetic Ideal 1910–1922* (1967), 164.

[7] J. Press, *A Map of Modern English Verse* (Oxford, 1969), 108.

[8] Ibid. 135.   [9] Ibid. 132.   [10] Ibid. 139.

[11] P. Fussell, *The Great War and Modern Memory* (Oxford, 1975), 250.

[12] C. K. Stead, *The New Poetic: Yeats to Eliot* (1964), 51.   [13] Ibid. 77.

[14] P. Howarth, *Play Up and Play the Game: The Heroes of Popular Fiction* (1973), 14.

[15] Ibid. 5.

'Banality is perhaps the most pervasive quality of his verse'.[16] This chapter looks beyond these criticisms to discover why Newbolt has been the target for such vociferous aesthetic and moral complaints and to see if, after all, he wrote any good poetry.

Newbolt, like Rupert Brooke, has acquired a reputation beyond that which he would seem to warrant; twentieth-century criticism seems to have blown both of them out of proportion. Also like Brooke, Newbolt has come to be known by one poem only, by which he is recognized and judged, 'Vitai Lampada':

> There's a breathless hush in the Close tonight—
> Ten to make and the match to win—
> A bumping pitch and a blinding light,
> An hour to play and the last man in.
> And it's not for the sake of a ribboned coat,
> Or the selfish hope of a season's fame,
> But his Captain's hand on his shoulder smote—
> 'Play up! play up! and play the game!'

The cricket match is used to expound a philosophy which is selfless in its loyalty to an ideal, and to a notion of the correct manner of conduct regardless of individual circumstances. Personal achievement is set aside in favour of fidelity to the intrinsic value of the game itself. The poem demonstrates the significance of a method: it is the way of behaving which is important, not the final result.

It is interesting that Newbolt's vision of chaos should find expression in the image of 'the wreck of a square that broke', where the collapse of perfect lineal order is the direct cause of death. This sense is heightened by the pun on 'square', which establishes an analogue with the cricket square of the first stanza. The rallying cry ' "Play up! play up! and play the game!" ' in this context emphasizes the importance of lessons learned at school, to which the poem returns:

> This is the word that year by year,
> While in her place the School is set,
> Every one of her sons must hear,
> And none that hears it dare forget.

The institution becomes a quasi-religious place of learning where the sacred text is passed on from generation to generation, keeping alive tradition and preserving the continuity of experience. Even

---

[16] Ibid. 4.

the line 'While in her place the School is set' is an image of order, recalling the square of the ranks on the battlefield, and the square of the cricket match with its strictly hierarchical batting order, 'last man in', its numerical continuity, 'ten to win', and its chronological sequence, 'an hour to play'.

The principle of hierarchy and regulated continuity expressed in 'Vitai Lampada' takes on a ritualistic significance with the refrain ' "Play up! play up! and play the game!" ' Cricket might be said to be the most ritualistic of sports, the most ordered by regulations prescribed before the action begins. The philosophy of the poem is learned at school, not in the classroom but on the sports field outside, probably because Newbolt, along with Baden-Powell, saw the schoolboy as being trained primarily for service of a physical nature, and especially for war.

Critics will probably continue to object to the poem, arguing that it is oppressively hearty, that it smacks of élitism and forced cameraderie, and that as a philosophy it is uselessly simplistic. Yet it is Newbolt's point that times of crisis demand direct action which in its very urgency is instinctive, and here 'Vitai Lampada' could be compared with prose works about heroism which are recognized as major literature of the period, such as Conrad's *The Nigger of The 'Narcissus'*, and Crane's *The Red Badge of Courage*. Note also that Newbolt's exhortation is for those who are naturally weaker: 'the last man in' is always the least able batsman. To discuss the poem in this way is to shift the emphasis back to its original sense. As one critic remarks , 'The debasement of the phrase "playing the game" does not invalidate its proper meaning.'[17] Released for a moment from the exaggeration of twentieth-century criticism, 'Vitai Lampada' can be seen as essentially a schoolboy fantasy of service in action.

Many of the characteristics of Newbolt's verse can be shown by reference to 'Vitai Lampada'; it clearly draws upon a particular conception of human life, one which Newbolt has himself eluci-dated:

It was a Roman rule, peculiarly fitted to the needs of the English schoolboy . . . demanding of us the virtues of leadership, courage and independence; the sacrifice of selfish interests to the ideal of fellowship and the future of the race. In response we gave enthusiastically but we gave something rather different: we set up a 'good form', a standard of our own. 'To be in all things decent, orderly, self-mastering: in action to

---

[17] P. Dickinson, *Selected Poems of Henry Newbolt* (1981), 13.

follow up the coolest common sense with the most unflinching endurance: in public affairs to be devoted as a matter of course.'[18]

This is surprisingly adult for a schoolboy; they seem to have taken themselves very seriously and to have had a finely tuned sense of their moral responsibilities. The stoicism, self-reliance, and exaggerated respect for authority are qualities imbued by the public schools of the late nineteenth century, and they seem peculiarly English. It is doughty in a stiff and mechanical way, a schoolboy's parody of fortitude and masculinity. The characteristically Edwardian note is Newbolt's concern for 'the future of the race'. What fourteen-year-old is worried about the future of the race? Edwardians felt that the chivalrous Englishman was in danger of degenerating into an urban surrogate, and that he needed to be preserved by nourishment at the wells of rural England. The higher echelons of society needed to maintain a good stock, to replenish the seed of empire. Newbolt's school was Clifton College, where he lived a life reminiscent of Kipling's *Stalky and Co.* (1899) with its predilection for violence and its attention to 'the sterner and more robust virtues'.[19] Newbolt won a classical scholarship to Corpus Christi College but he found Oxford a disappointment after Clifton:

I had hoped and believed that Oxford would be a second Clifton, with every kind of opportunity and contest and pleasure magnified in value. I found instead that there were differences, even defects . . . there was little to take the place of the ardent and imaginative school loyalty on which I had thriven.[20]

Above all, Newbolt laments the fact that there is no place for his sense of loyalty at university, his schoolboy partisanship can find no outlet: 'But the militant loyalty of the schoolboy—House against House, and School against School—this is not possible at a University, where the contests of life are imaged differently and upon a different scale.'[21] The scale of which Newbolt writes is surely that of the adult; there is no place for his uncritical schoolboy vassalage because he is no longer at school. Newbolt is reluctant to concede this. He chafes at having to grow up. Like a petulant Peter Pan he wants to remain a lad forever. Again there is a comparison with Rupert Brooke, who bitterly regretted the exigencies of sexual relationships, which threatened his innocent pubescent friendships.

---

[18] H. Newbolt, *My World as in My Time: Memoirs* (1932), 65.
[19] Ibid. 64.   [20] Ibid. 94.   [21] Ibid. 95.

Many of Newbolt's contemporaries served the Empire with their lives. His schoolfriends from Clifton College, Douglas Haig and Francis Younghusband, became soldiers and explorers. Haig made his reputation in the South African War (1899–1902) and for his military skill he received the brevet of colonel and the CB. His work in South Africa attracted the attention of Kitchener, Commander-in-Chief in India, who appointed Haig Inspector-General of cavalry. Haig was promoted to Major-General in 1904 at the age of 43, and he went on to serve England in the Great War. Francis Younghusband explored the mountains between Kashmir and China and accompanied the first British expedition to Tibet in 1902. He was the spirit behind the early attempts on Everest. Both Younghusband and Haig regarded the security of the Empire as their natural vocation, for, as Younghusband believed, 'thousands have willingly and joyously laid down their lives for her'.[22]

It is in the context of such contemporaries (and lifelong friends) that Newbolt's career should be considered. Newbolt chose to serve his country in verse, and 'England' became his theme. His poetry is a celebration of English history and English character. He is not the poet of an idealized province, Housman's Shropshire or Hardy's Wessex; Newbolt's England is historical and takes its character from heroes and personalities rather than from a particularized location. It is the England of *Richard II*: 'this sceptred isle ... This happy breed of men, this little world ... This blessed plot, this earth, this realm, this England' (ii, i. 40). The word 'England' echoes through Newbolt's poetry as a reliable, constant theme; its very recurrence is indicative of the poet's belief in national stability. The certainty with which he can rely upon 'England' is as unquestioning as the selfless sacrifices of soldiers such as Younghusband and Haig. 'England' is the talisman of Newbolt's poetry, as are the names of her national figures, and the incantation alone of those consecrated words is sometimes sufficient: 'Effingham, Grenville, Raleigh, Drake | Here's to the bold and the free | Benbow, Collingwood, Byron, Blake | Hail to the Kings of the Sea!' ('Admirals All').

There is scarcely a poem of Newbolt's in which the word 'England' does not appear. The speaker of 'The Quarter Gunner's Yarn' appeals 'That the days of old England may never be done', and the speaker of 'The Toy Band' is content 'As long as there's an Englishman to ask a tale of me'. The poem 'Northumberland'

[22] F. E. Younghusband, *England's Mission* (1920), 24.

begins 'When England sets her banner forth'; 'The Bright Medusa' will prosper 'till England's sun be set'; the heroes of 'Admirals All' perform their duty 'for England's sake'; 'For a Trafalgar Cenotaph' is addressed to the 'Lover of England'. The eponymous protagonist of 'A Ballad of John Nicholson' will command respect 'Were I the one last Englishman', and in 'The Fighting Temeraire' the ship of that name survives 'in England's song for ever'. Newbolt wrote one poem entitled simply 'England', and his verses to commemorate the coronation of Edward VII are called 'The King of England'. The sailors of 'Hawke' are successful for no better reason than because 'England was England'. This is tautological: Newbolt has reached the point where he cannot express himself beyond the repeated enunciation of the totemic word. Its utterance induces a kind of linguistic aneurism inhibiting further speech. As Newbolt wrote of his public school, 'my vision of Clifton Close is not a merely individual experience. It is a touch, a password between all those who have seen it.'[23] This emphasis on specific names and specific places should be seen as part of the Edwardian drive to express the essential England.

The turn-of-the-century period is characterized by celebrations of national identity; W. E. Henley published *For England's Sake* in 1900, William Watson's *For England* appeared in 1904, and Laurence Binyon's *England and Other Poems* in 1909. Even Edward Thomas wrote of 'This England', which once 'was called Merry' ('The Manor Farm'). C. F. G. Masterman published his account of *The Condition of England* in 1909, and Younghusband's pamphlet *England's Mission* (1920) explains that, concerning the nature of God, 'the right conception may perhaps be obtained by considering what we mean when we speak of "England" and of the relationship of Englishmen to "England" '.[24] The Poet Laureate of the Edwardian period serves as a useful comparison here, as a writer of verse on national subjects: 'In 1892 Mr Saintsbury had written: "Keep the seat ready (even with a dummy in it if better is not to be had)" ... and it was perhaps with some such provisional attitude that Lord Salisbury finally made his choice.'[25]

Alfred Austin was appointed Laureate in 1896, and in 1898 he published his first volume in his official capacity, *Songs of England*. Anyone who has dutifully read through Austin's collected poems could not fail to agree with John Lucas that 'the plain fact is that

[23] Newbolt, *Memoirs*, 46.   [24] Younghusband, *England's Mission*, 23–4.
[25] E. K. Broadus, *The Laureateship: A Study of the Office of Poet Laureate in England with Some Account of the Poets* (Oxford, 1921), 202.

he is a ridiculously bad poet'.[26] These poems treat the theme of 'England' with greater didacticism than those of Newbolt ('Austin was a prominent Conservative journalist'[27]) and include 'To England', 'In Praise of England', 'Why England is Conservative', and 'Who Would not Die for England!' Austin's use of the word 'England' is so prevalent that he feels it necessary to include the following 'Explanatory':

by 'England', for which no other appellation equally comprehensive and convenient has yet been discovered, it is intended to indicate not only Great Britain and Ireland, but Canada, Australia, South Africa, India, and every spot on earth where men feel an instantaneous thrill of imperial kinship at the very sound of the Name that lends its title to the opening poem in the present volume.[28]

The 'Name' to which Austin refers is 'Victoria', whose Empire he celebrates. Yet it is curious that he is reluctant to use the word 'Empire', which so obviously offers itself as the 'comprehensive and convenient' appellation Austin requires. This is possibly because the Laureate regards the dominions as possessions, and to place them all under the name 'England' is to deny their autonomy and independence; it is a form of cultural imperialism. Further, the name 'England' is the only thing which unites the disparate locations of the Empire; no single visual image which will synthesize the diversity of Canada, Australia, South Africa, and India. The dominions cannot be reconciled except by reference to 'England'; 'England' is abroad (in the sense of 'astray') and difficulties arise in trying to articulate it as a single idea, hence the necessary explanatory note. It is an indication of the astuteness of Edward Thomas as both a social and a literary commentator that he could write in 1909: 'What with Great Britain, the British Empire, Britons, Britishers, and the English-speaking world, the choice offered to whomsoever would be patriotic is embarrassing.'[29] These lines act as a commentary on Austin's interpretation of 'England', as does Thomas's observation that Edwardians, deprived of 'the small intelligible England of Elizabeth', have been 'given the word Imperialism instead'.[30] But depictions of the essential England were not the exclusive province of the imperialists, as we shall see.

[26] Lucas, *Modern English Poetry from Hardy to Hughes*, 50.   [27] Ibid. 203.

[28] A. Austin, *Songs of England* (1898).

[29] E. Thomas, *The South Country* (1909), 71.

[30] E. Thomas, *The Country* (1913), 6.

The character of Austin's 'England' is made amply clear at the outset of the poet's autobiography with the following encomium:

there are experiences in life that belong to the sanctuary of the soul, which no one has a right to invade. French biographies know no such self-imposed restraint, but it has generally been observed by Englishmen, at least by Englishmen of proper chivalrous instincts.[31]

Such xenophobic pronouncements are the forerunners of Philip Larkin's aversion to the cosmopolitan Modernism of 'Pound, Parker and Picasso'.[32] One critic has accused such writers of being 'celebrants at the ritual renewal of an ideological myth',[33] the myth being that English literature continues to evolve quite independently of foreign influences as if in cultural isolation. During the Edwardian period writers were anxious to publicize their pedigree; William Watson, for example, was at pains to describe himself as 'one who has prided himself on being peculiarly English in his sympathies and sentiments, and who comes of many generations of such Englishmen'.[34] The impact of the South African War (1899–1902) on the British Empire, and the recent death of Victoria and a passing therefore, to some extent, of a sense of national stability, contributed to anxieties about the national character. One study of Edwardian fiction argues that 'Synthetic pride' (a quotation from Henry James's 'The Third Person'), 'is an excellent phrase for the Edwardian rediscovery of England. There had to be a certain self-consciousness in the act, a certain wilfulness, a certain artificiality.'[35] This is surely true, and it is true because 'England', then as now, is an elusive concept which tends to defy any simple reductive definition. It was such a cultural identity for which many Edwardian writers were searching. It has been said of Alfred Austin that,

As he writes, he feels himself soothed, sustained, and magnified by the support of the landed gentlemen of England. He is not, he fancies, dipping his pen into the shallow well of egotism but into the inexhaustible springs of English sentiment.[36]

Almost all Edwardian poets tried to tap this spring at some point, and the effort to attain an English poetic identity which is both

---

[31] A. Austin, *The Autobiography of Alfred Austin*, 2 vols. (1911), 2.
[32] P. Larkin, *All What Jazz: A Record Diary 1961–1971* (2nd edn. rev., 1985), 22.
[33] S. Smith, *Edward Thomas* (1986), 12. Smith is describing Motion's book on Edward Thomas.
[34] W. Watson, *For England* (1904), 'Dedication'.
[35] J. Hunter, *Edwardian Fiction* (Cambridge, Mass., 1982), 164.
[36] S. P. Sherman, *On Contemporary Literature* (1923), 215.

personal and national is an essential part of their character. Edward Thomas's 'Lob' is a good expression of it, and Newbolt is trying, in his way, for the same thing.

The national consciousness of Edwardian England was framed by two wars, the South African War of 1899–1902 and the First World War. Following the latter, Henry Newbolt, President of the English Association founded in 1906, was commissioned to write a report on 'The Teaching of English in England':

The report argued that a national consciousness of pride in the language, similar to that shown by the French, had emerged in Britain as a result of the war, and that, if cultivated by the study of English, it could provide the basis for a lasting national unity.[37]

According to the Newbolt Report (1921) national pride at the English military success could be maintained and transmitted through the English language; 'English' would in this way become a tool for the development of political ideas. This report helped to establish the study of English as an independent faculty, but, it can be seen, for the wrong reasons.

A sense of difficulty in connection with 'England' is registered in Newbolt's poetry by the use of the word 'name'. 'The Vigil' begins with the exclamation:

> England! where the sacred flame
> Burns before the inmost shrine,
> Where lips that love thy name
> Consecrate their hopes and thine.

Simply to speak the revered word is sufficient homage, and his poetry need go no further. The activity of naming occupies an important place in Newbolt's poetry, as do 'words' and 'tales' and the 'voices' and 'lips' which convey them: ' 'Tis a name we remember from father to son | That the days of old England may never be done' ('The Quarter Gunner's Yarn'); 'Some heard him chanting, though but to himself | The old heroic names' ('The Non-Combatant'); 'England's self, whose thousand-year-old name | Burns in our blood' ('Epistle'). The combatants of 'The School at War', 'cheered the dead undying names', 'The Bright Medusa' it is said, 'shall bear her name by right', 'April on Waggon Hill' speaks of 'Your name, the name they cherish', and 'The Death of Admiral Blake' recounts its achievements 'Sweeping by shores where the names are the names of the victories of

---

[37] C. Baldick, *The Social Mission of English Criticism 1848–1932* (Oxford, 1983), 89–90.

England'. The activity of naming becomes a prime objective. On the foreign battlefield of 'Vitai Lampada', 'England's far, and Honour a name', a usage of 'name' which reveals that Newbolt was aware of its pejorative sense; he knew that something could come to exist in name only.

The degree of self-consciousness in Newbolt's 'naming' suggests its special value to his poetry. He is haunted by names whose importance is being forgotten, by words which are losing their significance: 'This is the word that year by year | While in her place the School is set | Every one of her sons must hear | And none that hears it dare forget' ('Vitai Lampada'). Despite this desperate warning, Newbolt's names are losing their totemic value and his words emptied of meaning: 'O Word whose meaning every sense hath sought' ('O Pulchritudo'). Proper nouns have a special significance in language because they refer to something unique and are not subject to the ambiguities of common words. It is for this reason that Edward Thomas is attracted to the function of names, and they hold for him a peculiar fascination: 'What I saw | Was Adlestrop—only the name' ('Adlestrop'). His poem 'Old Man' is famously eloquent on the subject of names:

> the names
> Half decorate, half perplex, the thing it is:
> At least, what that is clings not to the names
> In spite of time. And yet I like the names.

Newbolt's interest in names lies in the fact that they retain their value from earlier times, they are not so dangerously subject to etymological change. The names of his poetry stand against the processes of history which erode, displace, and obliterate the meanings of ordinary language. As Thomas expresses it in 'Bob's Lane', 'The name alone survives, Bob's Lane'. Newbolt's names are constant, unambiguous, and can be recognized by everyone. It is appropriate that he should have written a poem on the *Dictionary of National Biography* ('Minora Sidera'), an index of names whose function approaches that of Newbolt's poetry.

Newbolt's poetry is inundated with names: Obetello Bay, Quiberon Bay, Cadiz Bay, Cape St Vincent, Monte Video, Martinique, Trinidad—almost all are distant and exotic, the venue for battle and English victory. Only once does Newbolt permit himself to distinguish a province of his 'England': 'For me there's nought I would not leave | For the good Devon land' ('Laudabunt Alii'), and this is for the sake of its association with Drake and the conquering seed of empire. Newbolt himself was from Stafford-shire. Similarly his poems are crowded with dates, proving their historical verisimilitude, giving them a semblance of actuality: 'Hawke' begins 'In seventeen hundred and fifty nine', 'The Bright Medusa (1807)', 'The Guides at Cabul (1879)', 'Craven (Mobile Bay, 1864)', 'The Death of Admiral Blake (August 7th, 1657)', 'Sacramentum Supremum (Mukden, March 6th, 1905)', 'The King of England (June 24th, 1902)'. Newbolt prided himself on his historical accuracy, and a large proportion of his verse com-memorates specific events from English history; it is often based on fact.

At the same time of course, Newbolt's use of names suggests a crisis of identity which he is attempting to assuage by insistent repetition. The stability of his 'England' is illusory; it is perpetually engaged in battle, subduing foreign hucksters; only by alertness to insubordination can equilibrium be maintained. This vigilance, combined with his use of the word 'England' to the point where it scarcely has any meaning, is indicative of a desperate anxiety: 'As the real superiority of Britain over her rivals dwindled, so a neurotic desire for self-assertion became more voluble.'[38] This is apposite because Newbolt's verse belongs to the Edwardian period, that is to say after the South African War (1899–1902), which had delivered such a painful blow to the imperialist ego; there is a sense then in which his Edwardian patriotic writing is compensatory. Unlike Kipling, Henley, and Watson, Newbolt did not write throughout the 1890s; his first book was published in 1897 (*Admirals All, and Other Verses*), and he was Alfred Austin's junior by almost thirty years: Austin 1835–1913, Newbolt 1862–1938. Although Newbolt's verse appears to express a Victorian confidence, it has affinities with Tennyson's poetry on national heroes, which Peter Conrad has interpreted (in an article significantly entitled 'The Victim of Inheritance') as expressing the 'need to disown national parents'. Peter Conrad argues that Tennyson's 'Ode on the Death of the Duke of Wellington',

seems only too eager to inter and dispose of its subject. Wellington's eminence can only be sustained by verbal excess: 'Our greatest yet with least pretence | Great in council and great in war', or by the fatuity of repetition: '. . . with honour, honour, honour, honour to him | Eternal

---

[38] M. van Wyk Smith, *Drummer Hodge: The Poetry of the Anglo-Boer War (1899–1902)*, 43.

honour to his name' . . . Tennyson's four line epitaph for General Gordon is similarly parricidal.[39]

While Tennyson's use of repetition is dismissively curt, Newbolt's insistence on the value of his chosen names might be seen as an attempt to bolster faith and to find a language which remains constant through uncertainty. Newbolt's poetry is a quest for authority and expresses an eagerness to submit to it: the preacher of the poem 'Commemoration' warns the youth of his congregation, 'deem not thou | Thy life is thine alone | Thou bearest the will of ages'. Modern sensibilities are embarrassed and offended by Newbolt's national pride. John Bayley, although ostensibly concerned with the relationship between Edward Thomas and Philip Larkin, may have had Newbolt in mind when he wrote that 'The time of self-conscious "Englishness" in art and in public statement, at the beginning of this century, was a degenerate time, and vulgarised the concept.'[40]

Newbolt's verse is nostalgic for an England passed (like that of John Masefield) and it attempts to make tangible and preserve that which is being lost. This is a characteristic which Newbolt shares with Thomas Hardy and Edward Thomas. Twentieth-century poets such as Betjeman and Larkin were also engaged in a poetry of revivifying preservation, both in their subjects and their diction. Larkin's 'Going, Going' from *High Windows* is notable for making this intention explicit: 'And that will be England gone'.

It would be convenient to leave Newbolt here, as the guy to whom proponents of war poetry routinely turn when seeking to show the 'truth to life' of their subjects. But Newbolt is not so one-dimensional; many of his poems exhibit qualities quite different from the stirring exhortation of his narrative verse, qualities which have been discretely ignored by twentieth-century critics. As one recent commentator has pointed out, Newbolt's Christianity 'was of the muscular variety—though he was both more thoughtful and more intelligent than this may imply'.[41] 'Commemoration' for example, captures a moment of epiphany, presaging 'one like my own young phantom', and tentatively approaches an elusive intimation of the future:

[39] P. Conrad, 'The Victim of Inheritance', *Times Literary Supplement* (15 May 1982), 529.

[40] J. Bayley, 'English Equivocation', *Poetry Review*, 76 (June 1986), 4.

[41] P. Webb, 'Newbolt For Poets' Corner', *Spectator* (19/26 Dec., 1987), 55.

And the School passed; and I saw the living and dead
Set in their seats again,
And I longed to hear them speak of the word that was said,
But I knew that I longed in vain.
And they stretched forth their hands, and the wind of the spirit took
    them
Lightly as drifted leaves on an endless plain.

The poem harbours the moment's impulse to communicate, but it evades disclosure, leaving only a sense of loss. This moment is held with an intensity and sensitivity for which Newbolt is not usually credited. The final image is the natural and inevitable climax of the poem's carefully managed development, as the attempted physical embrace is thwarted, Housman-like, by departure and death. The lyrical force of 'Commemoration', in a 'war' context, has affinities too with Rupert Brooke's 'Fragment', beginning, 'I strayed about the deck, an hour, tonight.'

'Commemoration' is excellently restrained, it avoids explicit statement and succeeds by indirection, transfiguring its meaning into the final image 'as drifted leaves on an endless plain'. Despite Newbolt's reputation for didacticism, many of his poems elaborate the theme of not knowing, and of not being able to know. Newbolt shares this epistemological anxiety with Housman, who in *A Shropshire Lad* XXIII exclaims to the 'lads' at Ludlow fair, 'I wish one could know them, I wish there were tokens to tell', but finds that 'you can never discern' for 'there's nothing to scan'. Newbolt reserves elegiac understatement for 'The sons in exile on the eternal sea' in 'Outward Bound', where departure, removal, and loss acquire the significance of a personal crisis. The poem 'O Pulchritudo' attends a voice 'far off and faint' and intently seeks to discover the 'Word whose meaning every sense hath sought'. The poet enshrines the sense of concentration in reaching after something intangible and inexpressible. 'When I Remember' articulates the search for truth and the difficulties of interpretation which ultimately pass unresolved and undiscovered: 'Something there must be that I know not here | Or know too dimly through the symbols dear' (Newbolt's 'symbols' functioning as Housman's 'tokens' above). 'When I Remember' captures the fragility of the slightest of psychological moments, and Newbolt should be credited with the tact with which his poem refrains from disclosure. A similar uncertainty characterizes 'Gavotte', a poem which un-obtrusively suggests the presence of a ghostly female spectre, reminiscent of de la Mare's phantoms but without his frequent coyness. Some of these poems reveal the softening influence of de la Mare, whom Newbolt discovered while editor of the *Monthly Review* (1900–4). Newbolt's classical education, like that of Bridges (a fellow Corpus graduate), also has its effect on these lyrics; 'A Sower' for example has a Housmanesque epigrammatic compression: 'But the dumb fields | Desire his tread | And no earth yields | A wheat more red.'

Newbolt's best poems in this reticent style are 'The Middle Watch' and 'Messmates', which have a sombre and melancholy tone reflecting the beauty and the limitlessness of the sea. The imagery of 'The Middle Watch' is astrological:

> Like fleets along a cloudy shore
> The constellations creep,
> Like planets on the ocean floor
> Our silent course we keep.

The parallel movement of the stars brings to the human aspect of the poem a perspective which is overwhelming. The sailor laments the loss of a spacial and temporal perspective which is earthly and reassuring, but while the refrain calls for him to 'Watch , oh watch till ye find again | Life and the land of morn', the reply is austere and comfortless:

> From a dim West to a dark East
> Our lines unwavering head,
> As if their motion long has ceased
> And Time itself were dead.

The watchman's sense of complete suspension imbues the poem with a curiously detached tonal effect; 'The Middle Watch' has a poignancy which comes from the absence of authorial assertion. Despite the cosmic imagery, the poem is carefully understated, and this is the result of a modesty or absence of posture on the part of the poet. The withdrawal of intrusive comment reflects the sailor's abnegation.

A similar authorial detachment characterizes 'Messmates', a poem in which the speaking voice is absorbed in, or consumed by, the elemental vastness of the surroundings. The subject is a lighthouse-keeper, who is isolated, passive, and at the mercy of the environment:

> He's there alone with green seas rocking him
> For a thousand miles around;
> He's there alone with dumb things mocking him
> And we're homeward bound.

His physical and psychological separation are also expressed by the refrain 'And the great ships go by', which plays upon the idea of ships in the night, suggesting the tantalizing proximity but inaccessibility of human contact, a further Housmanesque theme. Newbolt's verses might be compared with Philip Larkin's poem about a lighthouse-keeper, in which 'liners | Grope like mad worlds westward' ('Livings'). 'Messmates' is technically accomplished, Newbolt's effective use of repetition and rhyme contributing to the impression of a dying fall which is both tidal and emotional:

> It's a long lone watch that he's a-keeping there,
> And a dead cold night that lags a-creeping there,
> While the months and the years roll over him
> And the great ships go by.

'The Middle Watch' and 'Messmates' concern those who fulfil a passive role; their function is vital but inactive; they preside over the safety of the society from which they are exiled. The authorial modesty or the lack of foregrounding of poetic voice by which this is achieved stands in strong contrast to the popular image of Newbolt's verse. He has not been credited with the self-effacing tonal subtlety which is these poems' distinctive feature.

The disparity between these pieces and Newbolt's emphatic ballads could hardly be more manifest. As an examination of one of Newbolt's notebooks in the archive of his Oxford college reveals, there is no chronological pattern to observe in their composition.[42] But it might be possible to propose a distinction on the basis of the public and the private worlds they evince. The split in Newbolt's poetry might be seen in terms of C. F. G. Masterman's 'two voyages':

Still two voyages are being accepted: a voyage without, in the actual encounter with primitive and hostile forces, and in a universe of salt and bracing challenges; and a voyage within, across distant horizons and to stranger countries than any visible to the actual senses.[43]

Although this is a general distinction, one which has been used for the purposes of a study of all poetry of the period 1880–1940,[44] it offers an especially close and accurate interpretation of the poetry of Henry Newbolt. This is perhaps because Masterman was concerned to describe Edwardian England, and Newbolt's verse is

---

[42] Corpus Christi College, Oxford, MSS 468, a notebook presented by Newbolt in 1912.

[43] C. F. G. Masterman, *The Condition of England* (repr. 1968), 188.

[44] V. de S. Pinto, *Crisis in English Poetry 1880–1940* (1951).

a product of that period. To place Newbolt as Edwardian and as one of a group of Edwardian poets is to recognize his verse as struggling with an identity crisis. That crisis is composed of a profound distrust of the imagination (a loss of faith in its transcendent potential), and an epistemological anxiety. Newbolt's autobiographical novel *The Twymans* (1911) is suggestive, in name at least, of duality, of a separated, not an integrated, personality. In this respect *The Twymans* might be seen in the context of contemporary works of *Doppelgänger* literature such as Stevenson's *Dr Jekyll and Mr Hyde* (1886) and Conrad's *The Secret Sharer* (1912).

Newbolt is not what could be called a modern poet, he does not make the kind of intellectual demands that modern poetry often does, and he does not challenge authority or literary decorum. His popularity is at odds with Modernism and he submits too readily to the needs of his audience. But the popular tradition of twentieth-century poetry is not without merit, and might include many of the Edwardians, as well as Kipling, Betjeman, and Philip Larkin, whose popularity has been noted by one critic with the words, 'He is the only sophisticated poet today who needs no sophisticated response from the reader'.[45] The work of each of these poets is accessible, often narrative, and preoccupied with traditional techniques of metre and rhyme; it is a tradition to which most Edwardian pre-Modernist poets belong, and it continues to flourish. John Betjeman acknowledged the Edwardian poet's accessibility when he wrote that 'Newbolt's poetry is easy to understand, rhythmical, and full of memorable lines', and yet 'he was an early admirer of Ezra Pound, T. S. Eliot and Peter Quennell'.[46] Such disparities, which must seem startling to a contemporary reader, are typical of the Edwardian period, and its transitional nature is well illustrated by the apparent incongruity of Newbolt's practice on the one hand and his critical sympathies on the other.

A brief consideration of the critical fate of Henry Newbolt serves as an instructive introduction to those whom Jimmy Porter called 'The old Edwardian brigade'. Newbolt's successes should not be overstated, but it is to be hoped that at the end of the twentieth century a dispassionate appraisal can now displace what was previously little more than vilification.

---

[45] J. Bayley, *Selected Essays* (Cambridge, 1984), 101.
[46] *Selected Poems of Henry Newbolt*, with an introduction by J. Betjeman (1940), p. xiv.

2

John Masefield: The Homesick Edwardian

JOHN MASEFIELD's first published work was *Salt-Water Ballads* (1902), a book of poems which portray the events of life at sea not as a historical survey of England's naval heritage, but from the perspective of the ordinary seaman. As the opening poem announces, Masefield sings 'Not of the princes and prelates with periwigged charioteers | Riding triumphantly laurelled to lap the fat of the years | Rather the scorned—the rejected—the men hemmed in with the spears' ('A Consecration'). True to this artistic and political claim, Masefield's first poems recount the everyday labours of ship crews, their physical hardships and technical skill, their dreams of shore-leave, exotic destinations, yarns, tales, and superstitions. Masefield also adopts the speech of his chosen characters and this gives the language of *Salt-Water Ballads* a robustness and vigour which is a departure from the aesthetic diction of the 1890s (although aligned with the practice of Kipling). The use of expletives, although limited, is surprisingly strong for the poetry of 1902: 'the bloody stay-at-homes', 'slower 'n a bloody snail', and 'The best cure known for fever chills is shovelling bloody coal' are three examples of colloquial language which the poet wryly explains in the 'Glossary' which accompanies these ballads: 'Bloody—an intensive derived from the substantive ' "blood" '. This unabashed directness is carried into the action of many of the poems; 'Burial Party', for example, is a poem which explains that a man buried at sea during the night will not sink, that his soul will stick in his throat and the corpse will swim all night with sharks gnawing at its flesh. Or consider the scenario of 'Evening—Regatta Day':

> And Stroke is lashing a bunch of keys to the buckle end a belt,
> And we're going to lay you over a chest and baste you till you melt.

This is clearly not the polite social verse which might be considered appropriate to a regatta, and nor is it the insipid narcissism fashionable among the poets of the 1890s. *Salt-Water Ballads* is refreshingly full of dramatic action and direct physical incident.

The book's prevailing mood is one of romantic adventure, and some of the best poems are those which express the inexplicable urge to travel and to face the elements in a primitive physical challenge. 'Sea-Fever' and 'Trade Winds' conjure a strong emotional impression from the minimum of technical resources, by their careful use of repetition and precise metrical and rhyming effects. 'Sea-Fever' uses repetition as its central structural device, to convey the strongly emotional or irrational nature of its impulse: 'I must go down to the seas again, for the call of the running tide | Is a wild call and a clear call that may not be denied.' The metre of the lines strikes a faintly elegiac note, and the refrain 'And all I ask' gives a sense of understatement which contributes to the poem's restraint, its quiet register. The final 'quiet sleep and a sweet dream' calls attention to the phantasmagoric quality of the poem, its sense of past experience suddenly overwhelming the speaker. 'Trade Winds' is a more muted representation of the mysterious attraction of foreign shores, expressed by the agency of the wind, which calls through the Spanish palm trees and which powers the sailing ships to their destinations: 'And in the ghostly palm-trees the sleepy tune | Of the quiet voice calling me, the long low croon | Of the steady Trade Winds blowing.' The form of three long lines ending with a shorter unrhymed line again contributes to an elegiac quality which is unobtrusive but distinctive. The 'wind' of the poem is not the fierce stormy weather which is a sailor's call to action but a 'cool and pleasant breeze' appropriate to a more relaxed and reflective tone; this distinction is the central issue of Conrad's *The Nigger of the 'Narcissus'* (1897), which, Jacques Berthoud has argued, represents a dialogue between 'The alternatives of diseased introspection and unreflecting action'.[1]

Salt-Water Ballads draws on an oral tradition of folklore and practical wisdom, those kinds of poetry which might be called specifically non-literary. This is a departure from the prevailing fashion of the 1890s, which was sometimes affectedly literary. Masefield's poetry originates among a small community, but not the kind of literary coterie which flourished among his contemporaries. The poet of *Salt-Water Ballads's* need to express himself arose from practical necessity:

No man need suffer much from introspection while opinions, ideals, and a sight of the most living of modern arts may be purchased for a few copper

---

[1] J. Conrad, *The Nigger of the 'Narcissus'* (Oxford, 1984), p. xxii.

coins. But at sea the individual must make his own amusement or become a victim of that brooding melancholy from which so many sailors suffer.[2]

Sailors' yarns were an established popular form developed during the 1890s by writers such as Kipling and Conrad to larger literary purposes. Kipling's *The Seven Seas and Other Verses* (1896) and *Captains Courageous: A Story of the Grand Banks* (1897) are experiments in this direction, and Conrad's tales recounted by Marlow, 'Youth' (1897), *Heart of Darkness* (1899), *Lord Jim* (1900), and *Chance* (1913) developed the form to accommodate sophisticated narrative purposes. Masefield's epigraph announces what is unique about his ballads: 'The mariners are a pleasant people, but little like those in towns, and they can speak no other language than that used in ships.'

Masefield utilizes a very small part of the range and variety of language available to him as a poet, focusing attention upon the particular violence done to ordinary grammar by sailor's speech, and demonstrating the liveliness which can be achieved by fidelity to it. He finds his voice by recognizing the potential of their language for ballad adaptation. The ballad is well suited to this kind of role-play and Masefield exploits it convincingly; his effects are vivid (if limited in number). The poet's speech becomes so saturated with nautical jargon that he must include a prose glossary at the end of the book with entries such as, 'D.B.S.— Distressed British Sailor. A term applied to those who are invalided home from foreign ports', and 'Crimp—a sort of scoundrelly land-shark preying upon sailors'. This kind of procedure is rare, demanding that the reader use the glossary to decipher the poems.

In Masefield's verse the strongest note is one of reflective melancholy and understated regret. It is a style which avoids the languor of much late nineteenth-century poetry by its close association with shipping's technical vocabulary, and by its fidelity to the wholly unromantic physical hardship of life at sea. Also, Masefield's use of the sailor's voice provides a sense of a story-telling tradition upon which he draws.

Given that *Salt-Water Ballads* was in some respects an original venture, quite different, for example, from most of the sea poems of Henry Newbolt, and considering its strong action and language, it is interesting to learn something of its contemporary reception. The title of the book was editorial, the idea not of Masefield but Grant Richards, and the publisher's choice proved an unfortunate

---

[2] 'In a Fo'c'sle', *A Tarpaulin Muster* (1907), 176–7.

one, suggesting a parallel with Kipling's *Barrack-Room Ballads* (1892) which many critics exploited to attack Masefield as purely derivative. L. A. G. Strong believes that Masefield's book 'attracted a good deal of attention' and cites 'the roughness and the deliberate crudity of language with which he challenged the taste of the time'.[3] But C. Biggane argues that *Salt-Water Ballads* 'seems to have attracted little attention at the time of its publication',[4] and Muriel Spark agrees that Masefield's first poems 'made an unspectacular appearance in 1902'.[5] Grant Richards has left a clue as to why Masefield did not become widely known:

Of the first edition of *Salt-Water Ballads* 500 copies were printed and the story is told in the trade that owing to a fire that took place in the warehouse of Leighton, Son and Hodge, the binders, the book was soon unprocurable. I believe this story of the fire to be an invention. My ledgers of that period in no way support it . . . the first binding was 300. In the first part of 1903 a further 150 were bound; and a further 50 were bound at a later date . . . Anyhow, the book became very much of a collector's item.[6]

Whether or not the story of the fire is true, the sale of 500 copies would not put Masefield in touch with a wide audience, and the status of 'collector's item' to which John Lane and Elkin Mathews had added prestige during the 1890s does not seem to have served Masefield well. In the opinion of one critic *Salt-Water Ballads* 'is undoubtedly meant to minister to the trapped spirit of the city clerk',[7] but still it does not seem to have been successful. Also, 1902 (immediately following the Boer War) was an unpropitious time for poetry which appeared to tell of the services. During the early Edwardian years, Kipling wrote chiefly about Sussex.

Kipling had created a precedent for Masefield's style, and the nature and extent of Masefield's indebtedness warrants a brief assessment.[8] Kipling's persona is a serviceman, but Masefield's is not; Kipling's poems are explicitly political but Masefield's honour the common workman without taking on board his patriotism or racism: Masefield's poetry is expository but not didactic. Masefield's ballads draw upon the musical element of the sea-chanty, but

---

[3] L. A. G. Strong, *John Masefield* (1952), 17–18.
[4] C. Biggane, *John Masefield* (1924), 1–2.
[5] M. Spark, *John Masefield* (1953), 61.
[6] G. Richards, *Author Hunting* (1934), 226.
[7] J. Lucas, *Modern English Poetry from Hardy to Hughes* (1986), 60.
[8] Kipling's *Barrack-Room Ballads and Other Verses* was published in London in 1892. Many of the poems had previously appeared in the *National Observer*, *St James's Gazette*, and the *Athenaeum*.

Kipling's are reminiscent of the music-hall. Kipling's poems use refrains extensively ('Tommy', 'Mandalay', 'Danny Deever'), but Masefield repeats only certain words and, occasionally, lines. The colloquialism of Kipling's ballads is based on the cockney accent ('moril', 'merricle', 'swaller'), but Masefield makes use of a specialized vocabulary of technical words. Kipling's poems have some notes to explain their occasional pidgin-Indian ('Panee lao!' in 'Gunga Din' for example), but the technical jargon of *Salt-Water Ballads* is more thorough and systematized. Masefield's language is extremely particular, but the heightened individuality of Kipling's *Barrack-Room Ballads* lies primarily in the sentiments it expresses.

Masefield's *Ballads*, published by Elkin Mathews in the Vigo Cabinet Series in 1903, illustrates the difficulties of expanding a range of theme and style without losing the individuality of expression achieved by his first publication. *Ballads* discards the colloquial language which contributed to the earlier poems' vitality and distinction, and relies heavily upon two traditional subjects, the English rural theme and the love sonnet. Unfortunately these are handled without the interest of a new perspective and the results are almost entirely conventional. Many poems depict an English landscape simply by enumerating every conceivable local feature (like some of the inert floral tapestry poems of William Morris). It is as if an effect might be achieved by their collective presence·

> The dawn comes cold; the haystack smokes,
> The green twigs crackle in the fire,
> The dew is dripping from the oaks,
> And sleepy men bear milking-yokes
> Slowly towards the cattle-byre.   ('Dawn')

The scene is not unlike that of some eighteenth-century landscape paintings, but in Masefield's poem the perspective is confused. The focus shifts too easily, too arbitrarily, and this destroys any sense of a central perception. This is the crucial factor which debars the poem from the success of the opening of Gray's 'Elegy Written in a Country Churchyard', where detached personal observation provides an important psychological dimension. Elsewhere in *Ballads* Masefield's attempts at insight and atmosphere are insipid and banal, most notably in 'The Wild Duck', where the rustic accessory cannot sustain the significance with which it is loaded: 'What things have the farm ducks seen | That they cry so—huddle and cry?'

Masefield's depiction of the love theme is little more felicitous; his group of sonnets in quatrains upon an idealized mistress begins with expressions such as 'When bony Death has chilled her gentle blood', 'Her heart is always doing lovely things', 'Being her friend, I do not care', 'Born for nought else, for nothing but for this', and 'Since I have learned Love's shining alphabet'. These inauspicious apostrophes introduce a devotion which is routinely sentimental; Masefield's use of courtly love conventions has not the personal urgency with which Rupert Brooke occasionally handled them. Also, they betray in their distance from the love object and their excessive sense of wonder, the influence of the early verse of Yeats; this is poetry which seems to lack sufficient linguistic resources to express itself precisely or directly. Masefield's personal friendship with Yeats at this time doubtless encouraged the young poet (he often visited Yeats at 18 Woburn Buildings and met Lady Gregory, Laurence Binyon, Arthur Symons, and Ernest Rhys), but in *Ballads* the signs are of distraction rather than inspiration. Deprived of its nautical context, Masefield's melancholy seems affected, the wistfulness of *Salt-Water Ballads* becomes self-conscious and contrived. The medievalism of *Ballads* has the ornateness of D. G. Rossetti rather than the realism of Malory, and the poem 'London Town' is a close imitation of Housman, especially poems XLI and L from *A Shropshire Lad* (1896). Most importantly, Masefield's metaphor for art in 'The Harper's Song' fulfils only a very minor and restricted function, as if the imagination were capable only of producing 'sweet mournful music filled with tears'.[9] Masefield's conception of his role as an artist underwent a radical and regressive transformation as the anxiety of influence shifted from Kipling to Yeats.

Masefield has two major problems. Despite the title *Ballads*, the poems of this collection are chiefly lyrical, and this seems to indicate that the poet is speaking with his own voice rather than adopting that of another. Technically this is much more difficult to achieve with success, demanding a confidence and maturity which it is difficult for a young poet to find. It is easier to speak convincingly through the voice of an assumed character. Secondly, Masefield's themes, rural, romantic, and sea-faring, lie uneasily together; they appear as separate voices, isolated and disunited. In attempting each of the subjects which he feels might hit upon a receptive audience, Masefield has sacrificed a credible human

[9] Cf. W. Gibson's first book, *Urlyn the Harper* (1902).

voice. The demands upon the reader of *Salt-Water Ballads* have been abandoned in the interests of commercial acceptability.

The exceptions to this disappointing development are two notable sea poems. 'The West Wind', beckoning the traveller to return home from foreign ports, conveys a tantalizingly intangible impression of an English rural landscape, one which is the feverish product of homesickness:

'Larks are singing in the west, brother, above the green wheat,
So will ye not come home, brother, and rest your tired feet?
I've a balm for bruised hearts, brother, sleep for aching eyes',
Says the warm wind, the west wind, full of birds' cries.

As with Tennyson's 'The Lotos-Eaters' the scene promises an idyllic release from struggle, hardship, and labour; but Masefield's poem is not a poem of escape in quite the same sense; it expresses the relief of home-coming with the same quiet insistence with which other poems convey the excitement of setting out. Another good sea poem, 'Cargoes', relies in part for its impact upon a response to exotic words, the meaning and significance of which may be entirely lost on the reader: 'Quinquireme of Nineveh from distant Ophir'. The attraction of the first stanza comes purely from the exotic sound and the foreign appeal of a roll-call of strange commodities: 'With a cargo of ivory, | And apes and peacocks, | Sandalwood, cedarwood, and sweet white wine.' The effect is not unlike the vowel music of the opening line of Coleridge's 'Kubla Khan': 'In Xanadu did Kubla Khan | A stately pleasure-dome decree'. But it is notable that 'Cargoes' offers a new inter-pretation of poetic subjects, in the form of the 'Dirty British coaster with a salt-caked smoke-stack', so that any working vessel may become the subject of poetry. There is something more vital in the description of the British ship, the consonants of 'Road-rail, pig-lead' playing off against the soft vowels sounds of 'Emeralds, amethysts'. Two distinct forms of aesthetic experience are juxta-posed without authorial comment, and the poem is an implicit restatement of Masefield's intention to render that which has traditionally been considered unfit for poetic treatment.

Perhaps because of the disappointing public response to his early verse, Masefield published no poetry between 1903 and 1911; he took a job with the *Manchester Guardian* for which he wrote a regular column, and supplemented his income by editing editions and anthologies and producing the occasional novel. Like his contemporaries John Davidson and Edward Thomas, Masefield's

Edwardian career was consumed by the need to survive financially on various forms of journalism and literary hack work, which left little time or energy for creative writing. Masefield wrote the notes for Binyon's edition of the poems of Keats (1903); edited and introduced *The Poems of Robert Herrick* (1906); introduced *The Travels of Marco Polo* (1908); produced an edition of *The Lyrics of Jonson, Beaumont and Fletcher* (1906); edited a selection of prose from the works of Defoe (1909); researched *Sea Life in Nelson's Time* (1905), and wrote the comprehensive survey *William Shakespeare* (1911). This resembles closely the activities and output of Edward Thomas, and while Thomas concentrated on the literature of the countryside, Masefield's special interest was the sea: *A Sailor's Garland* (1906) is an anthology of sea poetry, and *A Mainsail Haul* (1905) and *A Tarpaulin Muster* (1907) are collections of tales Masefield learned as an apprentice aboard a training ship and from his own personal experience. Among these Edwardian works are Masefield's novels *Captain Margaret* (1908) and *Lost Endeavour* (1910), and Masefield's experiments with play-writing, *The Tragedy of Nan* and *The Campden Wonder*, which were performed in London in 1907–8 under the direction of Granville-Barker. This is typical of the diversity of output of Edwardian men of letters such as Chesterton, Thomas, and Davidson.

By April 1909 Masefield was sufficiently well known to be the subject of a feature in the *Bookman* which followed an account of the poet's youth with the comment that 'We should look, I think, to all his hard work and these many hard knocks for the cause of that virility which is so marked a feature of Mr. Masefield's work.'[10] Since among his poems it was only of *Salt-Water Ballads* that 'virility' could be said to be a characteristic, it seems likely that the feature on Masefield in the *Bookman* was commissioned on the strength of his more recently acquired reputation, that is to say through his prose as much as through his poetry. Only when his name was reasonably established did critics begin to look back with interest at his first book of poetry. This argument is supported by the fact that in 1910 Masefield reprinted the verses of the 1902 and 1903 collections as *Ballads and Poems* without adding any new poems, probably to capitalize on his current popularity.

Masefield's early career illustrates the importance of journalism in the Edwardian writer's life, the function it fulfilled in providing both a remunerative outlet for writing and immediate access to a substantial reading public:

[10] A. Gibson, 'Mr. John Masefield', *Bookman*, 36 (Apr. 1909), 9.

For a serious writer coming to the fore in the 1900s worldly success was certainly a more ambiguous goal than it would have been two or three literary generations earlier. Nothing illustrates this more clearly, or indeed more notoriously, than the career of Arnold Bennett. It is a neat piece of inadvertent symbolism, as Walter Allen has pointed out, that Bennett should have made his journalistic debut by winning a competition in *Tit-Bits* and then followed this up by publishing a short story in the *Yellow Book*; from the very outset he was disconcertingly ready to switch roles, to appear now as a tradesman, now as a dedicated artist.[11]

The problems of artistic integrity were partially alleviated for Masefield by his belief that he wrote, from the beginning, for a popular audience: 'Not the ruler for me, but the ranker, the tramp of the road' ('A Consecration'). Despite his personal friendship with Yeats, Masefield was not a member of the Rhymers' Club and did not contribute to any of the little magazines of the contemporary coteries. Like many Edwardian poets he seems to have expected to establish a reputation largely on his own terms. Masefield had demonstrated his skill as a tradesman, but to what degree could he consider himself a dedicated artist?

Yeats was apparently fond of quoting Goethe's saying that we never learn to know ourselves by thought, only by action. Denis Donoghue explains that 'Thought is inclined to dispose its findings in some form of dualism, but action is unitary.'[12] Whether or not he was aware of Yeats's preoccupation, a similar dualism is present in many of Masefield's works. The emphatic rejection of literary pursuits in favour of direct action is the theme of a curious story called 'Edward Herries' published in *A Tarpaulin Muster* (1907). The eponymous protagonist ('hero' is significantly not the right term for this or most other Edwardian leading characters) is a poet corrupted by the self-indulgent excesses of Decadence:

He flung back the curtains, so that he might see better; and the moonlight, falling upon him, made yet more pale the paleness of his refined face, now wrung with sorrow. He took one of the silver candlesticks and held it so that the light might fall upon a portrait hanging in the window-nook. It was the portrait of a woman a little older than himself; and one had but to see the confident poise of the sweet head and the firm red line of the lips, and the delicate sharp cutting of the chin, to know that she was one of

[11] J. Gross, *The Rise and Fall of the Man of Letters: Aspects of English Literary Life Since 1800* (1969), 211–12.

[12] D. Donoghue, *Yeats* (1971), 95.

those queenly women before whom the hearts of the weak and the strong are as dust upon the road.[13] (pp. 11–12).

The moonlight, the wan complexion of our noble young writer harrowed by misfortune, and the agonizing futility of his love for an unattainable woman, are all symptoms of the debility to which a preoccupation with literature has reduced him. He exclaims to his mysteriously remote object of desire, 'Would I were a violet in the grass, hidden among the dead thorn leaves, that your passing foot might crush me' (p. 17). Unable to continue in this life of self-destructive enervation, Herries emerges from the shadows and sets out on a quest to discover that full participation in life which will make him a worthy suitor. After many trials, he returns:

He had changed much in the five years. He had been far from books, roving the world. He had grown sturdier, coarser, more self-assertive. He had been in battles and marches, at the sack of towns, at the boarding of ships at sea. He had many violent memories, memories of war and of anger, to lay by his memories of her beauty. (p. 31).

This interpretation of the *Bildungsroman* has affinities, especially in its nautical aspect, with William Golding's *Rites of Passage* (1980) and *Close Quarters* (1987). Herries's travels and adventures have cured the sickliness of his youthful disposition; he has acquired a new emotional confidence, 'more self-assertive', and his physical condition is fortified and tough, 'sturdier, coarser'. Art is insufficient, and the central character is transformed not by imaginative reflection but by physical ordeal. It comes as a surprise then that Herries does not win the lady with his new assurance and valour. He suddenly finds that his experiences have only vulgarized him in her eyes, reduced him to baseness. He creeps from her door 'ashamed and humbled' to consider again the value of his new character.

Masefield's story portrays literature and action as mutually exclusive activities. His conception of art is synonymous with passive contemplation and his action denotes only 'battles and marches' and other forms of violent physical combat. Having set out his possible routes, Masefield is unable to choose between them, and this causes a creative impasse. The story ends abruptly,

---

[13] The portrayal of Herries may owe something to the pervasive influence of J.–K. Huysmans's *A rebours* (1884); this is the novel Lord Henry Wotton lends the hero of Wilde's *The Picture of Dorian Gray* (1891), and which Symons described as 'the breviary of Decadence'. The feature that it shares with Masefield's story is the idea that those who are consumed by literature are also destroyed by it.

rejecting the easy moral to which it appeared to be leading. Masefield considers the merits of two entirely separate types of character, and both prove to be unsatisfactory.

This is the first of the stories in *A Tarpaulin Muster*, posing a dilemma between art and action which is not explicitly resolved. But it is notable that all of the following tales are concerned strictly with the exigencies of various types of direct action. 'A Raine's Law Arrest', for example, recounts an anecdote of police-bribing in a style reminiscent of Runyon, Chandler, or Hammet: 'As I entered I saw that one of the detectives was folding up a thick wad of green backs which the boss had just handed to him' (p. 211). The story of Herries is an analogue to Masefield's creative procedure, and the narrative of adventure is his artistic expedient for the imagination's potential excess. For Masefield, writing about immediate dramatic incident is the prime antidote to the kind of self-indulgence which art, for him, necessarily entails. It is also notable that most of these tales are non-fiction; they are either incidents from Masefield's own life or tales recounted by his fellow shipmates. In this sense they are not entirely products of Masefield's imagination, and this partially alleviates the anxieties of creative production and authority characteristic of much Edwardian poetry.

In a review in 1985, Neil Corcoran argued that although much of *The Everlasting Mercy* is 'lame and exasperating' the poem warranted inclusion in Masefield's selected poems on the grounds that it is a 'litmus paper for English literary taste before the First World War'.[14] Masefield's first long narrative poem was published in October 1911 in the *English Review*, a monthly publication edited by Austin Harrison which, also in 1911, carried short stories by E. M. Forster and D. H. Lawrence, and which in the issue containing Masefield's poem, concluded the serialization of Conrad's *Under Western Eyes*. Clearly this was a prestigious periodical, founded by Ford Madox Ford and partially funded by H. G. Wells. The editor's decision to publish Masefield's poem was a brave one, not because the poet was unknown, but because of the controversy he felt its racy language would arouse. W. H. Hamilton recalls the manner of the poem's impact:

I shall never forget that torrid day in 1911 when I languidly picked up a blue-covered copy of *The English Review* in a smoke-room, sank with it into

---

[14] N. Corcoran, 'Too Much of Green', *Times Literary Supplement* (26 Apr. 1985), 469.

a basket chair, lit my pipe, leisurely opened the magazine and got one of the shocks and surprises of my life.[15]

This is interesting for its (no doubt intentional) portrayal of precisely the affectation and mannerism to which Masefield offered an antidote. Robert Graves (who later rented the cottage at the bottom of Masefield's Boar's Hill garden), commented that '*The Everlasting Mercy* was a fresh wind that carried English poetry clear out of the Edwardian doldrums',[16] and it seems that the poem certainly had an immediate and profound effect on the literary scene. In his invaluable survey of early twentieth-century poetry R. H. Ross credits the poem with an important seminal value: 'It was Masefield's *Everlasting Mercy* [*sic*] which can fairly be said to have set the pre-war poetic renaissance in motion.'[17] To a modern reader Ross's favourable perception of *The Everlasting Mercy* would have seemed more appropriate to *Salt-Water Ballads* published nine years earlier. It suggests that the immediate pre-war years were a good time to reconstitute the close relationship between poetry and the public which had not existed since the death of Tennyson in 1892. The enormous popularity of Edward Marsh's *Georgian Poetry 1911–1912*, published in October 1912, seems to confirm this. James Reeves concludes that the success of *The Everlasting Mercy* 'indicated there was a wider public prepared to accept new things in poetry, provided they were made easily available'.[18] Masefield had suddenly and dramatically discovered his poetic voice, and a huge new audience.

It is almost impossible now, at the opposite end of the twentieth century, to appreciate the poem's intrinsic merit; its attempts at 'realism' seem quaint and innocuous, and any cause for controversy passes unnoticed by modern readers. *The Everlasting Mercy* belongs to the time when there was a large public appetite for rural salt-of-the-earth archetypes who would provide the stock to resist the flood of the 'people of the abyss'[19] (see Edward Thomas's 'Lob' and Kipling's Sussex poetry for formulations of this quintessential Englishman). The poem is little more than a period piece; Donald Stanford omitted it entirely from his *Selected Poems of John Masefield* (1984).

[15] W. H. Hamilton, *John Masefield: A Critical Study* (1922), 82.

[16] R. Graves, 'Robert Graves on John Masefield', *Times Literary Supplement* (22 June 1967), 568.

[17] R. H. Ross, *The Georgian Revolt: Rise and Fall of a Poetic Ideal 1910–1922* (1967), 51.

[18] *Georgian Poetry*, selected and introduced by J. Reeves (1962), p. xii.

[19] Cf. J. London's *The People of the Abyss* (1903), and C. F. G. Masterman's anonymous pamphlet about slum life *From The Abyss* (1902).

Masefield wants his subject both ways; he is eager to write about Saul Kane as a low-life hoodlum in a style which is convincingly realistic ('I drunk, I fought, I poached, I whored'), but at the same time he hopes to expound the wonders of rural beauty in a way which credits his uneducated protagonist with sensitivity and introspection ('And summat made me think of things'). There is nothing wrong with this (there is a whole tradition of writing which portrays working-class heroes possessed of distinguishing qualities), but Masefield's poem pulls in opposite directions; its doggerel often seems false, and its artistic sensibility seems artificially imposed. The redeeming spiritual or mystical dimension which G. Wilson Knight expounds is unhappily divorced from the poem's naturalistic setting.[20] The device of conducting the poem as a flashback is the central structural problem which divides the poem into two separate accounts and deprives the action of dramatic tension:

> 'We'll fight after the harvest hum.
> And Silas Jones, that bookie wide,
> Will make a purse five pounds a side.'
> Those were the words, that was the place,
> By which God brought me into grace.

Saul Kane, the born-again evangelist, conducts a moralistic running commentary, which splits the poem into two narratives (not unlike those of Tennyson's 'The Two Voices'). One voice recounts action for its own sake while the other interprets action in a Christian context. This latter voice is a nuisance, qualifying every incident with post-enlightened exclamations of piety and remorse.

Perhaps the presentation of evil is commonly more engaging than the depiction of virtue (c.f. the debate on *Paradise Lost*), but in terms of Masefield's imagination the voices of *The Everlasting Mercy* represent his characteristic struggle between action and interpretation. The structural division of the voices is an analogy for the polarization of the dual roles of the writer as Masefield perceived them. It is significant then that the pre-conversion Kane is more vital, interesting, and credible (as material for poetry), than his didactic counterpart. Masefield's active/contemplative dilemma is not exploited to advantage here as it is elsewhere.

Masefield's exceptionally eventful adolescence and his initial concern to establish a new language for poetry, helped to distinguish

---

[20] G. Wilson Knight, *Neglected Powers* (1971), chapter on 'Masefield and Spiritualism', 260–92.

his Edwardian work, but it seems likely that his training as a ship-hand, his adventures in Chile, and his years as a workman in a Yonkers carpet factory (see *In the Mill*, 1941) created a nostalgia for the late-Victorian rural England he left behind, which coloured all his writing, even well into the twentieth century. This nostalgia for a lost country childhood (the effect of which is also felt in the poetry of Housman and Edward Thomas) prevented Masefield from making imaginative use of the urban landscapes of modern England, and made some aspects of his output seem anachronistic in comparison to the urgent social themes of Henley, Davidson, and Wilfred Gibson. This nostalgia is the subject of the best criticism written on Masefield, an essay by John Middleton Murry in *Aspects of Literature* (1920). Murry complains that Masefield suffers from 'an unconscious desire to convince himself that he is saturated in essential Englishness' and argues that his poetry betrays 'a nostalgia so conscious of separation that it cannot trust that any associations will be evoked without an unemphasised appeal'.[21] This sense of 'Overstrain' and 'desperation' is illuminated by a comparison with Chaucer: 'Chaucer is at home with his speech and at home with his world; by his side Mr Masefield seems nervous and uncertain about both.'[22] This is a strong allegation, and one which is difficult to refute. But the nature of Masefield's uncertainty, the relationship between poetic speech and the world of which it tells, is the essential quality by which his work should be understood. It is precisely this anxiety which produces both his best and his most flawed writing; it is the worry which sustains the individuality of *Salt-Water Ballads* and fuels the dramatic urgency of his novel *Multitude and Solitude* (1909). But it also led Masefield to indulge, often sentimentally, his regret for the passing of Merrie England and its minstrels and folk bards.

John Bayley has recently commented on Edwardian and Georgian insularity: 'The time of self-conscious "Englishness" in art and in public statement, at the beginning of this century, was a degenerate time, and vulgarised the concept.'[23] It seems likely that uncertainty as to what were the appropriate and recognized subjects for poetry in the early twentieth century prompted widespread recourse to national and rural myths, which could be handled with relative safety. There are two possible explanations for the popularity of Masefield's nostalgia, that it appealed to the homesickness of soldiers away on active service, and that it crystallized the fear

[21] J. M. Murry, *Aspects of Literature* (1920), 154.   [22] Ibid. 153.
[23] J. Bayley, 'English Equivocation', *Poetry Review*, 76 (June 1986), 4.

that the security of rural England could never entirely return. The modernization of war accompanied the urbanization of modern England and parted Edwardians irrevocably from their world. What John Bayley calls 'that bad time around 1900'[24] was a crisis of confidence in poetry which initiated all manner of artistic expedients. Yet there was one commonly accepted theme, 'England'. Masefield had a persistent desire to capture what was unique about the English character; it was an ambitious undertaking to embark upon, and one which, because of its scope, often made it difficult for him to sustain an identity as an artist.

Dauber (1913) reveals Masefield still worried by the relationship between artistic sensibility and physical action, but here he finds an exceptional solution. His hero is a ship's painter who is scorned and despised by the rest of the crew and derided for his creative aspirations, 'Bullied and damned at since the voyage began'. 'The Dauber' is a derogatory term for an artist whose imagination is rigidly confined by the immediate practical demands of the ship. The crew are a microcosm of society, each member fulfilling a function and providing a skill which contributes to the efficiency and survival of the community. The Edwardian public may have been aware of the significance of this point, following the sinking of the *Titanic* a year earlier in 1912. The role of the painter is potentially ambiguous, encompassing that of the tradesman and the artist. Dauber's ambition is to become a master of sea-scapes by sketching in his spare time, and it is this ambition which arouses the particular hostility of the crew. This kind of painting contributes in no way to the progress or fitness of the ship; it is a purely personal luxury of no practical value to the rest of the men. This is a sensitive issue for a poet such as Masefield, his commitment to workers and artisans apparently compromised by personal literary aspirations (and poetry can seem the most useless bourgeois indulgence when considered in these terms). Dauber is the representative of art who, by winning the crew's respect, has the potential to refute this.

Like Masefield himself, Dauber misjudged the hardship of life at sea, seduced by its romantic associations:

> Down in his bunk the Dauber lay awake
> Thinking of his unfitness for the sea.
> Each failure, each derision, each mistake,
> There in the life not made for such as he.

[24] J. Bayley, 'English Equivocation', *Poetry Review*, 76 (June 1986), 4.

Against the gruelling regime of daily tasks, Dauber's only consolation is his art, 'It is most proud, whatever pain it brings'. The condemnation of the crew, sanctioned by the authority of the captain, is unequivocal:

> Spit brown, my son, and get a hairy breast;
> Get shoulders on you at the crojick braces,
> And let this painting business go to blazes.

Dauber's painting enables him to redeem his drudgery and make sense of the arbitrary tasks to which he is assigned. Yet it might be said that given the arduous routine of the ship, and the pastimes of the other crew members (knitting etc.), Dauber's painting does seem surprising, perhaps even irresponsible. In some respects he is certainly a nuisance, storing his canvases in the longboat. The balance of sympathies is carefully held, Dauber's passion distracting him from his proper business, and the brutality of his shipmates warranting moral censure.

Dauber's sense of personal pride insists that he should meet the crew on their own terms, and soon he acquits himself working the topsails in a storm rounding Cape Horn. He earns their respect, but he remains adamant that his painting will continue. For a brief spell he achieves a degree of integration, enjoying both the respect of the crew and the pleasure of knowing he has not surrendered his self-respect. But this does not last long; in his next outing he slips from the yard-arm and is killed. Dauber's artistic potential is never realized, he succeeds as a sailor but not as a painter, and the manner of his death, in heroic physical circumstances, would seem to endorse the view that art must be relinquished. Action wins, again at the expense of art, and this implies that Masefield finds it difficult to discover the appropriate metaphor for his own activities as a poet. This is a recurrence of the anxiety that his product has no material value.

At the same time, Dauber's death is the perfect expedient for Masefield, removing the problem of a very difficult thematic reconciliation by elevating the hero to the status of tragic failure. His death transmutes his struggle into a symbol of unattainable personal achievement. As Muriel Spark points out, there is a parallel with Henry James's story 'Owen Wingrave' (1892):

Owen Wingrave's death occurs in the process of 'proving' his courage. The tragic element of the story is the same as that of *Dauber*. It is this: the fatal error of both Wingrave and the Dauber was the attempt to justify their existence in a manner alien to them.[25]

What the narratives of James and Masefield share is that their protagonists die in tests of physical valour which are unnatural to them; intellectual and artistic aspirations are defeated by grotesque fatal accidents.

Dauber's talent is unfulfilled, and his dying words 'It will go on' (acquiring for this poem the significance of Kurtz's 'The horror, the horror') would seem to refer to the continuation of artistic endeavour in other mens' lives. But the manner of the poem's ending leaves this in doubt. The elucidation of numerous diverse actions after the painter's death formally reduces its impact and implies the context of a larger perspective. The ship sails on, and our attention must move with it: *Dauber* is not simply its protagonist's narrative. This is a very classical effect, successfully creating the context of cosmic inevitability with which Chaucer concludes *Troilus and Criseyde*. Again Masefield's narrative suggests affinities with Conrad: Lord Jim also dies from aspiring too high ('to be a saint' by forgiving Brown).

It is Masefield's technical accomplishment in *Dauber* which holds in abeyance the judgement that art is useless. The incessant progress of the ship provides Masefield with an excellent vehicle for his special talent. The sense of constant movement frames the sailor's life as profoundly as the confines of his vessel:

> The wester came as steady as the Trades;
> Brightly it blew, and still the ship did shoulder
> The brilliance of the water's white cockades
> Into the milky green of smoky smoulder.
> The sky grew bluer and the air grew colder.
> Southward she thundered while the westers held,
> Proud, with taut bridles, pawing, but compelled.

This larger sense of fated inevitability is underpinned by the detailed account of the handling of the ship's tackle which occupies the crew almost continually. This intense preoccupation with human action gives the poem its dramatic urgency. In this way Masefield testifies to the efficacy of the painter's ambition; on one occasion Dauber senses,

---

[25] Spark, *John Masefield*, 126.

That this, and so much like it, of man's toil,
Compassed by naked manhood in strange places,
Was all heroic, but outside the coil
Within which modern art gleams or grimaces;
That if he drew that line of sailors' faces
Sweating the sail, their passionate play and change,
It would be new, and wonderful, and strange.

Artistic fidelity to physical action is the means by which Masefield hopes to achieve his individual synthesis of qualities and values, simultaneously invigorating art and celebrating primitive impulses. The poem achieves that which its protagonist does not. *Dauber* is Masefield's most successful poem because it creates art from the confrontation of the issues which dominate his imaginative career. The poem is not dishonest because it fails to reconcile those issues, it is a graphic demonstration of the intractability of Masefield's twofold creative instinct.

Despite his interest in martial and heroic qualities, Masefield wrote only one poem about the War, 'August, 1914', and it is a surprisingly disappointing exercise in vaguely patriotic rhetoric, entirely devoid of dramatic urgency or immediate action. Like many Edwardian responses to the war (Brooke's sonnets for example), Masefield's poem registers the sense of a distant challenge or threat, and perhaps understandably, cannot imagine the consequences of international conflict. 'August, 1914' was written at a time when Masefield 'was putting into verse his deepest ruminations and spiritual gropings',[26] and the epithets of inexactness are appropriate to this poem, conducted entirely in the past tense, and seeming in its retrospection incapable of grasping the urgency and importance of the event which occasions it. The poem's historical subjects 'Who, century after century, held these farms', provide an analogue for Masefield's condition:

> Yet heard the news, and went discouraged home,
> And brooded by the fire with heavy mind,
> With such dumb loving of the Berkshire loam
> As breaks the dumb hearts of the English kind.

These pensive but inarticulate characters are archetypes of English stoicism and restraint who,

---

[26] C. Babington-Smith, *John Masefield: A Life* (1978), 121.

> died (uncouthly, most) in foreign lands
> For some idea but dimly understood
> Of an English city never built by hands
> Which love of England prompted and made good.

The syntactical confusion of these lines is an inadvertent parallel to the failure of speech depicted at the poem's centre. The sense of something which cannot be expressed pervades 'August, 1914', inhibiting it from finding the satisfactory mythological context which makes successful war poetry both specific to the historical event and capable of expressing something larger. Masefield simply aligns himself with those who have been customarily dumb-struck.

Masefield was 36 at the outbreak of the First World War, too old for the army, so in February 1915 he chose to join the British Red Cross as an orderly tending to French wounded near Chaumont, sixty miles from the front. It would be wrong to assume that Masefield shirked the brutal realities of the conflict:

As you know, I've seen pretty nearly every kind of wound, including some which took a stout heart to look at, but the burns easily surpassed anything I've ever seen. There were people with the tops of their heads burnt off and stinking like frizzled meat, and the top all red and dripping pus, and their faces all gone, and their arms just covered with a kind of gauntlet of raw meat, and perhaps their whole bodies, from their knees to their shoulders, without any semblance of skin. One can't describe such wounds, they have to be seen to be believed.[27]

This quotation comes from a letter written by the poet on 12 October 1916, and it is typical of the unflinching detail with which many of his letters recount the squalor, suffering, humiliation, and loss of dignity, that he regarded as the most pressing aspects of war. These letters provide very precise descriptions of the human waste and physical destruction which resulted from military engagements:

The battlefield is a bedevilled and desolate and awful place, still heaped, here and there, with dead Germans, and all littered and skinned and gouged, till it looks like the country of the moon. Here there is a heap of picks, there a coil of wire, here a body or a leg, there a bomb or two, a rifle, a smashed helmet, a few dozen cartridges, then some boots with feet in them, a mess of old coats and straps and leather work, all smashed and smothered in a litter of mud and mess, and great big stinking pools and

---

[27] J. Masefield, *Letters from the Front, 1915–1917*, ed. P. Vansittart (1984), 180.

old dud shells, burnt trees, and powdered bricks and iron. It cannot be described nor imagined.[28]

The collections *Letters from the Front* and *Letters to Margaret Bridges* (daughter of the poet, Robert), are undoubtedly a significant contribution to the literature of the First World War. Most revealingly for the study of Masefield as a writer, these letters are packed with information recording the material circumstances and physical conditions of wartime existence. It is precisely this visual realization that his poetry of this period lacks. The poems *Lollingdon Downs, and Other Poems, with Sonnets* (1917) are affectedly abstract and philosophical; they deal only with concepts and ideas.

The implication of this dichotomy of written texts and styles is that Masefield's poetry, as he conceived it, was incapable of accommodating his new experience. Despite the realism of his Edwardian writing, the reality of war was not a fit subject for his verse. A similar divergence characterizes Rupert Brooke's more limited experience of war; contrary to the suggestion of poems such as 'A Channel Passage' and 'Jealousy' his poetry was ultimately disinclined to take imaginative possession of sordid physical circumstances. Brooke chose to write about the evacuation of Antwerp only in his letters, and Masefield also recoiled from writing publicly about unedifying personal situations. While his letters are full of intimately detailed horrors, his poetry of this period is innocuous and woolly. This is a telling failure of imagination which reflects poorly on the Edwardian conception of poetry and its sense of proper subjects for poetic treatment. It gives an indication of the full value of the innovations of Owen and others, and demonstrates the constriction of imagination which can occur through subservience to outmoded notions of decorum and restraint.

Masefield's *Collected Poems* (1923) sold 80,000 copies, and *Sard Harker* (1924) and *Odtaa* (1926) sold almost as many again. In 1930 George V and Ramsay MacDonald (head of a Labour Government) appointed Masefield Poet Laureate; it was an obvious choice and a good one. Like Kipling and Betjeman, Masefield briefly restored poetry to a wide readership, and he remained a celebrity although no longer in the literary vanguard. After the war Masefield became increasingly cut off from the new and exciting developments taking place in the poetry of Eliot and

---

[28] J. Masefield, *Letters to Margaret Bridges (1915–1919)*, ed. D. Stanford (Manchester, 1984), 28.

Auden. Masefield was 52 in 1930 and there are signs that his nostalgia grew worse as he grew older. This is not to say that he became a recluse, but his creative writing continued to evoke the spirit of rural England long after it had ceased to be relevant to modern experience, and at a time when narrative had been completely abandoned as a legitimate vehicle for serious poetry ('Reynard The Fox', 'Right Royal').

Martin Dodsworth has recently recommended Masefield's *William Shakespeare* (1911) on the grounds that 'its quality of decisive personal engagement with Shakespeare's play . . . is of a kind singularly lacking in comparable general surveys of our own day',[29] and a revival of interest is apparent in the four separate volumes of Masefield letters published recently: *Letters to Margaret Bridges 1915–1919* (1984); *Letters From the Front 1915–1917* (1984); *Letters To Reyna* (1983); *Letters to Florence Lamont* (1979). Although Masefield continued to write until his death in 1967, interest centres on his early career because it shows how his pragmatic commitment to a literature designed to curb the excesses of imaginative indulgence governed his development, and because this theme is an indication of the pressures inherent in Edwardian literature; Masefield created his best work in coming to terms with them.

[29] M. Dodsworth, 'The Editorial Miscellany', *English* (summer 1986), 188–9.

3

Hardy's *The Dynasts*: 'words . . . to hold the imagination'

The Dynasts occupies an anomalous position in Hardy studies; while his standing as a poet has improved in the later part of the twentieth century, this revaluation has yet to reach his epic work on the Napoleonic Wars. The poem has been called 'the indispensable culmination of his work'[1] and 'the final fruit and major event of his creative life',[2] but *The Dynasts* receives no thorough treatment in Donald Davie's *Thomas Hardy and British Poetry* (1973), in Tom Paulin's *Thomas Hardy: The Poetry of Perception* (1975), or John Bayley's *An Essay on Hardy* (1978), and criticism seems impervious to the belief that Hardy 'took pride in it as the greatest of all his literary achievements'.[3] *The Dynasts* belongs to the stage in Hardy's career when he had repudiated fiction and was devoting his whole attention to poetry; Part First was published in 1904, Part Second in 1906, and Part Third in 1908; *The Dynasts* represents a major contribution to the character of Edwardian poetry. The poem has often been considered in the context of Hardy's career; this chapter hopes to show that it is useful to regard the poem in the context of its period, as part of a response to the problem of poetry in the early twentieth century, which Hardy shared with Housman, Thomas, and the Edwardians. It also tries to show the relation of *The Dynasts* to Hardy's other poetry, in a move towards 'the unity and wholeness of Hardy's vision, regardless of the genre in which he chose to write'.[4]

In choosing the Napoleonic Wars of 1805–15 as the subject of his major poetic work Hardy put his imagination at the service of history. This decision necessarily limited the scope of artistic creation before he began, for 'he did not here create out of his own

---

[1] R. A. Scott-James, *Thomas Hardy* (1951), 35.
[2] A. Chakravarty, The Dynasts *and the Post-War Age in Poetry: A Study in Modern Ideas* (1938), 11.
[3] H. Orel, *Thomas Hardy's Epic-Drama: A Study of* The Dynasts (Lawrence, Kan., 1963), 102.
[4] H. E. Gerber and W. E. Davis, *Thomas Hardy: An Annotated Bibliography of Writings about him* (1973), 18.

imagination that material with which he worked'.[5] Moreover,
Hardy is not at liberty to shape his material for his idiosyncratic
purposes but strives throughout for historical accuracy, to the
extent that 'Whenever any evidence of the words really spoken or
written by the characters in their various situations was attainable,
as close a paraphrase was aimed at as was compatible with the
form chosen' (Preface). Hardy's eagerness to achieve historical
verisimilitude involved him in extensive researches, such that, as
he wrote to Henry Newbolt, 'In the *Dynasts* I was obliged to
condense so strictly that I could not give a twentieth part of the
detail I should have liked to give.'[6] Hardy compensates for these
omissions and compressions by demanding from the reader some
prior knowledge of the historical background; his submission to
historical precedent is so complete that he must in part abdicate
conventional authorial responsibilities: 'the subject is familiar to
all; and foreknowledge is assumed to fill in the junctions required
to combine the scenes into an artistic unity' (Preface). The col-
laborative effort calls for a knowledge of the major historical
events, a requirement which is sometimes onerous. This is especially
true of Hardy's presentation of affairs in Spain in Part Third,
which necessitates a familiarity with Spanish history of the early
nineteenth century. This is a difficulty with the poem 'taking its
unity simply from the actual logic of historical events'.[7] The
degree to which the action of the poem is prescribed by historical
precedent acts as a curb to imaginative indulgence; in *The Dynasts*
imagination is subjugated to rigorous empirical constraints. The
scope of historical record which the poem compasses serves to
qualify severely the possible hazards of imaginative freedom.

The pressure of historical precedent is felt throughout the poem,
in the formal structure with its brief and quickly moving scenes,
and in the smallest details where the poet, in footnotes, needlessly
explains of a minor character 'that both her children grew up and
did well' (3. i. iv). Such notes are included to support the sense of
historical authenticity, and reveal Hardy as a writer unwilling to
relinquish the fruits of his research for the sake of artistic economy.
The intrusiveness of his historical sense is felt when he unnecessarily
comments, 'The writer is able to recall the picturesque effect of
this uniform' (3. ii. i); or that at one point 'the writer has in the
main followed Thiers' (1. ii. ii); or when he informs the reader that

[5] W. R. Rutland, *Thomas Hardy: A Study of his Writings and their Background* (1938), 291.

[6] H. Newbolt, *My World as in My Time: Memoirs* (1932), 283.

[7] L. Abercrombie, *Thomas Hardy: A Critical Study* (1912), 185.

'The remains of the lonely hut . . . are still visible on the elevated spot referred to' (1. ii. v); or when he comments that the Gloucester Lodge 'is but little altered' (1. iv. i). The pointlessness of these asides becomes obvious when he provides a footnote for the rose allegedly given by Napoleon to Queen Louisa of Prussia, to the effect that the gift 'is not quite matter of certainty' (2. i. viii), and when he portrays Madame Metternich's rejection of Napoleon's offer of marriage with the qualification 'So Madame Metternich to her husband in reporting this interview. But who shall say!' (2. v. i). These obtrusive and irrelevant notes (and there are many) are of little interest except as a guide to Hardy's faithful reproduction of historically accurate detail. They hinder the progress of the narrative and interrupt 'that "willing suspension of disbelief" ' which Hardy had called for in his Preface. The poet's submission to prescribed authority is indicative of an anxiety for the trustworthiness of imagination and the effort to produce an historically sound record is such that imagination fulfils a lesser role than elsewhere in Hardy's works. As one critic expresses it, 'The more history has to say the less chance has imagination . . . to get a word in'.[8] In the thoroughness of its submission to historical precedent *The Dynasts* is, in a sense, an indictment of the faculty of imagination.

In an early scene in Part First, Pitt outlines an important distinction for *The Dynasts*:

> To use imagination as the ground
> Of chronicle, take myth and merry tale
> As texts for prophecy, is not my gift,
> Being but a person primed with simple fact,
> Unprinked by jewelled art.
>
> (1. i. iii)

Is *The Dynasts* a work of 'imagination' or 'chronicle', of 'myth' or 'prophecy', of 'simple fact' or 'jewelled art'? Pitt argues for an honest relationship between speaker, subject, and audience; he asks that communication should not simply draw attention to the orator and his art. His speech is an attack on Sheridan's empty rhetoric, a mere 'device | Of drollery . . . Mouthed and maintained without a thought or care | If germane to the theme, or not at all'. Sheridan's facility is exposed at the Pavilion at Brighton when the Prince of Wales finds that he cannot repeat the eloquence of an earlier speech: 'What shall I say to fit their feelings here? | Damn me, that other speech has stumped me quite!' (2. iv. vii). The

[8] J. C. Bailey, *The Continuity of Letters* (Oxford, 1923), 234.

Prince, too eager to satisfy his audience's demands, calls on Sheridan for an appropriate metaphor, and as he rehearses it, the following exchange takes place:

A NOBLE LORD (*aside to Sheridan*). Prinny's outpouring tastes suspiciously like your brew, Sheridan. I'll be damned if it is his own concoction. How d'ye sell it a gallon?
SHERIDAN. I don't deal that way nowadays. I give the recipe, and charge a duty on the gauging. It is more artistic, and saves trouble. (2. iv. viii).

The products of imagination are open to abuse, and Sheridan's rhetoric serves as a warning that eloquence is not necessarily a measure of sincerity. His corruption of that which is 'artistic' is reminiscent of Touchstone's argument in *As You Like It*, that 'the truest poetry is the most feigning' (III. iii. 17). Sheridan's cynical manipulation of imaginative devices confirms Hardy's endorsement of Pitt's belief in 'simple fact'.

The word 'fact', acting as a synonym for the empiricism of *The Dynasts*, occurs only a few times in the poem, and chiefly in close succession in Part First. Nelson greets Collingwood's interpretation of the French Armada's feint to the West Indies with 'So far your thoughtful and sagacious words | Have hit the facts' (1. ii. i). Collingwood's suspicions are entirely borne out by subsequent events. Similarly Decrès's report to Napoleon of Villeneuve's inaction is expressed by the words 'featless facts' which, the action confirms, are indisputable, incontrovertible, and undeniable. The other important use of 'facts' comes from Villeneuve himself, who faces numerous possible contingencies:

> Rather I'll stand, and face Napoleon's rage
> When he shall learn what mean the ambiguous lines
> That facts have forced from me.
>
> (1. ii. ii)

Villeneuve learns that 'facts', when crowded upon one another, demand selection and interpretation, and here originate the 'ambiguous lines' of his text. As one critic expresses it, 'those facts have to be interpreted, and interpretation is a conversional process by which facts become metaphors'.[9] Villeneuve's words are a lesson in exegesis, showing that empiricism alone is inadequate and that interpretation begins at an early stage, when 'facts' are to be reconciled and acted upon. The attendant ambiguity disrupts and subverts Pitt's notion of 'simple fact'. Hardy's poem cannot

---

[9] W. E. Buckler, *The Poetry of Thomas Hardy: A Study in Art and Ideas* (1983), 120.

but elucidate and interpret, yet it is the function of his historical material to hold imagination in check, to prevent it from designing 'ambiguous lines'. Of Pitt's speech on the death of Nelson, the Spirit of the Years says:

> For words were never winged with apter grace,
> Or blent with happier choice of time and place,
> To hold the imagination of this strenuous race.

(1. v. vi)

Pitt's speech captivates a nation, but his eloquence springs from the aptness of his historical subject, Nelson, and in so doing yokes imagination to 'fact'. In this sense the word 'hold' carries connotations of restraint, of not allowing free rein.

Imagination in *The Dynasts* is consistently characterized as dangerous and untrustworthy. During the scene at a London club (2. v. iv) there are three pointed references to the speciousness of composed words: Josephine 'had learnt her speech by heart, but that did not help her'; Pitt's speech in Parliament was 'a brilliant peroration' but 'it was all learnt beforehand, of course'; and the debate to which Pitt contributes is 'only like the Liturgy on a Sunday—known beforehand to all the congregation'. Each of these orations is disparaged because it is not spontaneous and sincere but contrived and premeditated for particular dramatic effect. This distrust of imaginative stratagems extends to the common people of Wessex who burn an effigy of Napoleon. A rustic has walked miles to witness the occasion, but he is distraught upon discovering that it is not Napoleon himself but a 'mommet' or representation, and he indignantly exclaims, 'Then there's no honesty left in Wessex folk nowadays at all!' (3. v. vi). The poem allows the rustic's complaint a good deal of credence— he had thought that the Emperor had been captured,

> and brought to Casterbridge Jail, the natural retreat of malefactors!—
> False deceivers—making me lose a quarter who can ill afford it; and all
> for nothing! (3. v. vi)

The distress caused by the substitution of an artistic likeness for the real thing is permitted, even here, a serious expression. The syntax of speech is used so that the accusation 'False deceivers' reflects on both 'malefactors' and the locals responsible for the jape, thus equating that which is evil and criminal with an innocuous practical joke. This strongly moral treatment brings to mind Auden's criticism of *Twelfth Night*, that it was written 'in a mood of puritanical aversion to all those pleasing illusions which men cherish and by which they lead their lives'.[10]

Hardy's anxiety for the honesty of language is articulated by King George III who, in his madness, is comforted by a doctor with the news of the English victory at Albuera:

> He says I have won a battle? But I thought
> I was a poor afflicted captive here,
> In darkness lingering out my lonely days
>
> .   .   .   .
>
> —And yet he says
> That I have won a battle! Oh God, curse, damn!
> When will the speech of the world accord with truth,
> And men's tongues roll sincerely!
>
> (2. vi. v)

The capacity of a mere figure of speech to inflict acute personal anguish parallels the hardship suffered by the rustic of Casterbridge, who discovers the consequences of artistic deception. These incidents share a profound and obsessive suspicion of casual affectation which is consistently portrayed throughout *The Dynasts*; Hardy confirms this interpretation with an anonymous gentleman's aside on King George's outburst: 'Faith, 'twould seem | As if the madman were the sanest here!'

The portrayal of imagination and the various shapes it finds in *The Dynasts* only rarely takes the form of an affirmation. Chiefly the poem recognizes the autonomy of language as a self-sufficient system, and it is this autonomy wherein the danger lies. This is a modern characteristic which Hardy shares with other Edwardian poets. The poetry of Edward Thomas can be seen as a series of negotiations with the intractable nature of language, his faith in names supplying a measure of security to an otherwise uncertain linguistic world. Similarly Henry Newbolt's totemic incantations evince an uneasy disparity between language and things, and Housman's verse is consistently undercut by the poet's awareness of its duplicity as a linguistic construction. For one critic the effect of this is to erode the '*sense of meaningfulness* associated with poetic rhetoric', and the ultimate consequence is to 'produce a mental stillness so complete that no voice disturbs it'.[11] This interpretation of what Thurley believes is a uniquely English style receives assent from the poetry of Hardy, Edward Thomas, and Housman, and at

---

[10] W. H. Auden, *The Dyer's Hand* (1963); paperback edn. (1975), 520.
[11] G. Thurley, *The Ironic Harvest: English Poetry in the Twentieth Century* (1974), 34.

times from Brooke and Newbolt too, each of whom creates a verse which rests on the absence of an identifiable speaking persona. This is the Thomas of 'Lights Out', the Brooke of 'Fragment', and the lyrical Newbolt who wrote 'Commemoration' and 'Messmates'. Thomas Hardy's shorter poems would require a separate analysis here, but a poem such as 'Afterwards' is notable for its ability to extinguish the personality of its author, the man 'who used to notice such things'. Hardy's poems often enact a drama of self-erasure in which the writer is 'dissolved to existlessness' ('The Voice').

The most demonstrable expression of imagination as an independent faculty in *The Dynasts* is the Will which creates all things, Its 'Eternal artistries in Circumstance | Whose patterns' are the source of every action and every thought in the human drama. The Will represents the ultimate creative freedom or poetic sublimity which, without vision or reason, spins out Its web indulgently, arbitrarily, and without constraint of any kind. The Will governs all human lives, 'moving them to Its inexplicable artistries' (3. i. i). But although It is supreme, It is not transcendent but 'Immanent':

> Thus do the mindless minions of the spell
> In mechanised enchantment sway and show
> A Will that wills above the will of each,
> Yet but the will of all conjunctively;
> A fabric of excitement, web of rage,
> That permeates as one stuff the weltering whole.

(3. i. v)

The Will is a creative principle which is not intelligent but unconscious, not omniscient but inherent, and the 'Phantom Intelligences' are merely the choric aspect of the Will. Like the voices of Hardy's poem 'The Subalterns' they are powerless to influence events. The cosmic scope of the Will is such that Its perspective casts even dynasts of Napoleon's power as 'Like meanest insects on obscurest leaves' (3. vii. ix). This is brutal in its diminution of the protagonist's stature, and it is part of the immense artistic challenge Hardy sets himself in *The Dynasts* to maintain this overview convincingly and yet conceive scenes of human life which by their urgency will affirm (albeit momentarily) the value and status of their subjects. It is in this achievement that the poetry of *The Dynasts* consists.

The Will of *The Dynasts* is not completely without purpose; the

last lines of the poem herald the sound of 'Consciousness the Will
informing, till It fashion all things fair!' (After Scene). This
apparently belated confidence in the power of evolutionary meliorism has been criticized on the grounds that Hardy added it as a
platitudinous afterthought, but, apart from the fact that such a
technique is not characteristic of Hardy, the idea of awakening
consciousness is consistently dramatized throughout the poem.
When Gevrillière approaches Fox with the plan to assassinate
Napoleon, he is rebuffed in the belief that,

> we see
> Good reason still to hope that broadening views,
> Politer wisdom, now is helping him
> To saner guidance of his arrogant car.
>
> (2. i. i)

This is not simply poor judgement. Fox astutely observes
the operation of consciousness in others, and the absence of
it in Gevrillière: 'The man's indifference to his own vague
doom | Beamed out as one exalted trait in him' (2. i. i). Fox's
conviction in the power of noble virtue leads him to believe that
Napoleon will be cured by benevolent forces. Fox rejects the
assassination plan in the considered opinion that Napoleon will, in
the end, see sense.

The evolving self-knowledge of the Will is reflected in that of the
human characters who are Its 'outshaping', and in this way *The
Dynasts* should be seen as a drama of consciousness. The self-
consciousness exhibited by some of the leading figures is a measure of
that imagination which they share with the Will, it is an expression,
in small, of the creative principle of Hardy's universe, one which
can never be complete but which constantly reaches towards
poetic sublimity. Nelson is distinguished by the broadness of his
perspective, and a measure of his intelligent perception is registered
in his analysis of the man who shoots him:

> He was, no doubt, a man
> Who in simplicity and sheer good faith
> Strove but to serve his country. Rest be to him!
> And may his wife, his friends, his little ones,
> If such he had, be tided through their loss,
> And soothed amid the sorrow brought by me.
>
> (1. v. iv)

This is both generous and shrewd; Nelson understands perfectly
the equivocal vicissitudes of war. He is not distracted by personal

antagonism towards his adversaries but sees the role of the individual within the larger scheme. This ability is an intimation of the
cosmic perspective of the Will. Before the battle at Trafalgar,
Nelson is worried by 'Strange warnings . . . That my effective
hours are shortening here'. Collingwood dismisses such fears and
expresses the confidence that the Admiral has a charmed life, but
Nelson will not be patronized:

> I have a feeling here of dying fires,
> A sense of strong and deep unworded censure,
> Which, compassing about my private life,
> Makes all my public service lustreless
> In my own eyes . . .
> He who is with himself dissatisfied,
> Though all the world find satisfaction in him,
> Is like a rainbow-coloured bird gone blind,
> That gives delight it shares not. Happiness?
> It's the philosopher's stone no alchemy
> Shall light on in this world I am weary of,

> > (I. ii. i)

Nelson's self-consciousness, enabling him in a detached manner to
distinguish between his private and public lives, acts as a momentary intimation of the ultimate detachment of the Will. His
creative impulse in coining the image of the 'rainbow-coloured
bird' is a sudden recognition of his own place as part of the Will's
anatomy, and therefore of his imminent death. In the drama of
consciousness, Nelson is endowed with a glimpse of the Prime
Mover at the moment It conceives his demise; Nelson dies fulfilling
his role with consummate efficiency: 'I'm satisfied. Thank God, I
have done my duty!' (I. v. iv).

The key to the theme of self-consciousness in *The Dynasts* lies
with the unlikely figure of hapless Villeneuve, whose first words
reveal his imaginative turn of mind: 'Do I this | Or do I that,
success, that loves to jilt | Her anxious wooer for some careless
blade | Will not reward me' (I. ii. ii). Following immediately upon
Nelson's speech about the 'rainbow-coloured bird' Villeneuve's
petulant despondency is intended as an illustration of that kind of
leader 'who is with himself dissatisfied' and who has consequently
lost his military vision. One critic of the poem remarks that 'Free
and effective action always becomes more difficult if a person
allows an image of himself to come between him and what has to
be done.'[12] Villeneuve suffers from a consuming self-concern

---

[12] R. Morrell, *Thomas Hardy: The Will and the Way* (Singapore, 1965), 78.

which inhibits direct and emphatic action; his intense preoccupation with how his behaviour might appear to others prevents him from executing his duty. In Morrell's words, 'Concern for this image of himself, in his own and others' eyes, destroyed his ability to act freely and effectively in the service of France.'[13] Villeneuve uses imagination as a way to self-assessment, but unchecked it turns to self-indulgence.

Villeneuve's self-consciousness does not only inhibit action, it contributes directly to his death. Hardy accompanies Villeneuve's suicide with two important images of self-awareness. As he paces up and down the room at Rennes 'He sees himself in the glass as he passes', and addressing himself in the mirror he exclaims:

> O happy lack, that I should have no child
> To come into my hideous heritage,
> And groan beneath the burden of my name!
>
> (1. v. vi)

Villeneuve projects his reputation through subsequent generations by means of the metaphor of progeny, and he rejoices that no image of himself, 'no child', shall keep alive his ignominy. That he addresses himself in such a direct way is indicative of the advanced and deluding self-consciousness from which he suffers. This view is given support by Decrès's opinion of Villeneuve, and by the manner of its expression:

> Yet no less
> Is it his drawback that he sees too far.
> And there are times, Sire, when a shorter sight
> Charms Fortune more.
>
> (1. iii. i)

Villeneuve's consciousness is, paradoxically, too wide; he is aware of so many contingencies that he becomes incapable of committing himself decisively to any single one. Decrès remarks that a limited vision is unclouded by irrelevant possibilities, and the metaphor of role-play is extended:

> A headstrong blindness to contingencies
> Carries the actor on, and serves him well
> In some nice issues clearer sight would mar.
> Such eyeless bravery Villeneuve has not;
> But, Sire, he is no coward.
>
> (1. iii. i)

---

[13] R. Morrell, *Thomas Hardy: The Will and the Way* (Singapore, 1965), 79.

Villeneuve's defect was not cowardice but fear of appearing a coward. The image of the actor is a good one; Villeneuve was too conscious of an audience to play his part effectively. He is self-conscious to the point of becoming incapacitated. In the context of the debate about imagination in *The Dynasts*, Villeneuve's morbid self-consciousness is a further warning against the dangerous excesses of creative indulgence. This is further evidence that it is the purpose of Hardy's style in the poem not to allow imagination free rein. His poem is composed of 'words . . . to hold the imagination'.

Napoleon too is obsessed with the idea of progeny, but he is unique among the players of the drama. When Maria Louisa is suffering the pains of childbirth, Napoleon appeals to the physician's sense of professional identity, and asks him to suspend his self-consciousness:

> Fancy that you are merely standing by
> A shop-wife's couch, say, in the Rue Saint
> Denis.

(2. vi. iii)

Napoleon has the key to effective and successful action, and at the point of emergency he knows better than to contemplate the wider ramifications; circumspection must be curtailed for urgent action to take place. Only the correct measure of consciousness facilitates action in accord with the consciousness of the Will. Napoleon's consciousness must be at a minimum for the forces of the Will to work through him. As one critic said of another prominent leader, 'Wellington does not take the successes personally. It is less important for him, the agent, to be upheld than for the impersonal principle to be borne out.'[14] This is true; in the larger scheme of things, individuals are irrelevant.

Napoleon is exceptional because he shows some understanding of his relationship to the Will, and because his leadership is egotistical: he serves not France but his own ambition. The Spirit of the Years says of Napoleon, 'He's of the few in Europe who discern | The working of the Will' (2. i. viii), and Napoleon confirms this by speaking in a metaphorical language redolent of the Spirits themselves: 'We are but thistle globes on Heaven's high gales | And whither blown, or when, or how or why | Can choose us not at all!' (2. ii. vi). English statesmen are the agents of their

---

[14] S. Dean, *Hardy's Poetic Vision in* The Dynasts: *The Diorama of a Dream* (Princeton, NJ, 1977), 130.

country, but Napoleon is the instrument of the Will, and, crucially, he is aware of this:

> The force I then felt move me moves me on
> Whether I will or no; and oftentimes
> Against my better mind . . . Why am I here?
> —By laws imposed on me inexorably!
> History makes use of me to weave her web.
>
> (3. i. i)

Yet despite his military successes, the progress of Napoleon's career in *The Dynasts* is constantly hampered by his increasingly exaggerated sense of his own importance. He never loses his awareness of the Will, but he comes to overestimate his individual value: 'Instead of *doing*, he becomes conscious of *being*'.[15] Napoleon's errors are the result of a growing obsession with his own image, and his self-indulgence, like that of Villeneuve, takes the form of contemplating immortality, securing a hold upon the time in which he cannot live:

> I must send down shoots to future time
> Who'll plant my standard and my story there.
>
> (2. v. i)

What elsewhere Napoleon calls 'The launching of a lineal progeny' (2. i. viii), and what Josephine describes as 'this craze for home-made manikins' (2. ii. vi), is a vanity the magnitude of which exceeds his real importance. Napoleon is doomed when his self-consciousness reaches a certain pitch, at the Tuileries: 'My thanks; though, gentlemen, upon my soul | You might have drawn the line at the Messiah. | But I excuse you' (2. vi. iii). Napoleon confesses the ludicrous inflation of his self-esteem as his end draws near: 'To shoulder Christ from out the topmost niche | In human fame, as once I fondly felt, | Was not for me' (3. vii. ix). The connectedness of the themes of self-consciousness and imagination is illustrated when Napoleon parades his troops before a portrait of his son:

> Yes, my soldier-sons
> Must gaze upon this son of mine own house
> In art's presentment!
>
> (3. i. iv)

---

[15] Morrell, *Thomas Hardy: The Will and the Way*, 79.

This incident, 'a pathetic egocentric lapse just before the whole tide of the disastrous Russian campaign turns against him',[16] identifies the fatally corrupting agency of imagination and the various forms it takes: the picture is 'a portrait of the young King of Rome playing at cup-and-ball, the ball being represented as the globe' (3. i. iv). Here, art and gratuitous self-indulgence become synonymous. Free of empirical constraints, imagination is dangerously uncontrolled.

Napoleon is a distinctively Edwardian hero, that is to say, not a hero at all in the traditional sense, but one who is neutered by the conditions of his existence like those other Edwardians, Axel Heyst and Mr Polly. This is not only because his every action is set within the cosmic context of the Will which by Its scope diminishes all human activity. As early as Part First, Act One, Hardy writes that 'The Emperor looks well, but is growing fat' (1. i. vii). This inauspicious adumbration comes surprisingly early in the campaign. Considering Hardy's over-zealous attention to historical detail elsewhere, *The Dynasts* is often curiously reluctant to concede to Napoleon the achievements which history proves undeniable. The poem undercuts the Emperor's progress with disparaging asides, such as that at Astorga which sketches 'his unhealthy face and stoutening figure' (2. iii. ii). It is a demeanour which later 'bears no resemblance to anything dignified or official' (2. iv. ii). At the banks of the Nieman on the march to Moscow, Napoleon 'shifts his weight from one puffed calf to the other' (3. i. i). The Emperor's physical degeneration is the counterpart to his spiritual descent, as if he is flawed by indulgence of both mind and body. Hardy is correct to characterize Napoleon with a tyrant's necessary ruthlessness; at the Satschan Lake he orders the massacre of two thousand fugitives 'with a vulpine smile' (1. vi. iv). It is curious how often French successes under Napoleon's direction are presented not from the victor's point of view but from that of the defeated, a perspective which hardly allows Napoleon his hour of glory. In his final soliloquy in the wood of Bossu, he says:

> Great men are meteors that consume themselves
> To light the earth. This is my burnt-out hour.

(3. vii. ix)

Napoleon is depicted throughout the course of *The Dynasts* as if in a 'burnt-out hour', and this is characteristic of the Edwardian period's loss of faith in heroic models.

[16] Ibid. 79.

The real hero of *The Dynasts* is not Napoleon but England. In his Preface Hardy complains of 'the slight regard paid to English influence and action throughout the struggle' by previous European writers, and Hardy's poem can be seen partly as an attempt to rectify what he felt was an imbalance in the presentation of the role of England in subduing the French dictator. The dual purpose of *The Dynasts* has been succinctly identified by C. A. Garrison: 'Hardy's reasons for dramatising these events are corrective: to right the wrong impression of England's part in the wars . . . and to destroy the concept of a heroic Napoleon.'[17] The poem begins in a sense with Napoleon's defeat, by England at Trafalgar (the culmination of the early action), and although Napoleon dreams throughout of conquering England, Hardy has already shown the hollowness of these rhetorical boasts. Napoleon's most cherished ambition can never be fulfilled. Hardy might have concurred with Pitt that England's role was to 'save Europe by her example' (1. v. v), or with the Prince Regent in the belief that Napoleon 'owes his fall to his ambition to humble England' (3. iv. viii). England occupies the central place by virtue of Napoleon's obsessive tirades against her, and by his assertion that 'The English only are my enemies' (1. iv. v). This historical distortion is instructive.

Unlike some Edwardian patriotic verse *The Dynasts* does not advocate war but enumerates 'the foul obscenities of carnage',[18] yet the poem shares with Newbolt, Austin, Watson, Masefield, and Edward Thomas in a major explication of the theme of England. *The Dynasts* is a presentation of history in a patriotic vein which might be usefully compared with Thackeray's *Vanity Fair* (1847–8), a work which leads to the same historical event without celebrating it. As an Edwardian patriotic poem *The Dynasts* is usefully considered in the context of contemporary efforts to give a single unified expression to the subject of 'England'.

The self-deception of Villeneuve and Napoleon is the result of an over-imaginative concern for their own reputations. The critic Geoffrey Thurley has commented on this form of creative activity:

Self-deception is certainly incompatible with the writing of poetry, but we need not necessarily conclude that the object of poetry is therefore self-knowledge. The idea of self-knowledge might be quite irrelevant to the aims and purposes of a great poet. He may quite simply, have something

---

[17] C. A. Garrison, *The Vast Venture: Hardy's Epic-Drama* The Dynasts (Salzburg, 1973), 86.

[18] H. C. Duffin, *Thomas Hardy: A Study of the Wessex Novels, the Poems, and* The Dynasts (3rd edn., Manchester, 1937), 265.

more important to communicate, something which needs to be able to take its own honesty and integrity for granted. To posit self-knowledge (as irony) as an end may ultimately be corrupting and stultifying.[19]

This is precisely what happens to Villeneuve and Napoleon; each of them is consumed by the desire to know only himself to the exclusion of the world in which he moves. In so doing he denies the governing perspective of the Will, and this proves fatal: self-knowledge cannot suffice as an end in itself. This is the origin of the distrust of imagination in *The Dynasts*; Hardy fears that it may be a way to self-delusion.

Such was the situation in the early twentieth century that Edwardian poetry was largely unable 'to take its own honesty and integrity for granted' but set out to discover and affirm its identity and voice. This verse is exploratory rather than didactic. The poetry of Hardy, Housman, and Edward Thomas is often concerned with the fragility of human personality and the elusiveness of that language which purports to express it. It is the severe impersonality of their treatment of the self, the formal externalization of Thomas's 'The Other', and the fictive indeterminacy of 'A' Shropshire 'Lad', which prevents their verse from falling into what Donald Davie has called 'various kinds of sterile self-congratulation'.[20]

This discourse of checks and balances, the tendency to attach the imagination to empirically verifiable fact, is a common Edwardian characteristic which can be traced in the syntax of Edward Thomas, in Henry Newbolt's use of historical material for poetry, and in Housman's anxiety about the corrupting potential of imagination. John Masefield's depiction of physical action serves a similar purpose in restricting the excesses of creative indulgence. Each of these poets submits their imaginative impulse to external phenomena and to the rational structures of argument. Geoffrey Thurley has argued that this is a distinctively English procedure: 'Leavis's emphases upon self-knowledge, humility, modesty and integrity *in fact* have had the effect of limiting the scope of the poetic imagination.'[21]

These epithets apply almost perfectly to the poetry of Edward Thomas, as they might to Philip Larkin. A more recent critic has defended this kind of verse as 'the poetry of equipoise'[22] and

---

[19] Thurley, *The Ironic Harvest*, 25.
[20] D. Davie, 'A Voice from the Fifties', *Times Literary Supplement* (8 Aug. 1975), 899.
[21] Thurley, *The Ironic Harvest*, 25.
[22] G. Harvey, *The Romantic Tradition in Modern English Poetry: Rhetoric and Experience* (1986), 8.

identified Wordsworth, Hardy, Betjeman, and Larkin as its chief exponents. But does *The Dynasts*, in its epic scope, rise above the limiting strictures of empiricism? Does the poem express a faith in imagination sufficient to allow it access to the realm of great poetry?

Imagination is not possessed exclusively by the commanding figures of *The Dynasts*, the creative leap made possible by the use of a metaphor is accessible to all, to the servant for example, who asks, 'Dost know what a metaphor is, comrade? I brim with them at this historic time!' Upon receiving an imperfect reply, he continues:

Your imagination will be your ruin some day, my man! It happens to be a weapon of wisdom used by me. My metaphor is one may'st have met with on the rare times when th'hast been in good society. Here it is: The storm which roots the pine spares the p-s-b-d . Now do ye see? (3. iv. iii)[23]

The distinction of this kind of imaginative activity is that it enables the speaker to understand the larger scheme of things directly; he learns something not just about himself but about the nature of the world in which he lives. Imagination is not always a route simply to self-knowledge but to the servant's broader 'wisdom'. This amounts to a contradiction of Hynes's argument that 'Metaphor is a mode of knowing, and since man cannot know, he can speak only in flat, discursive, unmetaphorical language'.[24] Even the anonymous citizens of Vienna are capable of highly developed metaphorical expression:

> Ere passing down the Ring, the Archduke paused
> And gave the soldiers speech, enkindling them
> As sunrise a confronting throng of panes
> That glaze a many-windowed east façade:
> Hot volunteers vamp in from vill and plain.
>
> (2. iii. v)

This extended metaphor is proof that the imagination can operate in a liberating fashion in *The Dynasts*, enabling even the lesser figures to make creative connections between different kinds of experience and so take a small step towards the unifying perspective of the Will. Imagination here is not purely self-reflexive (serving to develop simply the individual's sense of personal identity), and it is not disablingly internalized. The

[23] The 'p-s-b-d' is a piss-a-bed, a folk name for the dandelion.
[24] S. Hynes, *The Pattern of Hardy's Poetry* (Chapel Hill, NC, 1961), 166.

metaphor is evidence of a genuinely expanding consciousness, and since imagination is not quantitative, this constitutes a leap of faith, and in the context of *The Dynasts*, poetic faith. Other similar imaginative connections are made by the gentleman who says of the subduing of Napoleon, 'Yet this man is a volcano | And proven 'tis, by God, volcanoes choked | Have ere now turned to earthquakes!' (1. i. v); by Castlereagh who says, 'I know no more what villainy's afoot | Or virtue either, than an anchoret | Who mortifies the flesh in some lone cave' (2. iv. vii); by Villeneuve's officer who says of the English fleet, 'Their overcrowded sails | Bulge like blown bladders in a tripeman's shop | The market-morning after slaughterday!' (1. v. i); and by Napoleon, who describes 'toadstools like the putrid lungs of men' (1. iv. v). There are very few uses of metaphor in *The Dynasts* and most, but not all, are attributed to the leaders who succeed by virtue of their imagination.

The theme of self-consciousness in *The Dynasts* is reflected by the poem's self-consciousness of artistic form. *The Dynasts* is notable for the dispersal of its authorial voice through the medium of stage directions, dumb shows, and various Spirit voices. Rather than a central governing omniscient persona, the poem has a variety of commenting phantoms, and their unresolved debate constitutes the second level of the drama. Critics have argued that the Spirits Sinister and Ironic represent the voice of Hardy, simply because they express a consistently ironic view.[25] But other remarks are commensurate with the Hardy of the Wessex novels: 'all joy is but sorrow waived awhile' (2. ii. vi); 'Nature's a dial whose shade no hand puts back' (2. ii. vi). These comments are uttered by Josephine and Napoleon respectively. At the Commons, Pitt warns, 'Times are they fraught with peril, trouble, gloom | We have to mark their lourings, and to face them' (1. i. iii). This might be Hardy also, the Hardy of 'In Tenebris II': 'if way to the Better there be, it exacts a full look at the Worst'. Likewise Moore's stoicism might be claimed as the true expression of the author's point of view in *The Dynasts*.[26] The search for a single authorial persuasion in *The Dynasts* is a fruitless one; it is a special formal

[25] 'It is the Spirit Ironic who attacks war as absurd, and so speaks for Hardy on this point'. J. O. Bailey, *Thomas Hardy and the Cosmic Mind: A New Reading of* The Dynasts (Chapel Hill, NC, 1956), 71.

[26] 'Moore's success . . . reminds us of the type of action to which Hardy gives, perhaps, final emphasis'. Morrell, *Thomas Hardy: The Will and the Way*, 82. But W. F. Wright believes that 'Villeneuve is in philosophic outlook most like the poet himself', W. F. Wright, *The Shaping of* The Dynasts: *A Study in Thomas Hardy* (Lincoln, Nebr., 1967), 170.

characteristic of the poem that there is none, and this is not surprising given that the poem is a 'drama'. This is to concur with Harold Orel, who writes that 'We cannot say for a certainty which speeches of the Spirits in *The Dynasts* represent Hardy's personal doctrine'.[27] More than any other of Hardy's works, *The Dynasts* is at pains to disguise authorial intention, as well it might, coming after the *Tess* and *Jude* débâcles. The debate between the Spirit of the Pities and the Spirits Sinister and Ironic is the central interpretative dialogue, but it is one which the author restrains from definitively resolving. This is the reason for the poem's impression of being remote and inaccessible, the reader is given no clear and reliable directions.

However, this is not to say that there is no point of view in *The Dynasts*; a strong controlling influence is exercised by the poem's 'dumb shows' which place the scenes before the reader's attention in a distinctive manner: 'A moving stratum of summer cloud beneath the point of view covers up the spectacle like an awning' (2. ii. v). The guidance of the reader's vision by means of precise optical arrangements is a highly developed technique, used to determine what is seen and how: 'The eye of the spectator rakes the road from the interior of a cellar' (2. iii. i). This mode of authorial direction is oblique, but nevertheless governs the arrangement of the reader's perspective: 'The town, harbour, and hills at the back are viewed from an aerial point to the north' (2. ii. iii). This visual positioning is not static but free-moving, and the mobility thus afforded is the real omniscience of the poem. It is embodied by the ranging 'eye' which dictates a series of optical movements:

> The north horizon at the back of the bird's-eye prospect is the high ground stretching from the Bisamberg on the left to the plateau of Wagram on the right. In front of these elevations spreads the wide plain of the Marchfeld . . . In the foreground the Danube crosses the scene . . . immediately under the eye, is the Lobau . . . On this island can be discerned . . . Lifting our eyes to discover . . . we perceive . . . A species of simmer which pervades the living spectacle. (2. iv. ii)

This intensely visual technique suggests a stylistic continuity between *The Dynasts* and Hardy's novels, 'the recurrent motif of spying in his fiction',[28] but more importantly, in its physical detachment it parallels the Spirits' mode of perceiving. The

---

[27] Orel, *Thomas Hardy's Epic-Drama: A Study of* The Dynasts, 24–5.
[28] J. H. Miller, *Thomas Hardy: Distance and Desire* (1970), 7.

powerlessness of the Spirits to influence the course of events corresponds to the formal restraint from authorial speech, and despite both provinces of interpretation, the drama proceeds regardless. Detachment endows a clear-sighted view of the whole picture, but it deprives the beholder of the power to act. This is true in Hardy of both physical detachment, removed from the point of action, and of temporal detachment, represented by powerless hindsight.

As the young Maria Louisa and her ladies leave Vienna by coach, 'they glance at the moist spring scenes which pass without in a perspective distorted by the rain-drops that slide down the panes, and by the blurring effect of the travellers' breathings' (2. iv. i). Louisa's perspective is caught up in the human interpretative processes of perception and in the very qualities of the scene she views. Although she is in a position to take action, she lacks the clear-sightedness which facilitates action in accordance with the Will. Her vision is clouded, literally, by the very fact that she is human; Louisa's perspective cannot be disentangled from the obscuring effect of 'the travellers' breathings'. The imperfection of the young ladies' view has something in common with that of the artist of Hardy's lyric 'The Figure in the Scene' who sketches in the rain:

> But I kept on, despite the drifting wet
>   That fell and stained
> My draught, leaving for curious quizzings yet
>   The blots engrained.

The way in which artistic representations are marred, or their 'perspective distorted', by the inherent imperfections of the scene they depict, contributes (paradoxically) to their fidelity. Hardy's visual style includes a provision to the effect that each is conditioned by the mode or the circumstances of perception. In other words, the poem makes an important allowance for human frailty in the act of seeing, 'both what they half create | And what perceive' (Wordsworth's 'Tintern Abbey').

The formal structure of *The Dynasts* alternates between the two perspectives illustrated above: one has the power of clear vision but no ability to act, and the other has the power to take action but is unsighted. The achievement of the poem is the convincingly sustained presentation of both views despite one another; it represents an opposition between the impersonal process of historical evolution and the human suffering of which

that process is composed. John Bayley has expressed the belief
that the two spheres are 'isolated from each other, so that each can
be enjoyed and reflected on in a manner appropriate to its own
nature',[29] but I would argue that it is in the very struggle between
the divergent positions that the poetry of *The Dynasts* consists. At
the bridge of the Beresina for example, where thousands of French
are drowned in the freezing water, the poem focuses not upon the
vast Grand Army's disintegration, but on the attendant women
and their final gestures of desperation:

Then women are seen in the waterflow—limply bearing their infants
between wizened white arms stretching above; Yea, motherhood, sheerly
sublime in her last despairing, and lighting her darkest declension with
limitless love. (3. i. x)

The sight of women carrying their children at arm's length above
the consuming waters is an appallingly vivid image of human
suffering and the struggle with adversity, one which acquires its
significance partly by its opposition to the cosmic drama. The
scene is quickly counterpointed by an expression of nature's
eternal endurance: 'darkness mantles all, nothing continuing but
the purl of the river and the clickings of floating ice' (3. i. x). Once
the desecration is over, the waters progress unperturbed.

The best example of this technique is the discovery by the
Russians of the remnants of Napoleon's Grand Army:

> They all sit
> As they were living still, but stiff as horns;
> And even the colour has not left their cheeks,
> Whereon the tears remain in strings of ice.—
> It was a marvel they were not consumed:
> Their clothes are cindered by the fire in front,
> While at their back the frost has caked them hard.
>
> (3. i. xi)

This macabre group of corpses, perished in extremities of heat and
cold, provides a pictorial set piece which momentarily arrests the
conduct of narrative and history and defies the perspective of the
Will, whose interpolations argue that these scenes are without
importance. Such portraits of human suffering are static close-ups
set in opposition to the ranging omniscient movements elsewhere;
this technique exchanges the panoramic sweep for an intimate
focus which can accommodate the smallest of details, contrary to

---

[29] J. Bayley, *An Essay on Hardy* (Cambridge, 1978), 229.

imposing spectral directions. Like the poems of Wilfred Owen, these cinematic 'stills' slow down the progress of events as a means of exercising a degree of control over them, and to concentrate the visual attention with an intensity which evokes compassion. Within the context of *The Dynasts* these are moments of epiphany, what Edward Thomas called 'moments of everlastingness', which evince an abiding faith in human character, and in the force of poetry to convey them.

A greater artistic success than C. M. Doughty's *The Dawn In Britain* (1906) or John Davidson's *Testaments* (1901–8), *The Dynasts* is the major poetic work of the Edwardian period, giving shape and focus to the character of English pre-war verse. For Abercrombie writing in 1912, *The Dynasts* 'attains to something that the age of Tennyson and Browning quite failed to effect',[30] and it is the distinctively modern impetus of the poem which separates it from its Victorian predecessors and aligns it with the twentieth-century verse of Hardy's contemporaries.

---

[30] Abercrombie, *Thomas Hardy: A Critical Study*, 188.

4

A. E. Housman and the 'perils of cheat and charmer'

THE problems of evaluating the poetry of A. E. Housman begin with chronology; born in 1859, he published only two collections of verse in his lifetime, *A Shropshire Lad* (1896) and *Last Poems* (1922), and he died in 1936. Most of *A Shropshire Lad* dates from 1895, *Last Poems* was written predominantly during the period 1895–1910, and the poems later collected from private notebooks by Housman's brother Laurence range across the poet's writing life. The study of Housman thus encompasses the years which saw the publication of *The Bad Child's Book of Beasts* by Hilaire Belloc, and *The Waste Land*. Chronology is made more problematical by the discovery that, as with Hardy, early poems occur in later publications. Also like Hardy, and another contemporary, Edward Thomas, Housman was already an accomplished prose writer when he published his first poems; he came to poetry with a well-practised voice which shows little trace of technical development. Critical problems are aggravated by the difficulty of locating Housman within a recognized literary context. To what period or movement does he belong? Housman declined Marsh's invitation to be included in *Georgian Poetry 1911–1912*, excusing himself on the grounds that 'I do not really belong to your "new era"; and none even of my few unpublished poems have been written within the last two years.'[1] But neither did Housman regard himself as a poet of the 1890s; he refused to be included in A. J. A. Symons's *A Book of Nineties Verse* (1928).

An obvious distinction between Housman and his contemporaries is his professional career. It was unusual in the late Victorian and Edwardian period (though common later in the twentieth century) for poets to be scholars, although Housman had an important precursor in Gray. It has been said of Housman that 'he saw himself as a professional scholar who occasionally strayed into writing English verse'.[2] As a classicist Housman's

---

[1] *The Letters of A. E. Housman*, ed. H. Maas (1971), 125.
[2] N. Page, *A. E. Housman: A Critical Biography* (1983), 162.

special province was the fallibility of written documents; his critical essays are expositions of literary corruption, of interpretation and exegesis, and of the exercise of intelligent judgement in dealing with language as an autonomous system. These intellectual qualities are combined with a personal reticence which became legendary.[3] Given Housman's intimacy with linguistic corruption and his craving for textual accuracy, it is perhaps surprising that he wrote poetry at all.

While it has been argued that Housman conforms decisively to the spirit of the 1890s in his 'fastidiousness of expression . . . the choice of minor poetic forms and the note of weary disillusionment',[4] this chapter tries to show that Housman's reluctance to commit himself to the jeopardy of self-expression separates him from his Victorian predecessors and places him as a distinctively modern poet. Housman wrote during the present century and published his *Last Poems* in 1922; his career belongs to the twentieth century in a way which that of Arthur Symons, for example, who lived and wrote until 1945, does not.

In *A Shropshire Lad* LI 'Loitering with a vacant eye', the poet encounters a Greek statue at a time when he is seeking consolation and encouragement 'brooding on my heavy ill', a time which is especially propitious for discovering wisdom, and in an environment conducive to philosophical reflection. The potential receptivity of the poet is signalled by the readiness of his 'vacant eye' as he peruses the models of endurance. The central event of the poem, the revelation of the wisdom of the ancients, is framed by the poet's interpretative response in the form of 'I thought the look would say' and 'So I thought his look would say', which introduces a provisional or conditional note into the discovery. The emphasis on the poet's imaginative processes reveals that in a sense the words of the statue are strictly the poet's own invention. The framing technique serves to qualify the value of the lesson thus imparted.

The placing of the poem's moral guidance within a precise suppositious construction tends to support an interpretation of the last lines as ironic:

> And I stept out in flesh and bone
> Manful like the man of stone.

[3] See for example W. H. Auden's 'A. E. Housman' who 'Kept tears like dirty postcards in a drawer'.
[4] I. Scott-Kilvert, *A. E. Housman*, Writers and their Work, 69 (1955), 25.

Here stoicism reaches insensibility; the transference of qualities cannot succeed without the human character becoming inanimate; he hopes to give to a living anatomy the virtues of a dead one. This reinforces the observation that the statue has no real psychological resilience to impart because it is completely devoid of rational perception. The drama of emotional recovery takes place only within the mind of the poet himself. That there can be no genuine exchange is illustrated by the opposition of qualities in the final couplet: that which is stone-like cannot be human. As with the 'stone | To trouble the living stream' of Yeats's 'Easter 1916', the poet can only attain the status of immortality by relinquishing his living human personality. Here it might be noted that the statue's advice ''tis not for long' is manifestly inadequate in a human context, again undermining the portentous revelation of the poem. These points each detract from the poem's apparent sense of psychological resolution.

The statue is itself a work of art, perhaps commissioned likewise to mitigate grief or other adversity, and this gives the poem a certain self-reflexive quality as regards the workings of imagination. In a sense the poet is duped by his own creative transposition, a deception which is expressed by the statue's complaint:

> I too survey that endless line
> Of men whose thoughts are not as mine.

Caution must be exercised in taking comfort from works of art. Each spectator finds the moral which he seeks, and although prompted by art, that consolation remains purely individual, even liable to mislead.

The same relationship between stoic philosophy and physical action is the source of *Last Poems* II 'As I gird on for fighting' in which the combatant braces himself for battle with austere impassivity: 'What evil luck soever | For me remains in store, | 'Tis sure much finer fellows | Have fared much worse before'. The exaggerated detachment of this attitude is due to the speaker's attainment of a very broad philosophical perspective, one which encompasses all those who have previously suffered 'the round world over'. Such a perspective encourages a belief in determinism and diminishes the sense of the individual's free will:

> So here are things to think on
> That ought to make me brave,
> As I strap on for fighting
> My sword that will not save.

As with the previous poem the provisional tense (in the form of 'ought') operates to qualify the value of discovered wisdom, while 'make me brave' rhyming with 'will not save' undermines the earlier impression of psychological resilience. In the context of the final line 'My sword that will not save' the poem's stoicism is irrelevant. This resignation is contrary to the speaker's desperately marshalled resolution. As with the earlier poem, action and thought are at odds, and in the context of the human adversity which these poems dramatize, the value of stoic philosophy is severely compromised. The exalted expression of stoicism in the first three stanzas of 'As I gird on for fighting' is rebutted, as if to confirm philosophy's inadequacy in the face of immediate action. The speaker is not wholly convinced, perhaps, by his own rhetoric. The theme is developed by *A Shropshire Lad* XXX, 'Others, I am not the first', in which the speaker concurs, 'More than I, if truth were told | Have stood and sweated hot and cold'. Here, enduring restlessness after death qualifies the philosophical perspective which provided fortitude and courage during life:

> But from my grave across my brow
> Plays no wind of healing now,
> And fire and ice within me fight
> Beneath the suffocating night.

Stoicism is proven misfounded and anxiety pursues this lad to his grave. That which is sufficient to sustain endurance during life may be inadequate in a more cosmic context, and death is not necessarily a complete release from quotidian sufferings. The linguistic arguments are restricted in their value for they sustain faith only while speech is available. Each of these poems manipulate forms of rhetoric which have only limited application; their practical value is confined to a particular occasion, which may have no use beyond the immediate context. What might be called the rhetoric of stoicism is subverted and debunked, turning the drama into something disturbing and suspicious.

David Daiches has drawn attention to Housman's 'mood of stoicism, of heroic endurance for its own sake' and commented that 'the value lies in endurance rather than any moral end that is to be attained by that endurance'.[5] This is true, but only if Housman's presentation of stoicism is accepted at face value and the sincerity of his exhortations is taken for granted. The equivocal style of his poetry, its dissembling tendency, suggests something

[5] D. Daiches, *Some Late Victorian Attitudes* (1969), 11.

more subtle. Housman's dramatization of the act of speech implies
an impersonal handling of the rhetoric of stoicism which is more
detached and more malleable than Daiches gives it credit for. The
characteristic technique of Housman's verse is to frame acts of
speech within a context which qualifies or undermines them. Once
he is recognized as a mischievous purveyor of dramatic utterances
which are not necessarily his own, Housman's position becomes
more mercurial and more flexible than has hitherto been allowed.

The quintessential expression of Housman's stoicism is the
poem 'Shot? so quick, so clean an ending?' (*A Shropshire Lad*
XLIV), which takes Victorian manliness to its logical conclusion
by endorsing the strength of character required to 'Put the pistol to
your head'. This poem seems unequivocal in its advocation of
suicide:

> Shot? so quick, so clean an ending?
> Oh that was right, lad, that was brave:
> Yours was not an ill for mending,
> 'Twas best to take it to the grave.

As with the previous poems, there is a particular urgency in the
anticipation of death, a relish at the prospect of extinction which
takes the dramatic form of wilful destructiveness. Death is seized
upon as a necessary and even worthy expedient, and the poem's
stoicism lies in the wilfulness and self-consciousness of its approbation: 'Oh lad, you died as fits a man.'

More recently it has been discovered that the poem is in fact a
tribute to a Woolwich cadet who committed suicide in August
1895.[6] A newspaper cutting establishes the source of Housman's
inspiration to be the text of his suicide note, which was printed in
full in the *Malvern News*. Although it is not entirely true that 'Parts
of that poem come close to paraphrasing the boy's letter'[7] (can
a poem 'paraphrase' anything?), there are undoubtedly close
parallels between the two written documents. The Woolwich
cadet's words 'better than a long series of sorrows and disgraces'
are similar to Housman's 'After long disgrace and scorn'; the
suicide's sense of relief that 'I have not morally injured . . . anyone
else', is similar to Housman's 'You would not live to wrong your
brothers'; and the poem's sense of hopelessness is to be found in

---

[6] J. M. Nosworthy, 'A. E. Housman and the Woolwich Cadet', *Notes and Queries*, 17/
9 (Sept. 1970), 351–3. All of the following quotations from the suicide note are taken
from this article.

[7] Page, *A. E. Housman: A Critical Biography*, 84.

the dead man's complaint that 'There is only one thing in this world which would make me thoroughly happy; that one thing, I have no earthly hope of attaining.' The sentiments of both suicide note and poem are demonstrably the same, and they reveal certain linguistic parallels. Housman might have been attracted by the articulate eloquence of such a personal piece of writing.

The boy's suicide in August 1895 followed closely after the trial and imprisonment of Oscar Wilde in May 1895 which made current the issue of homosexuality in late Victorian England. Although it is conceded that 'Housman (perhaps wrongly) attributed the depression to a recognition of irresistible homosexual tendencies',[8] the poem may nevertheless be read as a surreptitious formal sanction of something which the poet could not acknowledge explicitly:

> Now to your grave shall friend and stranger
>   With ruth and some with envy come:
> Undishonoured, clear of danger,
>   Clean of guilt, pass hence and home.

The poet's lines, if they are fitting, act as a testament to the dead man's courage; Housman offers his poetic efforts as a monument to that anxiety and suffering which would not otherwise receive tribute. The poem enshrines the cause of those troubles: what Housman and the Woolwich cadet share is a participation in subterfuge as well as a sense of moral transgression. The urgency of 'And here, man, here's the wreath I've made', testifies to the special value of this particular artistic endeavour. The poet uses his art not as a means of self-expression, but as a vehicle for impulses which must otherwise remain hidden. Further, the young man is removed from sexual temptation, 'clear of danger', by death, while at the same time becoming a 'martyr' and therefore a suitable subject for the purposes of poetry. If such a central tenet as Housman's stoicism is to be treated with the circumspection which these observations encourage, then the way is open for a different approach to his poetry, one which examines the text as an autonomous written document, liable to the corruption and duplicity which is the inheritance of the poet's medium, language.

The difficulties of interpretation play a special role in the poem 'Along the field as we came by' (*A Shropshire Lad* XXVI), in which the poet is initially capable of deciphering the message told in the trees because it is spoken especially for his benefit. The aspens say:

[8] Nosworthy, 'A. E. Housman and the Woolwich Cadet', 352.

> 'And time shall put them both to bed,
> But she will lie with earth above,
> And he beside another love.'

The prophecy proves true, but then the discourse is broken and the poet can no longer interpret the sound: 'And I spell nothing in their stir, | But now perhaps they speak to her.' Like the advice of the Grecian statue, the words of the aspens find a receptive audience because, it is implied, there is a degree of complicity in the act of imaginative interpretation. The poet's skill to unscramble the hidden significance might be recognized as a gesture towards the desired outcome. If the fate he envisages is borne out, then perhaps it was premeditated? The report of the trees returns to mere noise, 'rainy-sounding silver leaves', once the prophecy is realized, and there is cause for anxiety in the poet's foreboding incomprehension:

> And I spell nothing in their stir,
> But now perhaps they speak to her,
> And plain for her to understand
> They talk about a time at hand
> When I shall sleep with clover clad,
> And she beside another lad.

The failure of imagination is potentially fatal, as it proved for the lover of the poem's first stanza. Imminent death attends those who lose the power to scan their environment for intimations of the future. Edward Thomas might have been aware of this poem when he wrote 'Aspens', in which those trees also have the special ability to speak to those who are receptive: 'Aspens must shake their leaves and men may hear | But need not listen, more than to my rhymes.' In the diminished poetic rhetoric of the Edwardians, the writer's claim on the attention of his readers is reduced to a whisper.

The importance of the act of interpretation in the drama of Housman's poem suggests a minute self-consciousness in the handling of language and warrants a special vigilance. It is instructive to compare 'The lads in their hundreds to Ludlow come in for the fair' (*A Shropshire Lad* XXIII), which also expresses regret at the loss of imaginative foresight:

> I wish one could know them, I wish there were tokens to tell,
>   The fortunate fellows that now you can never discern;
> And then one could talk with them friendly and wish them farewell
>   And watch them depart on the way that they will not return.

But the fates of the country characters are not to be known, for the 'tokens' which elude the poet are those of imagination which elsewhere enable Housman to create encounters with the people of his artistic world. Here he discovers 'there's nothing to scan' and that the future of the individual lad is 'not to be told'. Recognition of this loss is made tantalizing and poignant because it is accompanied by a moment of physical contact, 'brushing your elbow', which does not compensate for a fuller embrace. The poem keeps its distance from the subject, refraining from invention but creating from this apparent failure a kind of fidelity which respects the 'otherness' of potential subjects for poetry. Communication is similarly disabled in the poem's companion piece, *A Shropshire Lad* XXII: 'What thoughts at heart have you and I | We cannot stop to tell.'

The same moment of creation is courted by 'From far, from eve and morning' (*A Shropshire Lad* XXXII) and with a similarly momentary poignance. Here the act of communication is synonymous with birth and death:

> Now—for a breath I tarry
>   Nor yet disperse apart—
> Take my hand quick and tell me,
>   What have you in your heart.

The economy of these lines is remarkable, and they convey a detailed and complex emotional appeal. The word 'breath' for example here stands as a metonym for life and as a metaphor for speech, uniting existence and expression as a single act. The physical embrace of 'take my hand' is an analogue to the emotional exchange of what is 'in your heart', and the presence of the word 'quick' not in its adverbial form but suggesting heightened sensitivity, unobtrusively emphasizes the special value of this encounter. The theme of communication is extended by the appeal to 'tell me', recalling the 'tokens to tell' above, thus placing utterance and revelation at the centre of the dramatic moment. This terse lyric is a highly charged entreaty to personal confession, perhaps made more attractive by the transience of the anonymous confessor. To unburden secrets to one such as this is perhaps to earn absolution: 'Speak now, and I will answer.'

The importance of the poem is that it represents a moment of intimacy with a stranger which is also a verbal or linguistic surrender; the phantom's plea to 'tell me' provides the opportunity for confessional release. *More Poems* XXXI, 'Because I liked you better | Than suits a man to say', develops the idea of personal utterance by dramatizing the value of reticence and fidelity, both personal and linguistic. The pressure of social propriety and decorum bears down upon this speaker who is inhibited by the attention of 'the world' and whose epithets 'stiff and dry' suggest the sterile rigidity of social convention. But despite these verbal signals, the poem calls attention to its linguistic coyness:

> If here, where clover whitens
>   The dead man's knoll, you pass,
> And no tall flower to meet you
>   Starts in the trefoiled grass,
>
> Halt by the headstone naming
>   The heart no longer stirred,
> And say the lad that loved you
>   Was one that kept his word.

The poem refuses to name or reveal, a procedure which preserves loyalty to the beloved at the expense of self-expression. This is an unorthodox method for a poem: it is a drama which tells of not telling. The incongruity of this strategy is matched by that of the impulse which gave rise to the poem, an inverse relationship between feeling and expression: 'Because I liked you better | Than suits a man to say.' Feeling is so strong that expression has to be curtailed. This is certainly a style which refutes the idea of poetry as the spontaneous overflow of powerful emotion. The poet of Housman's lines takes 'his word' to the grave and his life's passion passes without having been articulated. The poem is framed by two important utterances, the admission of love which discomfited the beloved in the first place, and the words on the poet's gravestone 'naming the heart no longer stirred'. Neither of these vital tokens of communication are made available by the poem; the poet here 'was one that kept his word'.

There is a sense in which the faithfulness of this poem parallels that of the Woolwich cadet, who kept his troubles to himself and at his death expressed relief that he had not 'morally injured (or "offended" as it is called in the Bible) anyone else'. Each of these poems is intensely preoccupied with the act of speech, and the verb 'to tell' occupies a central position in all of them. A heightened sensitivity is attached to the acts of utterance they portray, and so by analogy to the artistic utterance of the poet. In this sense these poems could be seen as dramatic deliberations about the writer's art and the degree of self-revelation to which it commits him.

Housman's poetry is like that of Edward Thomas whose dramatic encounters with the fragile and elusive world of language are similarly involved with their own limitations. Thomas's poetry sometimes expresses the desire not to be known, a paradox which Housman also entertains:

> Ask me no more, for fear I should reply;
>   Others have held their tongues, and so can I;
> Hundreds have died, and told no tale before:
>   Ask me no more, for fear I should reply—

This poem, unpublished in Housman's lifetime, pleads that the poet may be allowed to withold his lyrical eloquence, and the lines are composed from his intense feeling of reticence: the message is literally unspeakable. Elsewhere Housman offers his verse as an anodyne for future ills, 'But take it: if the smack is sour, | The better for the embittered hour' (*A Shropshire Lad* LXII) whereas the present poem protests that its import is overburdening for both speaker and listener. Nevertheless, as Housman must have realized, poetry demands that something be conveyed:

> How one was true and one was clean of stain
>   And one was braver than the heavens are high,
> And one was fond of me: and all are slain.
>   Ask me no more, for fear I should reply.

This brief moment of emotional release provides only limited relief; reticence not self-expression is the poem's creative source. Housman's affinity with Thomas is a close one, for both writers express a fear of self-exposure and engage themselves in linguistic strategies whose purpose is sometimes to restrict personal self-disclosure. A further analogue for Housman is the case of Oscar Wilde, of whose work Richard Ellmann has written, 'exposure or usually near-exposure is always the focal point in Wilde's plays'.[9] The predicament is inevitably more anxious for Housman because, as Norman Page points out, 'he is writing after, not before, the Wilde *débâcle*'.[10]

Each of the poems considered so far gives a special value to the activity of telling; they exhibit a marked reluctance to disclose or inform. The verb 'to tell' often occurs in the sense of 'to divulge or reveal' and perhaps, given the available range of words for utterance or speech, the recurrence of this verb is intended to carry

[9] R. Ellmann, 'Romantic Pantomime in Oscar Wilde', *Partisan Review*, 30 (1963), 352.
[10] Page, *A. E. Housman: A Critical Biography*, 187.

associations with 'telling on' or informing in the pejorative sense. The poem 'Ask me no more, for fear I should reply' only grudgingly yields its significance, and a similar appeal to withhold speech characterizes 'Tell me not here, it needs not saying' (*Last Poems* XL), where the verb 'to tell' is accompanied by two emphatic negatives. As with 'Because I liked you better | Than suits a man to say', this poem equates personal and linguistic fidelity in a way which attaches a special importance to the act of speech, and in a way which transforms the present poem into something exceptional. Although the poem manifestly reveals its emotional origin, there is a 'peculiar force derived from casting the poem in the form of a monologue from an old and cast-off lover to the young man who has succeeded him',[11] that is to say, the lover's complaint is loaded with the drama of its addressee's unspoken response. As with the previous poems , the dramatic situation gives a unique value to the act of speech itself, to the plea to 'Tell me not here'. The word 'here' in the context of Housman's verse comes to signify the unfolding event of the poem. The opening line is an announcement of imminent drama: it will be composed of the old lover's sad reminiscences, not from the new lover's sense of discovery. This situation endows the poem with its special tonal force:

> Possess, as I possessed a season,
>   The countries I resign,
> Where over elmy plains the highway
>   Would mount the hills and shine,
> And full of shade the pillared forest
>   Would murmur and be mine.

The use of the word 'season' is appropriate to describe a mistress who is systematically identified with Nature. Self-consciousness operates throughout the poem to bring together the act of love and the expression of it, and the role of art is signalled at the beginning of the poem by 'What tune the enchantress plays', showing that the poet's mistress has her own creative gifts to reveal, or to withold. The poem's resignation, what Empson called its 'tenderly hesitant'[12] tone, originates in its depiction of the breakdown of both fidelity and speech. The lyrical force of the poem comes from its effort not to speak, an impulse which is only overcome at what is

[11] C. Ricks, 'The Nature of Housman's Poetry', *A. E. Housman: A Collection of Critical Essays*, ed. C. Ricks (Princeton, NJ, 1968), 121.

[12] W. Empson, 'Rhythm and Imagery in English Poetry', *British Journal of Aesthetics* (1962), 41.

made to appear a considerable psychological expense. Speech contends with silence, and triumphs only with difficulty.

This poem is rare among Housman's verse in giving way almost completely to a romantic inclination for self-expression, which is made to appear emotionally therapeutic. More usually his poetry expresses a profound distrust of the beneficial workings of the imagination by surrounding its dramatized acts of speech with qualifications and ironies which render them almost impotent. *More Poems* XLII is ingeniously resourceful in the way it ekes out a deeply personal utterance by refusing to allow itself to speak. The poem is composed from a determination not to reveal the emotional impulse which precipitated writing: 'Unsaid the word must stay; | Last month was time enough, but now | The news must keep for aye.' Any sense of progression through the poem's five quatrains is illusory:

> The word unsaid will stay unsaid
>   Though there was much to say;
> Last month was time enough: he's dead,
>   The news must keep for aye.

This is perverse and can only be greeted with critical ambivalence: why do this poem and many like it take pleasure in defying the conventional lyric mode of self-surrender? It is difficult not to succumb to biographical speculations and adduce that the poem's title, 'A. J. J.', is a reference to Moses Jackson's brother Adalbert, with whom Housman lived in a Bayswater *ménage à trois* for nearly three years.[13] Again the nature of the relationship precludes open disclosure, but it should be recorded that Housman's reticence is shared by Edward Thomas and Thomas Hardy, writers who had no comparable fears.

The final effect is of a poetry inhibited by its own necessary procedures, and of this inhibition closing in decisively upon much of Housman's writing. As H. W. Garrod expressed it, 'Some god gave it to him to say what he suffers; but he would rather have been given the power to hold his tongue.'[14] Again, while Housman clearly has an affinity with Wilde, which helps to explain his fear of self-exposure, it is illuminating to compare the Edwardian reticence of Edward Thomas. Thomas's often deserted landscapes suggest that a tacit choice is being made between social involvement and personal liberty, a choice which is indicative of his ambivalence towards human relationships. There is a sense in which social

---

[13] Page, *A. E. Housman: A Critical Biography*, 53–6.
[14] H. W. Garrod, *The Profession of Poetry and Other Lectures* (Oxford, 1929), 219–20.

intercourse threatens his individuality. The poems to Thomas's
mother and wife, 'M. E. T.' and 'Helen', notably omit a sense of
reciprocation; the relationship is one of 'only gratitude | Instead of
love', and when he asks what is the most valuable asset he could
give, he finds the reply 'I would give you back yourself'. This
anxiety concerning the reciprocal aspect, the element of exchange,
colours much of Thomas's writing. The poem 'Aspens' demonstrates that in remaining faultlessly true to himself, Thomas
denies the needs of his public: the larger social dimension is set in
opposition to the individual speaker and the poem expresses a note
of antagonism towards the very people who should compose its
audience, the people of 'the inn, the smithy, and the shop'. For
Thomas, the poet's art, 'A language not to be betrayed', is the
cause of alienation rather than social integration, and it is a central
creative paradox that he frequently expresses the desire not to be
known, not to give himself away by his writing. It is this paradox
upon which much of Housman's verse is founded, although he
uses an ironic technique to cover his tracks. What Thomas and
Housman share with Hardy, especially *The Dynasts*, is the sense of
a crisis of creative authority; it is as if they are disabled by the
limitations of their chosen medium, by the indeterminacy of
language itself. Each poet tackles this problem in his individual
manner, but it might be recognized as an Edwardian characteristic,
and one which prefigures in a small way the innovations of the
more adventurous Modernists.

The vicissitudes of language, and particularly the idea of language
as a form of rhetoric to be employed in various ways for various
specific effects, is the predominant motif of Housman's poetry.
The operation of words as devices or instruments is the governing
idea which controls the conduct even of the most apparently direct
rural dialogues. The poem 'Oh see how thick the goldcup flowers'
(*A Shropshire Lad* V) is composed chiefly of the rhetoric of wooing,
which Housman acknowledges as a special kind of discourse with
its own techniques and conventions:

> Oh see how thick the goldcup flowers
>   Are lying in field and lane,
> With dandelions to tell the hours
>   That never are told again.
> Oh may I squire you round the meads
>   And pick you posies gay?
> —'Twill do no harm to take my arm.
>   'You may, young man, you may.'

The initial romantic introduction establishes the relationship upon which the young man hopes to build, and to begin with he has some success, the girl giving encouraging assent to his argument that 'spring was sent for lass and lad'. But as his approach becomes more direct the girl's compliance is rendered provisional:

> My love is true and all for you.
> 'Perhaps, young man, perhaps.'

The rhetoric of courtship is not always sincere, and while the reader must accept the charmer's seductive language as a necessary part of the drama, the girl can withold belief from his flattering attentions. The disparity between the reader's gullibility and the girl's shrewdness provides the dramatic impact of the last lines:

> —Ah, life, what is it but a flower?
> Why must true lovers sigh?
> Be kind, have pity, my own, my pretty,—
> 'Good-bye, young man, good-bye.'

This surprising reversal defeats reader expectations and dramatizes the disparity between passive compliance and detached critical awareness. Precisely the same moment of understanding is dramatized by the final lines of *A Shropshire Lad* XXVII, 'I cheer a dead man's sweetheart, | Never ask me whose.' Housman's mischievousness is evident in 'Oh see how thick the goldcup flowers' with the lines 'Oh, look in my eyes then, can you doubt? | — Why, 'tis a mile from town', which draws the couple together physically and indicates the distance they have wandered during the brief allurement. The proximity of their faces, juxtaposed with the remoteness of society, is conveyed with an economy reminiscent of the style of some eighteenth-century poetry in its use of alternating spacial perspectives. Thomas Gray's 'Ode on a Distant Prospect of Eton College', for example, describes the 'distant spires' which 'from the stately brow | Of Windsor's height the expanse below | Of grove, of lawn, of mead survey' (and note Housman's use of that word 'mead' in the poem presently under consideration). This use of spacial perspective is also a characteristic of Pope's *Windsor Forest*, Denham's *Cooper's Hill*, and James Thomson's *The Seasons*, but the obvious comparison is with Gray who, like Housman, was a classical scholar who produced a tiny output of very good English poems. Gray's 'Elegy Written in a Country Churchyard' has a compactness and subtlety which prefigures Housman's latinate style.

With the final line of 'Oh see how thick the goldcup flowers' the girl ceases to be persuaded by the wooer's enticing felicity, and her judgement depends upon her ability to recognize specious rhetoric. It is only the seduction of the reader which takes place. The allure of the poem consists in the charm of its linguistic and imaginative devices, but while the reader is fooled by the seducer's loquaciousness, the girl has already understood the potential for language to corrupt. 'Oh see how thick the goldcup flowers' is a skilfully understated exposition of rhetorical insincerity, revealing the corruption of language and suggesting the other forms of corruption to which it may lead. The degree to which reader expectation contributes to the effect of the poem may be judged from a consideration of the poem's counterpart 'Delight it is in youth and May' (*More Poems* XVIII), where another persuasive young man walks the same courting fields. There is no dialogue here, the deceptions of love and language are baldly stated, and the effect is not engagingly felt. Under cover of darkness the romantic associations of the nightingale are violated:

> Oh follow me where she is flown
> Into the leafy woods alone,
> And I will work you ill.

The comparative failure of the poem arises from the fact that it does not tell the reader lies and cannot work the reader ill. The menacing effect is more that of a murderer than a seducer, although for Housman there is possibly a dark equation in that.

The same drama of learning the value of language is recounted by 'When I was one-and-twenty' (*A. Shropshire Lad* XIII), where the rhetoric of courtship is replaced by the world-weary discourse which 'I heard a wise man say'. The lad of this poem comes, in the space of one year, to accept the value of a spoken language which he previously disregarded: 'But I was one-and-twenty | No use to talk to me.' The wise man's injunction to 'keep your fancy free' is heeded too late, and the lad must suffer the bitter consequences: 'And I am two-and-twenty | And oh, 'tis true, 'tis true.' This young man's naïvety or recklessness is the true counterpart to the shrewdness of the girl in 'Oh see how thick the goldcup flowers', who recognized a seductive entrapment. In both poems, different styles of persuasive language are tested against the experience of individuals. Many of Housman's poems operate somewhere along this scale, between a critical appreciation of the full value of words and an awareness of their potential misuse or artful designs. This might be recognized as a textual scholar's special province, the vicissitudes of lexical interpretation calling for the exercise of acute concentration and judgement. A similar warning about the corruption of language is issued by Pitt in Hardy's *The Dynasts*, who appeals for directness and honesty in speech:

> To use imagination as the ground
> Of chronicle, take myth and merry tale
> As texts for prophecy, is not my gift,
> Being but a person primed with simple fact,
> Unprinked by jewelled art.

(I. i. iii)

Housman's art suggests that this is a specious argument, which the very nature of language will tend to undermine. His poems work to vindicate the activity of taking 'myth and merry tale | As texts for prophecy' and strongly imply that where language is involved there can be no such thing as 'simple fact'. Pitt of course is only one character in Hardy's densely populated drama, but his words have a unique value for a poem which is eagerly in search of historical verisimilitude, using 'imagination as the ground | Of chronicle'. In its lack of clear authorial voice *The Dynasts* implies that writers should not distract attention from their 'chronicle'; Housman's view is completely the reverse; his poetry demonstrates again and again that there is no such thing as 'simple fact', that all meaning is dependent upon language, and that language is treacherous and unreliable. Such a fundamental difference in the relationship a writer has with his medium suggests that Hardy and Housman might not have as close an affinity as is commonly believed. John Crowe Ransom, comparing Housman with Hardy, finds that the latter 'does not even begin to let himself be led astray by the blandishments of rhetoric'.[15] These observations are also pertinent to Edward Thomas, and help to explain the nature of his search for 'A language not to be betrayed'.

The feature which these writers share is the sense of their poetry being deeply aware of its own artistic untruthfulness. Some of Housman's best poems call attention, by their formal patterning, to the constructed nature of poetry and its contrived artistic purpose. Opening lines such as 'Others, I am not the first' and 'Bring, in this timeless grave to throw, | No cypress' immediately signal the rhetorical design of their speech. This is even true of a lyric such as 'Loveliest of trees, the cherry now' (*A Shropshire Lad* II),

---

[15] J. C. Ransom, 'Honey and Gall', *Southern Review*, 6 (1940–1), 7.

in which the riddling numerical stanza and the verse's highly wrought formal arrangement debar the poem from a sense of conversational or natural utterance. Housman's verse is at times reminiscent of Milton, of his translation of Horace's Pyrrha ode, for example, which begins, 'What slender youth bedewed with liquid odours | Courts thee on roses in some pleasant cave, | Pyrrha for whom bind'st thou | In wreaths thy golden hair.' In a comment which seems apposite to the study of Housman, one critic has written of Milton's poem:

This is very far from colloquial English. But its latinate syntax and word-order give it a compactness and resiliency which could hardly have been attained in a more relaxed idiom. Admittedly, it has lost the ease of expression that Horace invariably preserves within his strict formal limits.[16]

These observations hold true for Housman's poetry too, except that his 'strict formal limits' consist partly of a desire not to speak at all, and some of the force of his verse comes from the effort of a natural taciturnity being painfully overcome.

The culmination of these devisive stratagems comes with *More Poems* VI:

> I to my perils
>   Of cheat and charmer
>   Came clad in armour
>   By stars benign.
> Hope lies to mortals
>   And most believe her,
>   But man's deceiver
>   Was never mine.
>
> The thoughts of others
>   Were light and fleeting,
>   Of lovers' meeting
>   Or luck or fame.
> Mine were of trouble,
>   And mine were steady,
>   So I was ready
>   When trouble came.

It is difficult to improve upon Christopher Ricks's analysis of this poem:

The poem says a dour glum cramping thing, but how does it say it? With gaiety and wit that are, if you like, utterly inappropriate. Instead of the

[16] J. D. Jump, *The Ode* (1974), 7.

'steady' tramp of military fortitude, there is the exquisite interlacing of a dance; instead of granite rhymes, there is a supple effrontery and insouciance that links 'charmer' and 'armour', and in so doing opposes something to the simple sturdiness, the indurated hopelessness, of armour. It says that 'The thoughts of others | Were light and fleeting' while 'Mine were of trouble', but whatever the poem may say (in its natural human wish to find armour for itself, to find steadiness), this cannot be the case. The movement itself is light and fleeting, and not just in the lines about others.[17]

Ricks, perhaps deliberately, neglects to point out just how appropriate this procedure is for a poem which avows to resist the 'perils | Of cheat and charmer'. This poem combines the dissembling of the charming young man in 'Oh see how thick the goldcup flowers', the lies of 'Delight it is in youth and May', and the collected deceptions of the literary imagination as portrayed in Housman's verse. 'I to my perils' is a mischievously self-conscious poem, and that is its unique pleasure.

The success of this poem awakens a suspicion of linguistic devices and larger rhetorical schemes while demonstrating the satisfactions of articulate formal control. Romantic impulses are held in check by classical convictions. This tension can be seen at work in other poets, notably Philip Larkin:

> The trees are coming into leaf
> Like something almost being said.

Like Housman's poetry, Larkin's 'The Trees' refutes the idea of poetry as the spontaneous overflow of powerful feelings and refrains from being completely explicit about its emotional origin: the poem describes 'something almost being said'. It is as if the poet cannot quite interpret the spring in terms which are personal to him, and so it becomes a metaphor for reticence. Both poets show signs of inhibiting or restricting their initial romantic impulse, in Larkin's poem a sense of yearly renewal suggesting something of Tennyson's 'In the spring a young man's fancy lightly turns to thoughts of love' ('Locksley Hall'). The act of expression in Larkin's 'The Trees' is not one of self-indulgent abandonment but something more Housmanesque: 'Their greenness is a kind of grief'. Larkin reviewed Norman Page's biography of Housman in 1984 and wrote that 'temperamentally he seems to have been·always on the defensive, as only one who knows his own

---

[17] Ricks, 'The Nature of Housman's Poetry', 109.

powerlessness in the face of emotion can be'.[18] These words could act as a gloss on Housman's poems 'Ask me no more', 'Tell me not here' and 'Because I liked you better'.

The rhetorical constructions of Housman's poetry include the persona who utters it, yet criticism has not often called attention to the fictive indeterminacy of 'A' Shropshire 'Lad'. In fact, critics almost habitually rename the collection 'The Shropshire Lad', an error which betrays a fundamental misunderstanding of the central creative device of Housman's poetry.[19] Housman was not a native of the district he made famous, he engaged in what his brother called the 'romantic falsification of local history'.[20] In fact the title *A Shropshire Lad* was the original suggestion of A. W. Pollard; Housman's proposed title was 'Poems by Terence Hearsay', which certainly 'suggests a deliberate distancing and disclaiming',[21] and implies a further qualification of the act of speech: these poems were not to be uttered at all, only overheard. The indefinite persona of *A Shropshire Lad* is significantly less fixed than, say, that of Geoffrey Hill's *Mercian Hymns* (1971), whose governing presence is King Offa and whose poems each describe a moment of his development.

This is hardly surprising, of course, because Housman was a Worcestershire lad for whom Shropshire represented a province just out of sight over the Malvern Hills; it is an imaginary landscape for which he has adopted real names. Or, as John Lucas expresses it, 'It is in fact a tourist's landscape'.[22] In the poem 'Hughley Steeple' Housman uses the landmark as the focal point for apparently personal nostalgic associations:

> The vane on Hughley steeple
>   Veers bright, a far-known sign,
> And there lie Hughley people,
>   And there lie friends of mine.

Given the detailed emotional response which this sight evokes, it is perhaps surprising to find that Housman wrote in 1925, 'Now that

---

[18] P. Larkin, 'Lost Content', *Observer* (29 Jan. 1984).

[19] E. Wilson is only one of numerous offenders in this respect: see his *The Triple Thinkers* (1938). See also Garrod, *The Profession of Poetry and Other Lectures*; C. Hassall, *Rupert Brooke: A Biography* (1964), 102; J. Lehmann, *Rupert Brooke: His Life and his Legend* (1980), 69.

[20] L. Housman, *A. E. H.: A Memoir* (1937), 82.

[21] Page, *A. E. Housman: A Critical Biography*, 85.

[22] J. Lucas, *Modern English Poetry from Hardy to Hughes* (1986), 68.

Hughley is burnt down it is curious to think that I never saw it.'[23]
This is testimony to Housman's gift for fiction, and to the impersonality of even his most emotional poems; contrary to the
apparent associations of the 'far-known sign' of 'Hughley Steeple',
it would appear that 'He merely liked its name'.[24] A similar
mythologizing process is at work in the poetry of Edward Thomas,
whose fascination with 'Adlestrop', or at least 'the name', is partly
due to the fact that in the poem he does not see the village, only its
railway station. Both Housman and Thomas use specific English
places to express a sense of absence from them. Philip Larkin has
written about 'The Importance of Elsewhere' and his poetry too
describes towns observed from the point of view of a railway
passenger: 'waking at the fumes | And furnace glares of Sheffield,
where I changed | And ate an awful pie' ('Dockery and Son').
Both 'Here' and 'The Whitsun Weddings' recount scenes of
English life observed from the train and anticipate arrival at
specific places, Hull and London, with a traveller's relish. John
Betjeman (who has written his own poem entitled 'A Shropshire
Lad') has also described a 'Distant View of a Provincial Town'
observed from a carriage on 'The old Great Western Railway', a
process repeated in his poem 'From The Great Western'; his verse
is full of English place-names, such as 'Cheltenham', where homely
security is disturbed as 'distant carriages jingled through | The
stuccoed afternoon'. Housman's poetry similarly gives the impression of having been written while 'through the wild green hills
of Wyre | The train ran' (*A Shropshire Lad* XXXVII). Each of
these poets discover specific English regions and locations with
the eye of an embryonic travel-writer. Names such as Ludlow,
Shrewsbury, and Bredon play an important part in *A Shropshire
Lad*, as they do in another poem of regional England, Rupert
Brooke's 'Grantchester', which has been described as 'a sort of
accumulated vomit from a stomach stuffed with place names'.[25]
Again the poem was significantly written from a distant vantage
point, in this case Berlin, a fact acknowledged by the poem's
original title ''The Sentimental Exile'. Many Edwardian poets
might be regarded as exiles whose ancestry or childhood is consistently portrayed as existing at one remove: Edward Thomas
from Wales, Masefield from Herefordshire, Davidson from Scotland.
Even Thomas Hardy's Victorian Wessex is disappearing around

[23] *The Letters of A. E. Housman*, ed. H. Maas, 233.
[24] F. L. Lucas, *The Greatest Problem and Other Essays* (1960), 203.
[25] G. Orwell, *Inside the Whale and Other Essays* (1940), 148.

him. The Edwardian poets' attempt to give the definitive expression
to their idea of England is bound up with a nostalgia for the places
of their childhood. Yet perhaps any attempt to fix national identity
in rhyme will seem, in retrospect, nostalgic? Only our privileged
view of the Edwardian period as curtailed by the guns of August
makes it possible for us to pass easy judgement on the period's
sustaining myths.

Many of Housman's poems articulate feelings of displacement
(*A Shropshire Lad* XL):

> Into my heart an air that kills
>   From yon far country blows:
> What are those blue remembered hills,
>   What spires, what farms are those?
>
> That is the land of lost content,
>   I see it shining plain,
> The happy highways where I went
>   And cannot come again.

This is Housman at his best, his technical skill working to maximum
effect within the confines of a formal discipline to give a very short
poem considerable emotional impact. Here the location is not
specified but topography is used to express a general statement of
loss which is both psychological (suggesting a romantic infatuation
with childhood) and physical: the poet's emotional life is closely
identified with a sense of place. Removal from home is frequently
used in Housman's poetry to give a dramatic focus to feelings of
emotional departure and loss. His characters complain, 'Now
through the friendless world we fare | And sigh upon the road' (*A
Shropshire Lad* XXXVIII); they have painfully understood that
'ere the circle homeward lies, | Far, far must it remove' (*A Shropshire
Lad* XXXVI); they have been advised 'Leave your home behind
you lad' ('The Recruit'), and have bid 'Farewell to barn and stack
and tree | Farewell to Severn shore' (*A Shropshire Lad* VIII), the
familiar landmarks having been replaced by remote foreign loca-
tions: 'It dawns in Asia, tombstones show | And Shropshire names
are read | And the Nile spills his overflow | Beside the Severn's
dead' ('1887'). Housman's poetry describes 'the land to which I
travel | The far dwelling' (*A Shropshire Lad* XI) and approaches a
metaphysical expression of alienation:

> I, a stranger and afraid
> In a world I never made.

These lines from *Last Poems* XII might be interpreted as the poet's complaint about the imaginative world he is impelled to inhabit, and as an expression of the anxiety attendant upon writing about a location and an emotional life which is invariably out of reach. The discomfort at finding himself in this artificially created environment might help to explain the poet's habitual reluctance to speak, and his wish for death, which in the context of poetry is a wish for the emotional turbulence of expression to cease. It is quite the opposite of Edward Thomas's relief at finding 'the inn where all were kind, | All were strangers' ('Over The Hills'). Stan Smith has argued that Thomas suffers from 'an incommunicable sense of exclusion which yearns for the ratifying womb of class, race, or tradition',[26] but this argument is more convincing when applied to Housman whose imaginary 'Shropshire' is an unsatisfactory substitute for all manner of unfulfilled emotional needs.

Housman's collections of verse conclude with the death of the narrator who speaks them. The final lines of the last poem of *A Shropshire Lad* hope that something will survive beyond their rhymes: 'And luckless lads will wear them | When I am dead and gone.' The last line of *More Poems* is counsel to 'sleep on, sleep sound', and the last of *Last Poems* is entitled 'Fancy's Knell' and dramatizes the death of the voice which sustained creative endeavour:

> Come, lads, and learn the dances
>   And praise the tune to-day.
> To-morrow, more's the pity,
>   Away we both must hie.
> To air the ditty,
>   And to earth I.

This note is that by which the poet relinquishes the imaginative device which made poetry possible, and so it signals the end of the poetic work. The verse might have extra importance for being the very last poem which Housman intended to publish. The surrender of voice at the close of a poem or poetic work has interesting parallels elsewhere in English poetry since Milton, whose *Lycidas* ends with its poet anticipating a new subject: 'At last he rose, and twitch'd his mantle blue: | Tomorrow to fresh woods and pastures new'. It is possible that Housman's use of 'Tomorrow' in 'Fancy's Knell' is an unconscious echo of Milton here. One scholar has shown that Housman's poem reveals other points of correspondence

---

[26] S. Smith, *Inviolable Voice: History and Twentieth Century Poetry* (Dublin, 1982), 51.

with *Lycidas*,[27] notably a duplication of the rhyme on 'mute | flute':
'Meanwhile the rural ditties were not mute, | Tempered to the
oaten flute, | Rough satyrs danced.' Milton's 'ditties' are those
which Housman relinquishes, 'To air the ditty | And to earth I'.
More recently the final poem of Auden's 1936–9 volume, coming
at the end of a decade (of a generation?) ended famously, 'We must
love one another or die', and Larkin, perhaps with Auden in mind,
concluded *The Whitsun Weddings* with the belief that 'What will
survive of us is love' ('An Arundel Tomb'). Similarly Seamus
Heaney's first book begins with an image of the poet holding a pen
poised for writing ('Digging') and ends with him gazing into a
well:

> Now to pry into roots, to finger slime,
> To stare, big-eyed Narcissus, into some spring
> Is beneath all adult dignity. I rhyme
> To see myself, to set the darkness echoing.

The self-affirmation without self-revelation of Heaney's 'Personal
Helicon' is apposite to Housman, illuminating the Edwardian
poet's obsession with the processes of writing and with dramatizing
moments of insight in a rhetorical style. Writing almost becomes
an end in itself, akin to the pleasure of Edward Thomas's poetry,
for which 'the journey and not the arrival provides him with the
wholeness he seeks, because it is there that self-consciousness is at
a minimum'.[28] One critic has argued that 'the structure of *A
Shropshire Lad* as a whole reinforces the theme of the persona's
movement from innocence to experience; that the ordering of
the poems is deliberate and meaningful.'[29] But the belief that
Housman's collections evince 'a progressive structure' disregards
the sense of artificiality which the poems themselves acknowledge
to be the prerogative of language; the development is of a progressive
sense of distrust. Housman's poetry may show signs of an expanding
consciousness but systematic development is unlikely given the
extent to which individual poems seem aware of their own fallibility
as flawed linguistic devices.

Verbal inconstancy (matching that of Housman's 'lads') produces many of the poet's most characteristic effects:

> The morning clocks will ring
> A neck God made for other use

[27] A. N. Marlow, *A. E. Housman: Scholar and Poet* (1958), 118.
[28] A. Motion, *The Poetry of Edward Thomas* (1980), 51.
[29] B. J. Leggett, *The Poetic Art of A. E. Housman: Theory and Practice* (Lincoln, Nebr.,
1978), 62.

There are two puns in this couplet from *A Shropshire Lad* IX, on ring/wring and morning/mourning, and the effect is to create a dense textual suggestiveness by means of confusing sound and sense. The homophone morning/mourning is Housman's favourite: 'Those are the tears of morning | That weeps' (*Last Poems* XXVII); 'He stood, and heard the steeple | Sprinkle the quarters on the morning town' ('Eight O'Clock'). These kinds of linguistic effects show that Housman was eager to exploit verbal ambiguity to give a resonance or depth to his brief lyrics. One critic has written of Edward Thomas that 'when a mode of writing works within a narrow range throughout yet still retains our attention, it is likely that variations are being played of a very subtle order indeed',[30] and this is true also for Housman whose subtleties tend to be of a lexical nature. The rewards of close analysis have been unveiled in a very detailed fashion by Randall Jarrell in his essay on 'It nods and curtseys and recovers' (*A Shropshire Lad* XVI) which points out that the three verbs of this opening line 'add up to *dance*'.[31] The nettle of the poem dances on the grave of the dead lover. Ricks elaborates the consequences of this in his own inimitable style: ' "Recovers" as a term in dancing; the dead man does not recover in this or any (unspoken) sense. 'Curtseys' as a part of the dance; but the curtsey is hardly a courtesy—indeed to dance on a grave is traditionally the extreme discourtesy.'[32] Reservations have been expressed concerning the convolutions of Ricks's style[33] which may seem over-ingenious at times but which serves to show the level at which Housman's dramatic scenes may be expounded. Ricks's obtrusive cleverness is oddly appropriate to the study of Housman; it is an indication of the textual allusiveness of Housman's poetry that it is capable of bearing such elaborate scrutiny.

Warnings about deceptive appearances abound in Housman's poetry, and he often hints self-consciously at his role as arch-deceiver. *A Shropshire Lad* VI illustrates the ease with which a mask may be assumed: 'Lovers' ills are all to buy: | The wan look, the

---

[30] J. P. Ward, 'The Solitary Note: Edward Thomas and Modernism', *Poetry Wales*, 13/4 (spring 1978), 71.

[31] R. Jarrell, 'Texts from Housman', *Kenyon Review*, 1 (1939), 268.

[32] Ricks, 'The Nature of Housman's Poetry', 118.

[33] One critic has described it as 'self consumingly self-referential and tends, like the cabbalistic serpent, to gobble up its tail . . . His most dazzling verbal effects are themselves small absurdist poems about the transmission of influence, and they wrap themselves round into a circularity from which there's no escape . . . Ricks himself operates within a closed field of echo and association, and it's there . . . that he incarcerates Tennyson.' P. Conrad, 'The Victim of Inheritance', *Times Literary Supplement* (15 May 1982), 530.

hollow tone, | The hung head, the sunken eye, | You can have
them for your own.' The rhetoric of courtship is comparable to the
facial disguise which accompanies it. A sense of the manipulative
artistry involved in a love relationship is given by *Last Poems* III,
'Her strong enchantments failing', in which the verb 'enchant' has
a special place; it is given by *Chambers's Dictionary* as 'to delight by
songs or rhymed formulas of sorcery', a definition describing the
kind of rhetoric to which Housman's poetry is uniquely susceptible.
As with many of Housman's poems, the collapse of imaginative
dissembling ('Her strong enchantments failing') is not simply
unfortunate or troublesome, it is in fact fatal: 'And I shall die to-
morrow | But you will die to-day.' The loss of creative ability
frequently leads directly to death, a consequence which attaches a
heightened importance to the faculty of imaginative perception.
Similarly the poet of *A Shropshire Lad* XVIII reveals how easily
such guises may be discarded; once 'the fancy passes by' his self
deception is over and 'I | Am quite myself again'. The lover of *A
Shropshire Lad* LV 'Makes the vow he will not keep', and 'The
Deserter' bids 'Farewell the vows that were', illustrating the ease
with which solemn promises may be repudiated, perhaps because
they are recognized as no more than verbal tokens of fidelity.
These Shropshire characters are no less trustworthy than the
lovesick faces and recruiting rhetoric which deceives them. For
Housman's poetry the persuasive appeal of recruiting sergeants is
synonymous with the seductive charms of lovers, as if to suggest
that all kinds of emotional approach should be treated with
extreme caution. The emotional life of the individual is sacrosanct,
but once committed to the fickle medium of language it becomes
treacherous and unreliable.

   Seamus Heaney's *Death of a Naturalist* identifies the poet with the
figure of 'big-eyed Narcissus' who stares into wells and whose
poetry is an important act of self-affirmation: 'I rhyme | To see
myself' ('Personal Helicon'). Housman's *A Shropshire Lad* includes
two such poems, 'Look not in my eyes' (XV) which depicts a
Grecian lad who 'Looked into a forest well | And never looked
away again', and poem XX in which the poet observes in the
water 'A silly lad that longs and looks | And wishes he were I'.
These dramatizations of self-reflection suggest a desire to create
an *alter ego* for psychological reasons, akin to that of Edward
Thomas's 'The Other' and Conrad's *The Secret Sharer*, as a means
to detached self-observation. For Housman the externalization of
the self may provide relief from the internalized martial resolve to

which his verse holds with such fastidiousness. For one critic it is probably evidence that Housman is 'tortured by the compulsive need for self-identity'.[34] The Narcissus theme can be an unhealthy one for a writer, implying a search for personal metaphor which is unsuccessful or incomplete. Oscar Wilde's *The Picture of Dorian Gray* (1891) is a major treatment of this theme contemporary with Housman, and it also makes an appearance in Wilde's 'The Young King' (1888) in which 'A laughing Narcissus in green bronze held a polished mirror above its head'. The intense pre-occupation with the vocation of the writer is sometimes indulgently combined with affectedly self-conscious artistry at the turn of the century; Douglas Jefferson writes of Henry James's 'The Death of the Lion' and 'The Next Time', as stories 'in which his sense of alienation from the great reading public finds a not altogether healthy expression'.[35] This might prove an analogue for Housman's equivocal style, as if in the absence of a full relationship with his audience, writing about writing became the only meaningful activity. But not all Edwardians renounced the public sphere: 'However critical of the established order, men like Shaw and Wells, Bennett and Chesterton put their trust in a popular audience; they might promulgate minority opinions, but not the idea of a minority culture.'[36]

This is true, but it prompts the question of how minority opinions are compatible with a popular audience. Eccentricity perhaps (in the case of Chesterton), but if these writers were endearingly singular then who represents the Edwardian main-stream? It must also be true that this kind of polarization affects poetry most adversely; twentieth-century criticism sometimes implies that popularity is at odds with artistic integrity, an argument which has inhibited appreciation of Masefield, Brooke, and John Betjeman, and has delayed recognition of Kipling. Their popularity is the corollary of their empiricism, of what one critic has called the 'emphasis on a sharable reality'.[37] Modernist critical criteria have eroded the idea of common and recognizable experience as the basis for poetry.

[34] J. W. Stevenson, 'The Martyr as Innocent: Housman's Lonely Lad', *South Atlantic Quarterly*, 57 (winter 1958), 84.

[35] H. James, *What Maisie Knew* (Oxford, 1966), ed. D. Jefferson, p. ix.

[36] J. Gross, *The Rise and Fall of the Man of Letters: Aspects of English Literary Life Since 1800* (1969); repr. Pelican books (1973), 232.

[37] G. Harvey, *The Romantic Tradition in Modern English Poetry: Rhetoric and Experience* (1986), 8.

A Shropshire Lad has been immensely popular, but not during the years immediately following its publication in 1896; George Orwell has written that 'during and immediately after the war, the writer who had the deepest hold upon the thinking young was almost certainly Housman'.[38] This is testimony to Housman's survival in the twentieth century, as is the quality of the critical attention he has received from modern critics such as Ransom, Jarrell, Brooks, Empson, and Ricks; as Page comments, few minor poets have impelled critics of this calibre.[39] Orwell offers his own suggestions for the continued interest in Housman but neglects to mention the poet's technical dexterity, and it is this which has fascinated modern commentators. Housman's critically detached treatment of language, his manipulation of words as units in a system of rhetoric, distinguishes him from his Victorian predecessors and is the source of contemporary interest. Housman's self-conscious awareness that human discourse can be undermined by the in-determinate nature of language itself supplies each of his poems with an elusiveness which subverts concepts as absolute as stoicism, determinism, pessimism. The depiction of the act of speech in Housman's poetry evades such categoric definition. It is the elasticity of Housman's relationship to language which qualifies his verse for the title 'modern'.

While Housman's self-consciousness is indicative of a new awareness of formal constraints in the composition of poetry, his verse does not accomplish a thoroughgoing exploitation of the possibilities he discovered. He lacks the range and variety of voices which Yeats successfully explored. Housman's sense of himself writing poetry intrudes into the verse more usually to inhibit than to facilitate writing. The metaphors he finds for his art do not radically extend its scope; he is too often concerned with denial for his own poetry to reach its potential fulfilment. Housman's doubt as to the efficacy of art is shared by his Edwardian contemporaries, and their distrust of the imagination constitutes a British modernism which might be usefully distinguished from the more radically self-conscious Modernism of Eliot and Pound, which clinched the demise of Romantic theories of writing as the passionate surrender of an essential self.

---

[38] Orwell, *Inside the Whale and Other Essays*, 146.
[39] Page, *A. E. Housman: A Critical Biography*, 182.

5

Edward Thomas and Modern Poetry

In a history of English poetry, the place of Edward Thomas is not immediately obvious. A contemporary of the Georgians and war poets, he does not fit decisively into either of these groups, and like them he shares a relationship with Thomas Hardy which has not yet been exhaustively explored. Donald Davie's study *Thomas Hardy and British Poetry* (1973) makes no reference to Thomas. Edward Thomas wrote 144 poems between 1914 and 1917 after ten years of debilitating literary hack work, but of his twenty-two months as a soldier all but seventy days were spent training in England, and he wrote only one poem in France, 'The sorrow of true love'. His poems were published in none of the *Georgian Anthologies* which ran from 1912 to 1922 and only oblique insights may be discovered by means of a comparison with trench poets such as Owen and Rosenberg. Although the most English of poets, Thomas's rightful context is made a little more difficult to identify because of his relationship with an American, Robert Frost. To concur with Edna Longley in an appendix to her edition of Thomas's poems:

One result of wholly repudiating a link between Thomas and the Georgians has been to leave him without any literary context whatsoever, apart from his alliance with Robert Frost. This is a paradoxical position, not only for a poet whose roots sink so deeply into the English tradition, but for one so well acquainted with the poetry of his own day.[1]

This chapter does repudiate the link between Thomas and the Georgians, but argues that it is possible to see Thomas in terms of a pre-war line of modern poetry, distinct from the radical advances of modernists such as Pound, Eliot, and Joyce, which provides him with a context which is both more accurate and more illuminating than 'Georgian' or 'war poet'. To locate Thomas within a broader English tradition is to establish him as a modern poet of major stature, as this chapter hopes to demonstrate.

Characteristically the Modernists behaved as though in order

---

[1] E. Thomas, *Poems and Last Poems*, ed. E. Longley (1973), 408.

to reflect fully a disordered world and a modern consciousness, the forms of art needed to be fundamentally reshaped. The Modernists freed themselves from the obligation to make their meaning immediately and manifestly obvious; the form of their art became, in a radically new sense, as important as the experience it conveyed. Denis Donoghue identifies this function when he writes that 'in the later chapters of *Ulysses* Joyce has come upon certain possibilities of language which, if fully exploited, would bring him far beyond anything that could be deemed to have communication as its first object.'[2] In poetry, the breaking-down of formal constraints resulted in disordered syntax and other technical difficulties, which made uncompromising demands upon the reader. Exploring the possibilities of artistic deployment became the new imperative. Thomas's style does not make these kinds of demands; but it may be said to use confusion thematically: his poems are often expressions of doubt which work towards a tentative solution. Unlike his early Modernist contemporaries, Thomas refuses to abandon rational structures, traditional forms, and comprehensible language, even when expressing feelings of crisis and despair ('Lights Out' for example, or his seven poems which are formal sonnets). These structures are often signalled by the use of conversational features, like that of 'The Barn', 'It's the turn of lesser things, I suppose',[3] which qualify Thomas's observations with their informality. His use of the interrogative is a key part of this strategy, exploiting an element of doubt which he has no intention of resolving: 'But if this be not happiness, who knows?' ('October'). The five consecutive questions which conclude 'The Glory' represent a bewildering range of options for the poet's potential development: 'Shall I now ... Or must I be ... And shall I ... And shall I . . . Or shall I perhaps . . . ?' The poet's awareness of possibilities creates a disabling helplessness which he cannot overcome, and so fulfilment is denied: 'I cannot bite the day to the core.' Similarly governed by a rational sequence is 'Beauty', the opening line of which asks simply and directly, 'What does it mean?'; the rest of the poem is an attempt to formulate a reply so that it may end with an answer, albeit oblique: 'Beauty is there.' These structures are controlled by feelings of scepticism and a reluctance to make definitive philosophical or moral statements. They often have a temporal design; the subject of 'April' is the loss

2 D. Donoghue, *Ferocious Alphabets* (1981), 63.
3 All quotations from *The Collected Poems of Edward Thomas* (Oxford, 1978), ed. R. G. Thomas.

of innocence and the discovery of maturity, and the corresponding construction reads, 'I thought at one time . . . but now I know', where the two stanzas of the poem represent a before/after progression. This is a dramatic technique which resembles very closely the style of A. E. Housman, especially poem XIII from *A Shropshire Lad* (1896), 'When I was one-and-twenty', where the temporal pattern gives dramatic poignancy to a sense of the passing of a year, 'And I am two-and-twenty | And oh, 'tis true, 'tis true.'

To interpret Thomas's poems as expressions of the very process of making sense or order is a view supported by the first lines of an important poem, 'Old Man', which are regulated by a tone which is quizzical:

> Old Man, or Lad's-love,—in the name there's nothing
> To one that knows not Lad's-love, or Old Man,
> The hoar-green feathery herb, almost a tree,
> Growing with rosemary and lavender.
> Even to one that knows it well, the names
> Half decorate, half perplex, the thing it is:
> At least, what that is clings not to the names
> In spite of time. And yet I like the names.

The final 'At least . . . And yet' phrasing is especially astute in its acceptance of that which may appear contradictory, and in its determination to avoid that which is pat or dogmatic. Thomas pursues his meaning with exemplary honesty, and these lines show him in the process of trying to judge and evaluate experience, rather than simply stating something which has been prescribed. In this sense it is worth noting that Thomas's poems are often dramatic utterances, and that his resolutions are achieved primarily by means of the poem's framework of philosophical inquiry. Thomas is preoccupied with the problems of discovering truth convincingly through poetry and the rational process of that discovery is an important part of his artistic identity.

It is perhaps in this sense that John Bayley believes that 'It is Thomas's syntax not his sentiments or his subject matter which is English',[4] a comment which defines Englishness for Bayley as that which is provisional or ambivalent. He argues that the syntax of equivocation is a uniquely English characteristic. It is important to recognize that this line of interpretation restricts the utterance of the English poet to a necessarily minor key; to concur with

[4] J. Bayley, 'English Equivocation', *Poetry Review*, 76 (June 1986), 4–6.

Bayley's 'English Equivocation' is to concede that Thomas's diffidence prevents him from attaining the status of a visionary or oracle in the high Romantic sense. Thomas seems to confirm this view when he writes in his *Maurice Maeterlinck* (1911) that,

> a poem of the old kind has a simple fundamental meaning which every sane reader can agree upon; above and beyond this each one builds as he can or must. In the new there is no basis of this kind; a poem means nothing unless its whole meaning has been grasped. (p. 21)

This distinction locates the vicissitudes of communicable sense at the centre of Thomas's poetic creed; it expresses his faith in a 'fundamental meaning' which is the basis of common consensus. It is a belief which distinguishes him clearly from the Modernists.

Stan Smith agrees with Bayley that 'Edward Thomas is the quintessentially English poet'[5] but he defines Thomas's Englishness in terms of an ideological gap between his 'accidentally Cockney nativity'[6] and his Welsh ancestry. Smith argues that 'The play between London birth and Welsh allegiance is the key to understanding the idea of England in Thomas's work.'[7] The suggestion is that Edward Thomas is not strictly speaking an English poet (any more than R. S. Thomas), but despite this qualification Smith's political approach gives back to Thomas's verse a status of which parochial notions of England have deprived it. Our conception of what is English will determine whether we see Thomas as the poet of personal equivocation or as the voice of Edwardian political anxiety. It is for this reason that the role of Robert Frost has come to acquire such importance; he disturbs the idea of Thomas as an exclusively English poet.

Although he has all the virtues of good prose, within the reasonably ordered formal confines of Thomas's poetry there exist moments of experience which, occasionally, defy rational explanation. These points are described in 'The Other' as 'Moments of everlastingness' and represent the kind of secular epiphanies which he discusses in detail during his studies of Maeterlinck and Jefferies, and which Stan Smith argues are indebted to the pragmatism of William James.[8] For Thomas these occurrences coincide with a shift in language and imagery which is dramatic and startling; the poem 'Adlestrop', for example, is quite

---

[5] S. Smith, *Edward Thomas* (1986), 11.
[6] J. Moore, *The Life and Letters of Edward Thomas* (1939), 277. The phrase is Thomas's own.
[7] Smith, *Edward Thomas*, 19.   [8] Ibid. 93.

straightforward in its directness of tone and its simplicity of diction:

> Yes. I remember Adlestrop—
> The name, because one afternoon
> Of heat the express-train drew up there
> Unwontedly. It was late June.
>
> The steam hissed. Someone cleared his throat.
> No one left and no one came
> On the bare platform. What I saw
> Was Adlestrop—only the name

But a marked contrast is provided by the following stanza, especially with the inversion of 'haycocks dry' and the phrase 'No whit less still and lonely fair | Than the high cloudlets in the sky' which draws upon a completely different realm of language, one which is more self-consciously poetic and archaic:

> And willows, willow-herb, and grass,
> And meadowsweet, and haycocks dry,
> No whit less still and lonely fair
> Than the high cloudlets in the sky.

The contrast of diction is part of the poem's technique, drawing linguistic attention to an experience which lasted only 'for that moment' but which was nevertheless the central event of the poem. This event is not defined but is registered in a shifting of the poet's relationship to language.

An even more marked change in diction occurs in 'This is no case of petty right or wrong', the first nine lines of which are relatively prosaic in their exposition of an argument, but which lead to imagery requiring close attention:

> Dinned
> With war and argument I read no more
> Than in the storm smoking along the wind
> Athwart the wood. Two witches' cauldrons roar.

Here the language moves from metaphor to symbol and is characteristically accompanied by the use of the poetic and archaic 'Athwart'. The poem returns to plain language with its oversimplified but logical conclusion that 'And as we love ourselves we hate her foe', but at the centre of the poem lies an image which perhaps can never be satisfactorily explained. Like the 'flying trickster' of Auden's 'Have a Good Time', Thomas's 'storm' deliberately witholds its precise meaning and forms a stylistic contrast with the expository tone of the poem. The metaphor moves into another dimension; it is different in kind. 'This is no case of petty right or wrong' makes an ostensible effort to explain itself, but in fact the poem's central moment entirely refutes the rational structure upon which the verse is constructed and which Thomas seems to rely upon for the poem's conduct and development.

There are many such moments in Thomas's poetry, like that of 'The Ash Grove': 'But the moment unveiled something unwilling to die | And I had what I most desired without search', or 'I never saw that land before', 'I neither expected anything | Nor yet remembered: but some goal | I touched then'. The crucial event, that which approaches complete personal fulfilment, comes unexpectedly. Within the dramatic context of these poems, the vital revelation is one which cannot be summoned. Thomas's epiphanies take place in spite of, not because of, his rational organization.

At another level, such moments represent crises in Thomas's already obsessive preoccupation with language. Modern British poets from Housman to Larkin are concerned with innovations of poetic diction. They aim to achieve an individual style by using words in a way which makes them personal to the poet: Housman's frequent use of the word 'lad' for example, to denote not one but a complex range of relationships. For Thomas, the interest in diction is part of a wider concern for the correlation between language and things, the signifier and the signified. His poems call attention to the apparently arbitrary assignation of words and often bring into question the referential nature of language. The poem ' "Home" ' (3) reveals the importance of this issue for human relationships:

> The word 'home' raised a smile in us all three,
> And one repeated it, smiling just so
> That all knew what he meant and none would say.
> Between three counties far apart that lay
> We were divided and looked strangely each
> At the other, and we knew we were not friends
> But fellows in a union that ends
> With the necessity for it, as it ought.

The poet uses inverted commas even in the title, to indicate that the word has no single objective meaning but signifies something different for each of them. This linguistic ambiguity highlights their essential separateness and shows that in defining his individual relationship to language, the poet necessarily commits himself to a degree of isolation. The linguistic disparity might be exaggerated by the differences in accent which would exist 'Between three counties far apart that lay'. With a crisis in the relationship to that which is signified, the poet relies increasingly upon the word alone, 'And then to me the word, only the word', and eventually the realm of language takes over completely: 'If I should ever more admit | Than the mere word, I could not endure it.' Thomas's relationship with language is a very special one, for occasionally it is capable of replacing human contact altogether as a source of value or fulfilment. In 'Adlestrop' the absence of human contact in the final stanza is compensated by a unique feeling of community with aspects of language: 'No whit less still and lonely fair'. The change in diction is a dramatic event and may to some extent explain the nature of Thomas's 'Moments of everlastingness'. To interpret 'The Other' as the poet's search for himself and 'Lob' as his search for social context is to see that 'the journey and not the arrival provides him with the wholeness he seeks, because it is there that self-consciousness is at a minimum'.[9] In the sense that Thomas's poems are dramatic events, they are all escapes from, as well as expressions of self-consciousness.

This crisis takes place again and again in Thomas's poetry as he struggles to define his relationship to language and reconcile its commonness with his individual use of it. With 'The Word' he identifies in the thrush's song a form of utterance which has no literal meaning, 'the name, only the name I hear', but which is given perpetual currency by the thrushes' reinterpretation of it (like Keats's nightingale). In 'Adlestrop' his attention is held not by the place but by the word, 'Adlestrop—only the name', and this distinction is made in 'Words' with 'From the names, and the things | No less'. The poem 'Bob's Lane' suggests that place-names might be more specific in their otherness; although there is a residual inaccuracy in language ('To name a thing beloved man sometimes fails') this form of word might have for Thomas a greater efficacy, 'The name alone survives, Bob's Lane'. The poem 'Beauty' begins by attempting to define the word, 'What does it mean?', and 'Up in the Wind', Thomas's first poem, devotes twenty-two lines to an inn's signboard, without which he could not tell that the building 'Was not a hermitage but a public house'. Even here the relationship between signs as forms of communication and the possibility of human contact is present:

---

[9] A. Motion, *The Poetry of Edward Thomas* (1980), 51.

'But if you had the sign | You might draw company.' Although this is a reference to a specific written signboard, it still admits the connotation of language at large and so reveals the intensely linguistic nature of his preoccupations and the extent to which, even in his first poem, he establishes a special relationship with language. Thomas's first notebook, showing the method by which his poems were written from certain paragraphs of prose chosen from among his earlier commissions, reveals that his poetry is carefully composed; it is written not directly from experience, so to speak, but created from previous written documents or texts. This procedure may well have intensified Thomas's sense of a relationship with language, the sense in his poetry that words are things in themselves.[10]

The opening lines of 'Old Man' demonstrate the need to recognize the element of imperfection in language:

> Even to one that knows it well, the names
> Half decorate, half perplex, the thing it is:
> At least, what that is clings not to the names
> In spite of time. And yet I like the names.

As Andrew Motion remarks, the lines express Thomas's belief 'that language cannot adequately re-create the object that it describes',[11] but it is also useful to understand that for Thomas, language represents an entirely separate mode of contact: there is a very special sense in which he inhabits the world of language. In 'Celandine' and 'Sedge-Warblers' stanzas of contrived literary artifice are followed by the expressions 'Yet rid of this dream' and 'But this was a dream'. Both poems make (not entirely successful) efforts to renounce a relationship with language as a substitute for a relationship with the things language denotes.

At the same time, Thomas seeks to preserve and extend the repertoire of poetic diction by giving old words a new currency and vitality. The first lines of 'Sedge-Warblers' appear uncharacteristically Parnassian:

> This beauty makes me dream there was a time
> Long past and irrecoverable, a clime
> Where river of such radiance racing clear
> Through buttercup and kingcup bright as brass
> But gentle, nourishing the meadowgrass

---

[10] This notebook is kept at the State University of New York at Buffalo. I have seen a copy by kind permission of Professor R. G. Thomas.
[11] Motion, *The Poetry of Edward Thomas*, 165.

That leans and scurries in the wind, would bear
Another beauty, divine and feminine,
Child of the sun, whose happy soul unstained
Could love all day, and never hate or tire,
Lover of mortal or immortal kin.

This ten-line stanza is a single sentence, the diction, alliteration, and syntactical cadence of which remove it immediately from any sense of common speech. But the poem's formal literary style is cultivated (as can be seen from a comparison with an earlier draft of the poem printed in Professor Thomas's edition), and it serves a thematic purpose. Edward Thomas's language in this poem symbolizes a breakdown of the capacity of words to convey meaning. The poet's song is an analogue to that of the sedge-warblers:

Their song that lacks all words, all melody,
All sweetness almost, was dearer now to me
Than sweetest voice that sings in tune sweet words

This is a failure of language to convey anything other than itself; the bird-song 'lacks all words' but is valued for its own sake above the sounds of intelligible communication. The collapse of the communicative function is reflected in the language of the poem: in 'Sedge-Warblers' the persona subsists in the world of words rather than in the 'otherness' or reality which those words signify. It is a rejection of rational processes which is expressed in the final line: the birds sing of 'What no man learnt yet, in or out of school'.

This has important consequences in helping to define Thomas's literary context, for it places him in relation to the epistemological crisis which characterizes the work of major writers of the period such as Conrad and James. Edward Thomas's diction is not a wholly outdated usage or a sign of arrested development but a distinctly modern stylistic feature: the poet redefining his relationship to formal structures, in Thomas's case the individual words themselves. This may distinguish him once and for all from certain of the Georgians. His use of language serves a specific dramatic purpose which is central to his theme and style (and this cannot be said of the Georgians). Thomas's achievement is comparable to that of Owen, who transformed conventionally poetic images by placing them in a new context. Consider 'Dulce Et Decorum Est' with its 'old beggars' and 'hags' which were the property of W. H. Davies but which in Owen's poem acquire entirely new significance: soldiers are 'Bent double like old beggars under sacks' and after a gas attack they are heard 'coughing like hags'.

Compare also Thomas's 'The Other' and Owen's 'Strange Meeting'
as manifestations of early twentieth-century *Doppelgänger* literature;
Thomas's task is 'To watch until myself I knew' and Owen's
counterpart reveals to him that 'Whatever hope is yours | Was my
life also'. Both poets could have read Conrad's *The Secret Sharer*
(1912) and would certainly have known Stevenson's *Dr Jekyll and
Mr Hyde* (1886), and both poets might have known Hardy's 'He
Follows Himself', but the contention here is that their adaptation
of poetic image and dramatic form is a unique reinterpretation of a
specifically English tradition. It is not that Thomas and Owen are
not 'war poets', but that they represent something more important
and more meaningful which is not confined to a single historical
moment. This might be called the advent of modern British
poetry.

   These innovations are developments primarily in the nature
and function of poetic diction. Like Hardy, Thomas and Owen do
not depart dramatically from earlier practices but aim to extend
possibilities inherent in the tradition of English poetry. They
reinterpreted in personal terms that which most of the Georgians
could only weakly imitate. A revived interest in diction was a
characteristic of British poetry of the 1950s; Donald Davie's *Purity
of Diction in English Verse* (1952) revived the issue of the language of
poetry for the poets of the Movement: he hoped that his work
'might help some practising poet to a poetry of urbane and
momentous statement'.[12] The poetry of Philip Larkin could certainly be examined in terms of his preoccupation with diction, his
use of words such as 'accoutred', 'frowsty', and 'simples' in
'Church Going' for example, and the way in which he succeeded in
establishing a relationship with language which at times became
mannered or stylized (the 'awful pie' of 'Dockery and Son' for
example). It is in this sense that Geoffrey Hill has described some
of Larkin's poetry as 'pawky'. The poetry of John Betjeman might
also be interpreted in terms of its use, in new contexts, of language
which seemed exhausted or outdated. Donald Davie's terms,
'a poetry of urbane and momentous statement', conspicuously
suggest the character of Thomas's achievement. Thomas himself
wrote that 'A great writer so uses the words of everyday that they
become a code of his own which the world is bound to learn and in
the end take unto itself.'[13] Critics of Thomas's poetry must be
especially alert to the dramatic context of lines such as 'No whit

[12] D. Davie, *Purity of Diction in English Verse* (1952), 107.
[13] E. Thomas, *The South Country* (1909), 136–7.

less still and lonely fair' ('Adlestrop'); 'some legendary or fancied place' ('The Path'); 'whisper my soul' ('I never saw that land before'); and 'only in the blossom's chalice lies' ('What Will They Do?'), because they represent the moments at which Thomas tries to redeem in a dramatic context aspects of the language of the nineteenth century and make them function successfully in new roles. They are more than simply 'a few awkward archaisms'.[14] As Edna Longley has expressed it, 'Inversion is a particularly marked feature of Thomas's syntax. By no means a reflex archaism, it serves both his back-and-forth trawls for meaning, and his historically bridging role.'[15]

It might be proposed that Thomas's poetry consists of a tension between the two elements broadly outlined above, the rational structure of argument and the irrational moment of revelation. In a recent book called *The Romantic Tradition in Modern English Poetry* (1986) Geoffrey Harvey traces this tension from Wordsworth and defines it in his study as 'a tradition which involves a romantic commitment to the exploration of some sense of transcendence counterbalanced by a classical restraint', and he designates this style as 'essentially English.'[16] Similarly Terry Whalen has described the same style as a 'tradition of empirically oriented poetry'.[17] For Edward Thomas the 'Moments of everlastingness' identified in 'The Other' are at the centre of this stylistic paradox:

> Once the name I gave to hours
> Like this was melancholy, when
> It was not happiness and powers
> Coming like exiles home again,
> And weakness quitting their bowers,
> Smiled and enjoyed, far off from men,
> Moments of everlastingness.
> And fortunate my search was then
> While what I sought, nevertheless,
> That I was seeking, I did not guess.

Although the poem follows a rational procedure in externalizing a crisis of personal identity, the language here reaches towards a symbolism which evades precise analysis. There is a measure of

---

[14] D. C. Walker, 'The Poetry of Edward Thomas', unpublished B. Litt. thesis, University of Oxford (1966), 57. Bodleian MS B. Litt. d. 1207.

[15] E. Longley, *Poetry in the Wars* (Newcastle, 1986), 43.

[16] G. Harvey, *The Romantic Tradition in Modern English Poetry: Rhetoric and Experience* (1986), 19.

[17] T. Whalen, *Philip Larkin and English Poetry* (1986), 98.

syntactical ambiguity which shifts the mode of expression from metaphor to symbol: the 'powers' and 'weakness' come to exist independently because they bear no direct and absolute relation to 'I'. This ambiguity is felt strongly at 'Smiled and enjoyed' which must refer back to 'I' but which is confused by 'far off from men' which, as a spacial reference, appears to connect back imaginatively to 'exiles'. The 'Moments of everlastingness' belong both to the first-person speaker and to the 'powers' which exist independently of a metaphorical relationship: they attain symbolic status. Thomas stretches the possibilities of metaphor and the stylistic change is a dramatic moment in the poem's conduct, comparable to those sudden and marked changes of diction noted earlier.

According to the edition of Professor Thomas, 'This stanza is on a separate sheet of paper and seems to have been inserted later into the poem'.[18] This is curious because it contains many key aspects of Thomas's style and theme: the significance of the activity of 'naming' for example, its struggle to convey rationally a moment of psychological integration by reconciling contradictory elements, and its oblique acknowledgement that what he seeks is that which cannot be understood, only experienced. His use of a symbolist technique and rhetorical cadence disrupts the logical relationship between concepts, liberates him from that which can be known, and enables him to articulate a moment of transcendence. That 'The Other' was only the sixth poem Thomas wrote is an indication of the extent to which his poetic identity was formed during his years as an Edwardian journalist.

It is instructive to compare this stanza with poems by Larkin (who has had the full benefit of Yeats's example). 'High Windows' for example employs precisely the same stylistic tension between the structure of argument, 'When I see a couple of kids | And guess he's fucking her', and the moment of revelation. Larkin's 'Moments of everlastingness' also find expression in what approaches a symbolist technique:

> Rather than words comes the thought of high windows:
> The sun-comprehending glass,
> And beyond it, the deep blue air, that shows
> Nothing, and is nowhere, and is endless.

As a symbol, Larkin's 'high windows' has a range of meaning which cannot be simply and categorically specified. His break-down of communicative sense, 'Rather than words', is a very close

---

[18] *The Collected Poems of Edward Thomas*, ed. R. G. Thomas, 30.

parallel to that of Thomas. Like Yeats's 'stone | To trouble the living stream' ('Easter 1916') and Thomas's 'powers' and 'weakness', Larkin's symbol achieves an independent existence, not absolutely fixed in a metaphorical context. At this level Thomas's poems represent a struggle between Yeats's heroic urge to defy time and Hardy's stoical acceptance of fate. Larkin professes to have renounced one for the other, 'the Celtic fever abated and the patient sleeping soundly' (Introduction to *The North Ship*), but his poems naturally work to exploit the best of both worlds. Between 1902 and 1909 Thomas reviewed Yeats's work favourably and was very sympathetic to its aims and methods; Vernon Scannell believes that 'Had he not been killed it seems likely that Thomas would have developed the narrative gifts shown in those longer and neglected poems "Lob", "Up in the Wind", and "Wind and Mist"',[19] but Longley points out that Thomas very rarely reviewed fiction, a fact which, for her, acts as 'an underlining of the trend of his own writing towards symbol rather than narrative'.[20] Thomas's poetry as we actually have it consists of a tension between Yeatsian symbolism and Hardyesque empiricism, which he had not time to resolve or develop but which represents in itself an art we can call modern.

Modern stylistic tensions can be seen at work in 'The Barn and the Down', a poem which is ostensibly concerned with the nature of perception and the way in which larger conclusions are drawn from that which is seen. Especially in its visual concentration, 'Before critical eyes', the poem is reminiscent of Hardy; 'At Middle-Field Gate in February', for example, where the poet stands at a threshold and surveys the scene. Hardy's 'Afterwards' is also a poem about the intellectual organization of visual perceptions. For Hardy and Edward Thomas the artful arrangement of that which is seen can be potentially beguiling. But Thomas's poem is perhaps not so straightforward:

> But far down and near barn and I
> Since then have smiled,
> Having seen my new cautiousness
> By itself beguiled

[19] V. Scannell, *Edward Thomas* (1963), 31.
[20] *A Language not to be Betrayed: Selected Prose of Edward Thomas* ed. E. Longley (Manchester, 1981), p. iii.

> To disdain what seemed the barn
> Till a few steps changed
> It past all doubt to the down;
> So the barn was avenged.

In contrast to the earlier stanzas, the line-units here are no longer complete and self-contained units of sense. The poem acquires a self-reflexiveness which confuses the subject and lends an ambiguity to 'By itself'. Where precisely is 'far down and near' and is it not a contradiction? These difficulties are heightened at the stanza break 'By itself beguiled | To disdain what seemed the barn', and compounded by the absence of punctuation. The poem is not entirely successful in achieving a symbolic meaning, but it does help to define that which is unique to Thomas. The poem returns to his characteristic directness with the last line, 'So the barn was avenged', but only a very careful reading would explain the significance here of the verb 'avenged'. The fixed inanimate object disconcertingly subverts the perceptions of an informed and mobile intelligence, and this allows Thomas a freedom of expression which is not dictated by logical deduction. It is interesting that the verb 'smiled' is used here and in that vital central stanza of 'The Other', as well as during the important section of ' "Home" ' (3) but very rarely elsewhere in Thomas's work. It signals Thomas's appreciation of the special experience taking place in these poems.

The occasionally bizarre effects of this freedom can be seen in 'The Hollow Wood' where the imagery acquires a macabre and surreal suggestive force:

> Out in the sun the goldfinch flits
> Along the thistle-tops, flits and twits
> Above the hollow wood
> Where birds swim like fish—
> Fish that laugh and shriek—
> To and fro, far below
> In the pale hollow wood.
>
> Lichen, ivy, and moss
> Keep evergreen the trees
> That stand half-flayed and dying,
> And the dead trees on their knees
> In dog's-mercury, ivy, and moss:
> And the bright twit of the goldfinch drops
> Down there as he flits on thistle-tops.

The poet has released himself from the demands of discursive exposition, hence the irregular rhyming and the image of fish swimming through the air laughing and shrieking. To paraphrase Donoghue's observation on *Ulysses*, this poem has something beyond simple communication as its first object.

The contradictory elements at the heart of 'The Other' help to explain the wider use of paradox and oxymoron throughout Thomas's poetry. He often achieves a resolution by combining opposites: 'This roaring peace' of 'Interval', 'Half a kiss, half a tear' which concludes 'Sowing', or the expression 'I'm bound away for ever' from 'Early One Morning'. Each of these poems has a poignance which comes from their careful suggestion of a human presence in a deserted landscape. A tacit choice is being made between social contact and personal freedom. Thomas does not wish to be compromised. For him it is a dilemma which highlights an intense ambivalence towards human relationships and a feeling that social intercourse threatens his individuality. Occasionally this is expressed in an extreme form: 'No man, woman or child alive could please me now' ('Beauty'), or 'Too sharp, too rude, had been the wisest or the dearest human voice' ('Melancholy'). Yet a measure of ambivalence is to be found at almost every point where a human figure enters his personal landscape. The war for example did not bring Thomas that sense of companionship which might have been expected; his fellow soldiers, with whom he has endured considerable hardship, 'were not friends | But fellows in a union that ends | With the necessity for it, as it ought' (' "Home" '3). The poet's austere honesty bars him from easy friendship (a point to which we must return). Consider the dialogue of 'May 23':

> 'Where did they come from, Jack?' 'Don't ask it,
> And you'll be told no lies.' 'Very well:
> Then I can't buy.' 'I don't want to sell.
> Take them and these flowers, too, free.
> Perhaps you have something to give me?
> Wait till next time. The better the day . . .
> The Lord couldn't make a better, I say;
> If he could, he never has done.'

This apparently happy and fortuitous meeting is given in terms of wily rural banter, but it is significant that the conversation proceeds by a series of disagreements; the dialogue is a set of statements and counter-statements, there is little genuine exchange. Perhaps the element of friction adds relish to the importance of the encounter: May 23 is 'The day Jack Norman disappeared'. The idea of moments of isolation endowed with special poignance is more openly explored in 'The Owl' where the poet writes of 'what I escaped | And others could not':

> And salted was my food, and my repose,
> Salted and sobered, too, by the bird's voice
> Speaking for all who lay under the stars,
> Soldiers and poor, unable to rejoice.

The word 'salted' introduces another psychological dimension into the poem, suggesting that his comfort is given relish by the thought of those who are comfortless. The reference to the war recalls 'As the team's head brass', the dialogue of which is dislocated as the ploughman passes back and forth before his interlocutor:

>   'Now if
> He had stayed here we should have moved the tree.'
> 'And I should not have sat here. Everything
> Would have been different. For it would have been
> Another world.' 'Ay, and a better, though
> If we could see all all might seem good.' Then
> The lovers came out of the wood again

The ploughman wishes for an earlier stability but the poet finds his security in the present and clearly does not want the hypothetical change in circumstance which would bring back the ploughman's mate. It is a difference of opinion which is felt in their respective use of the word 'here', and in their implicit contrast with the harmony of the lovers. Both this poem and 'The Owl' awaken feelings of guilt, and on close examination it is noticeable that Thomas's chance meetings with rural characters are rarely without a suggestion of awkwardness or difficulty. The poem 'Early One Morning', for example: 'A gate banged in a fence and in my head. | "A fine morning, sir", a shepherd said', where the tone lends a mocking and slightly sinister note to the greeting. In 'The New Year' the solitary human figure is presented entirely in terms of animals, an indication that Thomas finds difficulty in identifying with that which they have in common; he transposes the human in order to accommodate it. They speak briefly but only 'So far as I could hear through the trees' roar'. Everywhere in Thomas's poetry, personal dialogue is interrupted, disturbed, and unsatisfactory. Writing to Gordon Bottomley in 1904 Thomas complained that in his attempts at imaginary conversations there were 'two monologues to be heard, not one dialogue'.[21]

---

[21] *Letters from Edward Thomas to Gordon Bottomley*, ed. R. G. Thomas (1968), 61.

In this respect it is helpful to consider two poems about specific relationships, those with Thomas's mother and wife, 'M. E. T.' and 'Helen' respectively. The poem which Professor Thomas informs us was about the poet's mother,[22] beginning 'No one so much as you . . . ' ends with the image of 'A pine in solitude | Cradling a dove', where the tree is stately, insensate, singular, and cold, while the attributes of the bird are warmth and vulnerability. The tree provides involuntary protection and receives none of the warmth of the dove. A feeling of reciprocity is missing; the relationship is one of 'only gratitude | Instead of love'. It is precisely this reciprocal aspect, the element of exchange, which worries Thomas about relationships. In the poem addressed to his wife, he asks what is the most valuable thing he could give her, and finds the reply, 'I would give you back yourself'. The idealistic impossibility of this impulse is matched by the sense of insurmountable difficulty which characterizes Thomas's relationship with his father; his poem 'P. H. T.' begins, 'I may come near loving you | When you are dead.'

As was suggested earlier, Thomas's isolation is partly the result of his integrity and honesty, two vital qualities of his art. In ' "Home" ' (3) Thomas acknowledges that to be a poet is to use words in a way which is very particular, and in doing so he cuts himself off from the sense of community that comes from common talk. Language is common property, but Thomas's use of it is intensely personal. The poem 'Aspens' ends,

> And it would be the same were no houses near.
> Over all sorts of weather, men, and times,
> Aspens must shake their leaves and men may hear
> But need not listen, more than to my rhymes.
>
> Whatever wind blows, while they and I have leaves
> We cannot other than an aspen be
> That ceaselessly, unreasonably grieves,
> Or so men think who like a different tree.

The poem testifies to Thomas's personal integrity, 'We cannot other than an aspen be', and acknowledges the risk he takes in being misunderstood, 'Or so men think who like a different tree'. The quietness of the aspens is contrasted with man's noisy activity, but a choice between them is to some extent vitiated by the conviction that 'it would be the same were no houses near';

---

[22] *The Collected Poems of Edward Thomas*, ed. R. G. Thomas, 276. This is strongly contested by S. Smith in his *Edward Thomas*, 172.

Thomas would always remain faultlessly true to himself. It is characteristic of his poetry that the larger social dimension of 'Aspens' should be set in opposition to the individual speaker. The poem expresses an essential antagonism towards the very people who should compose its audience, the people of 'the inn, the smithy, and the shop'.

'I never saw that land before' similarly chooses personal fidelity at the expense of wider companionship:

> and if I could sing
> What would not even whisper my soul
> As I went on my journeying,
>
> I should use, as the trees and birds did,
> A language not to be betrayed;
> And what was hid should still be hid
> Excepting from those like me made
> Who answer when such whispers bid.

The poet's art is the source of alienation rather than social integration: his natural language of 'the trees and birds' stands in opposition to the rhetorical language of man which is capable of being 'betrayed'. Thomas's language has a fidelity beyond corruption, because it belongs to no one else. That his poetry is an intensely private utterance, and a mystical experience, is felt in the assertion that 'What was hid should still be hid | Excepting from those like me'. 'The long small room' also locates the issue of fidelity and corruption at the heart of Thomas's creative instinct. A recent critic has noticed 'how the shape of the room resembles a coffin',[23] a further point of correspondence with Philip Larkin, whose 'Mr Bleaney' is confined to 'one hired box' and who, in a particularly Thomasian attitude, lies on the bed in his boarding house, 'Telling himself that this was home'. Thomas's writing commits him to a degree of isolation, but at the same time acts as a permanent source of security:

> When I look back I am like moon, sparrow and mouse
> That witnessed what they never could understand
> Or alter or prevent in the dark house.
> One thing remains the same—this my right hand
>
> Crawling crab-like over the clean white page,
> Resting awhile each morning on the pillow,
> Then once more starting to crawl on towards age.
> The hundred last leaves stream upon the willow.

[23] M. Kirkham, *The Imagination of Edward Thomas* (Cambridge, 1986), 37.

Thomas's writing continues despite the lack of a human audience; his solitude is both relieved and intensified by his devotion to art. Its essential fidelity, 'One thing remains the same', recalls that of 'Aspens', 'we cannot other than an aspen be', and 'I never saw that land before', 'A language not to be betrayed'. The rhyme on 'page/age' signals the power of art to defeat time, but only through that which is impersonal and beyond knowing, 'what they could never understand' (c.f. Hardy's 'page/lineage' rhyme in 'The Jubilee of a Magazine', and Yeats's 'face/lineaments trace' rhyme in 'The Municipal Gallery Revisited'). Thomas's lines approach very closely the themes of Yeats's mature poems, as does the symbolist last line where the 'leaves' refer both to the writer's pages and the natural 'expression' of trees. Thomas's poem helps to illuminate the special individuality of a voice which can describe 'the inn where all were kind | All were strangers' ('Over The Hills'), and explain how for him 'The friendless town is friendly; homeless, I am not lost | Though I know none of these doors, and meet but strangers' eyes' ('Good-night'). It is perhaps the ultimate creative paradox that Thomas's poetry frequently expresses the desire not to be known; it is an ambivalence in his attitude to self-expression which naturally conditions all of his poetry. Stan Smith has argued that Thomas's poetry is characterized by 'an incommunicable sense of exclusion which yearns for the ratifying womb of class, race, or tradition',[24] but this poet's social impulse is far more provisional than Smith would have it. The attendant conditions Thomas places upon mutual exchange make social integration for him almost impossible. Thomas's sense of himself is too fragile to surrender any part of it.

'Aspens', 'I never saw that land before', and 'The long small room' are important statements of Thomas's artistic identity. Thomas's is a search for context and ratification through language. Again a glance at 'The Other' is instructive: Thomas's 'Moments of everlastingness' take place 'far off from men'. One critic has commented that 'certainly you will not find Thomas's kind of voice among the Edwardian poets, look where you will',[25] but the separation of the individual from the larger social context or institution is an important theme for much Edwardian poetry and is symptomatic of a wider political anxiety characteristic of the period. Andrew Motion, writing of Thomas as a war poet, has said that, 'Because all his poetry was written after the outbreak of war,

[24] S. Smith, *Inviolable Voice: History and Twentieth Century Poetry* (Dublin, 1982), 51.
[25] J. Lucas, *Modern British Poetry from Hardy to Hughes* (1986), 84.

it is all, in an important sense, war poetry. Behind every line, whether mentioned or not, lies imminent danger and disruption.'[26] The pressure of 'danger and disruption' is certainly felt very keenly in Thomas's poetry, but it would be too easy to attribute this entirely to the outbreak of war. All but one of Thomas's poems were written in England and he spent only seventy days in France before being killed, yet throughout the Edwardian decade he laboured under the burden of a kind of writing (and poverty) which contributed considerably to his sense of personal unworthiness. This feeling brought him in 1911 to the verge of nervous breakdown and suicide, but as early as September 1903 he had consulted a specialist about exhaustion, caused by his penurious existence as a writer. From the moment he left Oxford he was preoccupied with the problems of social alienation; in 1904 he wrote to Gordon Bottomley: 'A variety of social intercourse should be good: & I wish you were able to try it. But with me, social intercourse is only an intense form of solitude.'[27] One of the numerous 'superfluous men' who populate Thomas's prose complains in *The South Country* (1909):

I realise that I belong to the suburbs still. I belong to no class or race, and have no traditions. We of the suburbs are a muddy, confused, hesitating mass, of small courage though much endurance. As for myself, I am world-conscious and hence suffer unutterable loneliness.[28]

The separation of the individual from a sense of social community was a preoccupation Thomas shared with C. F. G. Masterman's *The Condition of England* (1909) and which Thomas identified in a review of Yeats in May 1908: 'The individual is everything in it: society has not been considered. But then society is not alive, it is a lump that exists. Reform society, not the artist.'[29]

These quotations give the impression that deracination, alienation, and isolation were feelings with which Thomas was familiar well before the outbreak of war; he commonly makes a distinction between the individual and the community. Thomas did not need war to make him feel anxious. In fact there is convincing evidence that the war worked to relieve his sense of oppression:

To understand Edward's mood at this time it is necessary to know that the war had brought him, in a curious fashion, a sense of relief . . . while

[26] Motion, *The Poetry of Edward Thomas*, 92.
[27] *Letters from Edward Thomas to Gordon Bottomley*, ed. R. G. Thomas, 53.
[28] *The South Country* (1909), 85.
[29] Review of *Discoveries* in *Daily Chronicle* (18 May 1908).

the war had not really solved any of his problems—in fact it had increased the difficulty of earning a living—it had at any rate relieved him of the necessity for worrying about them. It had not lessened his responsibility; but it had lessened his sense of responsibility.[30]

This is an important distinction which helps to explain Thomas's outpouring of verse after the outbreak of war; it has been expressed by another commentator with the words 'not war but specifically England at war is what concerns him'.[31] Thomas's poetry was in some measure an expression of a sense of freedom he had not felt since his undergraduate days more than ten years earlier.[32] This is a far more convincing explanation of Thomas's writing than that which suggests he wrote out of feelings of loss and regret; the original imaginative impulse is seldom a negative one. Larkin's practice may prove an analogue: 'The impulse for producing a poem is never negative; the most negative poem in the world is a very positive thing to have done.'[33] Larkin is a poet who has also written about finding a balance between personal integrity and social contact, notably in 'Vers de Société' and 'Faith Healing'. The anxiety heard in Thomas's voice is partly a pre-war or Edwardian characteristic and finds an echo in the poetry of John Davidson and Thomas Hardy. Hardy's *The Dynasts* (1908) is dominated by an authorial reticence which conditions the entire work and which is in some ways comparable to that of Thomas. Both the style of *The Dynasts* and the voice of Thomas's poems express the fear that an obtrusive technique will only obscure the 'simple fact' which they feel it is their obligation to convey.

Ezra Pound said of Thomas Hardy's *Collected Poems* in 1937, 'Now there is clarity. There is the harvest of having written twenty novels first,' and this might equally have been said of Edward Thomas. Correlations between Thomas and Hardy are worth pursuing briefly, especially their respective interpretations of the speaking voice:

> The cherry trees bend over and are shedding
> On the old road where all that passed are dead,
> Their petals, strewing the grass as if for a wedding
> This early May morn when there is none to wed.

This is Thomas's 'The Cherry Trees' in which there are two references to the absence of human life and a macabre rhyme

[30] Moore, *The Life and Letters of Edward Thomas*, 216.
[31] Kirkham, *The Imagination of Edward Thomas*, 120.
[32] See R. G. Thomas, *Edward Thomas: A Portrait* (Oxford, 1985), 73.
[33] 'A Conversation with Philip Larkin', *Tracks*, 1 (summer 1967), 8.

'dead/wed' to emphasize the emotional isolation of the poet (c.f. Housman's poem 'Loveliest of trees, the cherry now | Is hung with bloom along the bough' from *A Shropshire Lad*). The scene is recorded directly without obtrusive authorial interference, and little impression of the writer is allowed to emerge. But the sense of a personality is present in the poem's visual attentiveness. In the absence of an explicit first-person speaker the poem is at once highly self-conscious and self-less. This method of statement through self-erasure is the theme of Hardy's 'Afterwards' from *Moments of Vision* (1917), which is about the poet's reputation after his death. Not only does it concern his literal non-existence, but an accompanying extinction of human life takes place as the poem moves from 'neighbours' to 'a gazer' and then to simply 'one', 'those', and finally 'any'. Yet the poet's non-existence is successfully refuted by the studied faithfulness of his poem's visual detail; he was manifestly 'a man who used to notice such things'. Both poems resolve the problem of making authoritative statements in poetry by using a persona which has no remnant of Victorian self-confidence and assurance but which has withdrawn altogether behind a veil of negative propositions. In the light of this Edwardian reticence, Hardy and Thomas attempt a poetry of pure perception. 'Afterwards' and 'The Cherry Trees' strive for a form of impersonality, and this is a characteristically Edwardian procedure. It is an idea taken up and developed by T. S. Eliot in his essay 'Tradition and the Individual Talent'.

The landscape and community that Hardy preserved were those specifically of Wessex, but Thomas had suffered displacement and had no native countryside. Born in Lambeth and brought up in Wandsworth, he moved house six times before he joined up in 1915 and lived all his life in rented property. Perhaps as a result of this disorientation, what Thomas called his 'accidentally Cockney nativity',[34] there is something provincial or suburban in his use of the imagery of property like that of 'I built myself a house of glass' where it becomes a metaphor for the fragility of ostentatious outward show:

> No neighbour casts a stone
> From where he dwells, in tenement
> Or palace of glass, alone.

The poet's vulnerability goes unrecognized among neighbours of the same temperament; each of them is imprisoned by a splendid, polished, and superficial façade. The property image provides an immediate visual impact in 'Blenheim Oranges': 'Look at the old house | Outmoded, dignified | Dark and untenanted'. A note of desperation is introduced by the insistent refrain 'I am something like that', and the 'glass' metaphor is used again to convey his insecurity:

> Not one pane to reflect the sun,
> For the schoolboys to throw at—
> They have broken every one.

The fragile appearance has been shattered but this does not bring a new and genuine confidence, as the muted rhyme 'sun/one' indicates. Both poems employ the notion of a tenant, the special characteristic of which is that he has only temporary rights of occupation. In contrast 'The Other' describes a moment of personal integration in terms of 'A dark house' where the poet finds 'one peace | Held on an everlasting lease'. Poems such as 'The New House' and 'Two Houses' and Thomas's numerous roads, inns, forests, and gardens contribute to his evocation of an English rural environment, and an important feature of the war poetry of Hardy and Thomas is their portrayal of displacement from this scene: the 'foreign constellations' of 'Drummer Hodge' and the 'foreign clod' of Thomas's 'Bugle Call'. Thomas's sense of imminent removal from an English landscape and his feeling that he would probably not return helped to crystallize its value to him with poignant urgency. Walter de la Mare wrote in his preface to the *Collected Poems* that when Thomas was killed in Flanders 'a mirror of England was shattered of so pure and true a crystal that a clearer and tenderer reflection of it can be found no other where than in these poems'.

There seems to be currently under way, in certain quarters, a revision of the idea of Modernism, a feeling that it might have been, after all, a more isolated event than was realized, a foreign incursion which is now being absorbed into more traditional ways of thinking about English poetry. It has been suggested that young poets are returning to pre-Modernist writers for their inspiration, and Philip Larkin is often cited as the figure-head of this anti-Modernism. Blake Morrison has detected in Philip Larkin's 'MCMXIV' a note of literary nostalgia for 'a long standing English tradition of which the Georgians are the last representatives'[35] and tentatively outlines 'the tendency, common in the

[34] Moore, *The Life and Letters of Edward Thomas*, 277.
[35] B. Morrison, *The Movement: English Poetry and Fiction of the 1950s* (Oxford, 1980), 196.

Movement generation, to think of 1914 as the date at which an indigenous tradition in poetry ended, and at which the Modernist tradition began'.[36] Strictly speaking this notion is absurd; Larkin's poetry reveals at many points the influence of modern poetry,[37] and no contemporary writer can prosper without being cognizant of what has gone before, especially if it had the impact and artistic value of Modernism. But despite these qualifications, it can be argued that British poets of the pre-war or Edwardian period had evolved a modern art of their own, recognition of which has been eclipsed by the more obviously radical innovations of subsequent years. Whether or not contemporary poets are drawing on pre-Modernist models is not at issue here, but if they were, then Edward Thomas would be an excellent focus for their attention.

[36] B. Morrison, *The Movement: English Poetry and Fiction of the 1950s* (Oxford, 1980), 202.

[37] See especially B. Everett, 'Philip Larkin: After Symbolism', *Essays in Criticism*, 30 (1980), 227–42. Also Motion, *Philip Larkin*.

6

John Davidson: Scottish versus English

AN important characteristic of the Edwardian poets is their relation to a sense of England. Rupert Brooke, Henry Newbolt, Masefield, Hardy, A. E. Housman, and Edward Thomas each appear to cultivate a specifically English identity, one which is preoccupied with English diction, English history, and a distinctively English landscape. They can seem provincial and insular in comparison to Modernist cosmopolitanism. Terry Eagleton identified an important aspect of the Modernist character when he pointed out that 'With the exception of D. H. Lawrence, the heights of modern English literature have been dominated by foreigners and émigrés'.[1] This is true because writers such as Conrad and Eliot were able to bring to the English cultural identity they adopted 'a range of experience . . . which went beyond its parochial limits, and with which England could be fruitfully compared . . . it was a tension notably absent in the work of their contemporaries'.[2] In fairness to those contemporaries, many of whom are subjects of this book, the tensions of formulating an exclusively English identity are not necessarily less productive, but they do nevertheless limit the writer's range of vision. Eagleton has shown how, in Conrad's *Under Western Eyes*, 'The provincial pragmatism of English culture is sharply exposed, in the light of foreign currents of feeling with which it cannot deal.'[3] The result is a major technical advance in the handling of the position and authority of the omniscient narrator. This approach provides a valuable context for a consideration of John Davidson (1857–1909), who was born in Barrhead, now a suburb of Glasgow, and lived in Scotland until he was 33, when he moved to London. Davidson's early writings are characterized by their exploration of a Scottish cultural heritage (the Spasmodic poets, Carlyle, Stevenson, Burns, and Scott), which initially he seems to have endorsed. But Scottish literature alone became increasingly insufficient for Davidson as his talent and ambition developed. His early life is

---

[1] T. Eagleton, *Exiles and Émigrés: Studies in Modern Literature* (1970), 9.
[2] Ibid. 14.   [3] Ibid. 30.

also marked by his emphatic rejection of the creed of his father, a minister of the Evangelical Union. The Scottish poet's aversion to the austerity and self-denial of his father's Calvinism developed into a tendency to radical and independent thought which was almost programmatic. Davidson's move to London in 1890 is a watershed in his progress at which ostensibly he abandoned Scotland as a source of imaginative inspiration. He was a reluctant exile, however, and the poverty of his literary career intensified the isolation he felt as a Scot in Edwardian London. Only superficially did the poet experience what his biographer has called 'a fierce alienation from his native culture'.[4] This chapter tries to show that Davidson's sense of Scottish identity helped to sustain him in his creative enterprise despite public indifference, and argues that his cultural displacement characterizes him as perhaps unique among Edwardians, as one who anticipates some of the innovations of the Modernists.

Davidson's first work, *Bruce*, a play published in Glasgow in 1886, is in many respects a celebration of Scottish individuality, of separateness from England; it uses a directly historical subject to help define the young writer's artistic identity as Hardy used the Napoleonic Wars in *The Dynasts* (1908) to exorcise the anxiety of the European threat to Wessex, which had obsessed him since childhood. Davidson's play begins by announcing the location of its imaginative world with the words ' "Once more my lords the rude North claims our care" ' and proceeds as an historical record of struggle with the English, Bruce declaiming, ' "I am the heart of Scotland" '. The nature of the relationship between the English and the Scots is neatly identified by Bruce when he asks ' "What good knight was it, like a water-drop, | Lost shape and being in an English sea?" ' and he recounts a parable of Scottish resistance to English cultural imperialism to bolster his troops on the eve of the Battle of Bannockburn. The image of the water-drop becoming subsumed by a neighbouring flood, losing its 'shape and being', is at once personal and political; it is conscious of national characteristics and expresses the dangers of cultural adulteration. Although at this stage the theme does not represent what could be called an anxiety for Davidson, the play is an exploration of a sense of national identity, of ' "These fiery children of the North" '; the English confess, ' "We have never vanquished them in fight | Except where treachery assisted arms." ' The poet is

[4] J. B. Townsend, *John Davidson: Poet of Armageddon* (New Haven, Conn., 1961), 95.

clearly attracted to an image of heroic defiance, of character in action, and of those who attend the demands of their nature rather than social convention. He portrays integrity and honour as predominantly but not exclusively Scottish qualities. Such characterization is accompanied by the depiction of a Scottish landscape and climate, its uncultivated and inhospitable beauty clearly distinguishable from the restrained gentility of Georgian rural scenes, and from decorative Pre-Raphaelite floral tapestries. Davidson also experiments with the Scottish language ('cushats', 'sonsy', 'capercailzie'), as if testing his native tongue as a suitable vehicle for his artistic personality. Ultimately the play celebrates the Scottish victory at Bannockburn, at which point the drama ends abruptly. This might be compared to Hardy's *The Dynasts* which, as we have seen, ends with victory for the English at Waterloo.

Davidson demonstrates a very assured handling of blank verse in *Bruce*, his robust and vigorous language matching that of the characters and action. Although indebted to Shakespeare's histories, the poet's verse has the conviction of a genuine artistic discovery and achievement: ' "Edward of England, if one pure pulse beats | In that debauched and enervated core which was your conscience | I will make it ache." ' In this play it is the purpose of speech to strive for the maximum emotional impact.

Smith: A Tragedy (1888) develops the idea of Scottish integrity with a further image of virtuous diminution, ' "I would rather be | A shred of glass that sparkles in the sun | And keeps a lowly rainbow of its own" '. Again the importance of the Scottish location is emphasized, it is a stage 'remote from any breath of modern weariness' (an aside for the aesthetes of London), but more importantly it is the subject which makes the greatest demands upon Davidson's skill as a poet:

> 'Garth's in the North, a hamlet like a cave,
> Nestling unknown in tawny Merlin's side,
> A mount, brindled with scars amd waterways.
> The windows, Argus-eyed with knotted panes
> That under heavy brows of roses blink
> Blind guard, have never wept with hailstones stung;
> No antique, gnarled, and wrinkled, roundwood porch,
> Whiskered with hollyhocks in this old thorpe
> Has ever felt the razor of the East.'

The energy of the language is closely related to the innate violence of the environment in which the drama takes place. Davidson's protagonist, Smith, is a Byronic hero befitting the romantic vigour and isolation of this landscape, one who urges his lover to ' "Obey your nature, not authority" '. He commits suicide rather than be denied his bride by an authoritarian father. The other important character is Hallowes, an affected and world-weary poet, who also chooses suicide rather than (artistic) failure. In this way both romantic despair and romantic defiance end in death; both role models are unworkable because they are incomplete. This duality is characteristic of Stevenson's *The Master of Ballantrae* (1889) and identical to that of Masefield's story 'Edward Herries' (1907) in which the contemplative life and the active life are tested and found wanting, yet no middle way can be discovered; a 'dialogue' of this kind is the central matter of Conrad's *The Nigger of the 'Narcissus'*. Davidson's eponymous protagonist ends in failure, unable to find the *modus vivendi* appropriate to his time; he is a truly Edwardian creation, like Christopher Tietjens, Mr Polly, and even Nostromo, 'a hero in a world which has no role for him to play'.[5] Davidson's work is romantic melodrama, but an interpretation in terms of its duality redeems the play: his characters represent a complete mind/body split which is more than simply 'a fundamental contradiction of design which invalidates both the ideas and the comedy'.[6] This is an illustration of the way in which studying Davidson in the context of his contemporaries enables him to be better understood. The dualism of his play is found in the work of many Edwardian writers, Masefield, Brooke, and Newbolt among them. Davidson attaches ideas of integrity and honour to the act of suicide, drawing upon another turn-of-the-century characteristic, one elucidated by Daiches,[7] and found in the poetry of A. E. Housman, especially his poem 'Shot? so quick, so clean an ending? | Oh that was right, lad, that was brave: | Yours was not an ill for mending, | 'Twas best to take it to the grave' (*A Shropshire Lad* XLIV). Davidson's consistent advocacy of the right to take one's own life is a calculated contravention of religious dogma and a typically Schopenhauerian assertion of the individual will. For Davidson, suicide is the supreme expression of mind over matter.

The North Wall, published in Glasgow in 1885, is a very self-conscious piece of literary artifice in which romantic novels and those who read them are robustly lampooned. It is written specific-

---

[5] J. Batchelor, *The Edwardian Novelists* (1982), 23.

[6] Townsend, *John Davidson: Poet of Armageddon*, 126.

[7] D. Daiches, *Some Late Victorian Attitudes* (1969).

ally for a Scottish working-class audience, for those reading 'on the camp-stool of a Clyde steamer' (p. 148). The protagonist is 'A practical novelist' who sets out to demonstrate that ' "Practical joking is the new novel in its infancy" ' (p. 10), and indeed the entire work is a practical joke upon the reader, Davidson's characters throughout declaring themselves for mere caricatures and chastising us for expecting anything more in so unashamed an entertainment. The hero addresses the family lawyer with ' "Well sir, your contribution to this work is wholly unexpected, but likely to produce most interesting complications" ' (p. 88). The novelist advises his handsome young suitor, ' "Go in for dissipation: there's nothing like it for the cure of romance. Unworldly diseases need worldly remedies. And yet that's too common, especially with lady novelists" ' (p. 126). At one point it is reported that his daughter will die rather than marry against her will, at which romantic cliché the novelist complains: 'I am sorry her message is so commonplace. It indicates that her novel reading has not been eclectic, to say the least; and, which is worse, it lowers the tone of the present work' (p. 75).

Davidson's novel is comparable to Austen's *Northanger Abbey* in the exaggeration of its literary self-consciousness, and in the way in which it satirizes conventions while using them as a vehicle for fiction. It is an exuberant burlesque of Stevensonian romance, displaying the episodic style he employed in a later satirical novel *Earl Lavender* (1895). Like Austen's novel, *The North Wall* struggles affectionately with a literary parent from which it cannot quite detach itself, but the importance for Davidson is that he is already testing a Scottish literary vehicle and finding it insufficient for his wider artistic purposes. With *The North Wall* his dissatisfaction with received literary forms takes the shape of parody, and the subversive impetus is comically anarchic.

Scaramouch in Naxos (1888) is the last of Davidson's works written in Scotland, an experiment with the conventions of pantomime which represents, it has been claimed, 'a minor critical landmark in the development of classical English comedy from Jonson and Marston to Gilbert and Shaw'.[8] The humour originates in a confusion of roles between mortals and deities; Glaucus insists that he could pass as a god:

GLAUCUS. After all, I am a well made man; and Endymion looks no more.
IONE. But he is disguised.

---

[8] Townsend, *John Davidson: Poet of Armageddon*, 88.

GLAUCUS. It may be that I am disguised too.

IONE. I doubt it: no god could be disguised so completely as not to know his own identity.

GLAUCUS. Still, here is a god punished with dumbness: Jupiter may have punished me with oblivion of a brilliant past.

IONE. What god could you possibly be?

GLAUCUS. Probably just a god. Doubtless there are gods of nothing in particular, merely decorative.

(scene ii)

The play is a celebration of the freedom and perception which imagination endows, the gods bringing to mortals a sense of power of which they would not ordinarily be aware. In this way the theme of human identity is developed beyond national types. Although the play employs the traditional pantomime devices, Davidson's shifting between earthly and cosmic perspectives to combine contemporary social satire with intimations of a dimension beyond human knowledge anticipates the way in which he later uses an unearthly perspective to imply forces which are not mystical but economic, not benign but indifferent or malevolent. *Scaramouch in Naxos* turns upon a comic contrast between human and godly, where romantic transcendental sublimity is reserved only for Bacchus; Glaucus 'wants to be immortal in order to move up in the world (so to speak)'.[9] But as Davidson developed, the claim of the mortal characters, that man might supplant gods, becomes a serious central issue. The operation of the fantasy element in this play might be compared to that of *Peter Pan* (1904) and *The Man Who Was Thursday. A Nightmare* (1908), but Davidson is more seriously intent upon the innovative subversion of his chosen literary form than Barrie or Chesterton, and it is this formal development which is important.

In 1889 Davidson received a letter of encouragement from George Meredith and this determined him to move to London to try a literary career.[10] The immediate result was *In a Music Hall and Other Poems* (1891) most of which was written in Scotland and which includes many Scottish subjects, 'Winter in Strathearn', 'Ayrshire Jock', and 'Kinnoull Hill'. The book records his sense of separation from 'the banks of the busy Clyde' and his first encounter with the intense competition of London's literary scene ('Grub

⁹ M. O'Connor, *John Davidson* (Edinburgh, 1987), 21.

¹⁰ For the text of this letter see Townsend, p. 56. The young Scottish poet had been similarly encouraged by an English luminary when he met Swinburne in 1878.

Street').[11] Having given up various positions as a schoolmaster Davidson soon learned that 'hawking daily an edition | Of one's own poetry would tame | The very loftiest ambition' ('Ayrshire Jock'). The title sequence is a group of vignettes of music-hall performers, but the authentic note of a speaking voice eludes most of Davidson's attempts at ventriloquy. They possibly owe something of Kipling's *Barrack-Room Ballads*, the first of which, 'Danny Deever', had appeared in W. E. Henley's *Scots Observer* in February 1890.

A notable exception is the poem 'Ayrshire Jock' which addresses contemporary Scottish writing:

> They drink, and write their senseless rhymes,
> Tagged echoes of the lad of Kyle,
> In mongrel Scotch: didactic times
> In Englishing our Scottish style
> Have yet but scotched it: in a while
> Our bonny dialects may fade hence:
> And who will dare to coin a smile
> At those who grieve for their decadence.

Ayrshire Jock complains of the adulteration of his native language and prophesies its obsolescence, when this idiosyncratic and local manner of speech will seem like mere affectation. The pun on 'scotched' parallels 'Englishing' in making a verb from a proper noun and so suggests the way in which the language is maimed and reduced to a quaint ethnic curiosity. The cultural imperialism of Davidson's Scottish play *Bruce* is here presented as threatening the very language with which he speaks. This is a surprisingly Modernist anxiety, one given fuller expression in *A Portrait of the Artist as a Young Man*: 'His language, so familiar and so foreign, will always be for me an acquired speech. I have not made or accepted its words. My voice holds them at bay. My soul frets in the shadow of his language.'[12]

Joyce's 'Dublin Greek' is a synthetic language which circumvents this problem: Joyce did not write in Gaelic. Similarly, Ayrshire Jock uses a Scottish word 'plisky' (a mischievous trick), but only as a rhyme for 'Scottish whisky'. Davidson's speaker does not advocate a return to the dialect poetry of Burns, but says, 'I rhymed in English, catching tones | From Shelley and his great successors.' In this respect one critic has written of Davidson that

---

[11] Gissing's *New Grub Street* was also published in 1891.
[12] James Joyce, *A Portrait of The Artist as a Young Man* (1917), 249.

'He too recognised the exhaustion of the English high literary medium . . . but he refused to abandon it for a language more worn-out still, the low Burnsian Scots.'[13] 'Ayrshire Jock' is a good poem, successfully dramatizing the voice of Scottish low life, lugubrious and half-drunk. In a review of 1892 Yeats compared Davidson to Arthur Symons (whose cabaret sketches *London Nights* appeared in 1895).[14] Yeats noticed Davidson's search for new subject-matter and identified him with a new generation of young poets as 'an Alastor tired of his woods and longing for beer and skittles'.[15]

Davidson's first book of poetry was not a commercial success, but *Fleet Street Eclogues* (1893) published by Lane and Mathews, received some recognition 'among the cognoscenti'.[16] The work is typical of Davidson's minor innovations of literary form, an ironical association of Arcadian shepherds and newspaper hacks which contrasts urban and rural pursuits and counterpoints nostalgic innocence with modern corruption. As with other of Davidson's works this is a kind of literary joke, using contemporary satire to revivify an ironically appropriate form. These shepherds are under no illusions as to the practical value of their discourse: 'We review and report and invent, | In drivel our virtue is spent' ('New Year's Day'). This poem exemplifies Cyril Connolly's belief that the period was characterized by 'the struggle between literature and journalism'.[17]

1894 was a crucial year for Davidson's career; 'A Cinque Port' was published in the *Pall Mall Gazette* in March and 'In Romney Marsh' appeared in the *Speaker* in the same month; his 'Two Songs' was published in the first number of the *Yellow Book* in April 1894, 'Thirty Bob a Week' in the July number, and 'The Ballad of a Nun' in the *Yellow Book* of October 1894. Davidson's collected 1890s verse *Ballads and Songs* was published in November, and his collected *Plays* were reissued with a frontispiece by Beardsley, to capitalize on his current notoriety. 1894 was also the year Davidson met Yeats and became an associate, but not a full member, of the

---

[13] L. Dowling, *Language and Decadence in the Victorian Fin de Siècle* (Princeton, NJ, 1986), 229.

[14] Arthur Symons's debt is less to Davidson than to Browning and the French symbolists he was translating at this time. His first book was *An Introduction to the Study of Browning* (1885). See also his poetry *Silhouettes* (1892).

[15] W. B. Yeats, 'The Rhymers' Club', *Letters to the New Island* (Cambridge, Mass., 1934), 142, 146; repr. from the *Boston Pilot* (23 Apr. 1892).

[16] Townsend, *John Davidson: Poet of Armageddon*, 167. See also Grant Richards's comment that 'His *Fleet Street Eclogues* did the trick', *Author Hunting* (1934), 218.

[17] C. Connolly, *Enemies of Promise* (1938), 23.

Rhymers' Club. In 'The Tragic Generation' Yeats recalls that although Davidson attended meetings he felt that the group 'lacked "blood and guts"' and that he disrupted their unanimity by insisting on the election of four Scottish friends. The Club 'secretly resolved never to meet again'.[18] Yeats wrote of Davidson that 'his Scots jealousy kept him provincial and but half articulate', and it would seem that this sense of separateness led Davidson to join the Rhymers not as a sympathizer but as a lone devil's advocate. Despite his evident dissatisfaction with Yeats's group Davidson did not align himself with the poets of the 'Henley Regatta' even though he had written poetry worthy of them and might have found an affinity with Henley's combative manner.[19] Frank Harris records that Davidson 'could not stand Henley',[20] but it seems unlikely that the two poets ever met. Perhaps, as Yeats hints, Davidson's Scottishness contributed to his artistic isolation during his career in London. Lionel Johnson in the *Academy* of March 1895 recognized Davidson as 'half-jesting and half-despairing, yet defiant all the while', which neatly summarizes his cultural ambivalence and misanthropic individuality.

Ballads and Songs (1894) includes what are arguably Davidson's three most famous poems, 'In Romney Marsh', 'Thirty Bob a Week', and 'The Ballad of a Nun'. The first of these is a slight and rather inert rural poem, a scene observed from 'knolls where Norman churches stand', which strives for an impression of richness, for something jewelled and precious, but is rarely more than simply decorative. The poem's colours are Pre-Raphaelite regal, 'purple', 'sapphire', 'saffron', 'crimson', and its sense of elegy and epiphany is too obviously composed rather than discovered. The accompanying 'A Cinque Port' is better, using a more skilful stanza form and working towards a metaphorical conclusion:

> Below the down the stranded town
> Hears far away the rollers beat;
> About the wall the seabirds call;
> The salt wind murmurs through the street;
> Forlorn the sea's forsaken bride,
> Awaits the end that shall betide.

[18] W. B. Yeats, *Autobiographies* (1926). Quotation from Macmillan edn. (1970), 315–18.

[19] Davidson is not even mentioned in J. H. Buckley's *W. E. Henley: A Study in the 'Counter-Decadence' of the 'Nineties* (Princeton, NJ, 1945). See the chapter 'The Henley Regatta. London 1890–1894', 147–61.

[20] F. Harris, *Contemporary Portraits* (1915), 126.

The Scottish poet uses the ancient association of the Cinque Ports
and the image of desertion to conjure a nostalgic sense of English
history. The volume *Ballads and Songs* includes several other poems
suggestive of Kentish and Sussex downland; 'Spring' contains a
description of morris-dancing and wistfully asks, 'To England
shall we ever bring | The old mirth back?' There is a feeling of
English national pride here with which Kipling might have been
pleased, but which sounds incongruous in the mouth of a Scot who
had earlier asked, 'What good knight was it, like a water-drop, | Lost
shape and being in an English sea?' (*Bruce*). These proto-Georgian
rural lyrics are indicative of the extent to which Davidson became
Anglicized during the 1890s, conforming to English literary
fashion for the sake of popularity. It is an act of ventriloquy as
convincing as some of his earlier dramatic portraits.

'Thirty Bob a Week' is a rhyming ballad in which a Kiplingesque
suburban clerk laments his lot 'A-scheming how to count ten bob a
pound', and the poem extols a philosophy of private stoicism, even
heroism: 'It's walking on a string across a gulf | With millstones
fore-and-aft about your neck, | But the thing is daily done by many
and many a one | And we fall, face forward, fighting, on the deck.'
'Thirty Bob a Week' is an exercise in successfully imitating
another's style with sufficient aplomb for the poem not to seem
simply parodic. 'The Ballad of a Nun' is a narrative ballad,
a blasphemous tale attacking moral convention: 'Straight to
his house the nun he led | "Strange lady, what would you with
me?" | "Your love, your love, sweet lord", she said | "I bring you
my virginity." ' The poem achieved instant notoriety because the
nun who flees the convent for a debauched interlude receives
subsequent approbation from the Virgin Mary.

Although *Ballads and Songs* includes what are probably his three
best-known poems, it is 'A Ballad in Blank Verse of the Making of
a Poet' which demonstrates Davidson's originality. This poem has
something of Wordsworth's *The Prelude* in describing the awakening
of the creative personality with Romantic indulgence. Davidson's
poem is also reminiscent of Byron's *Manfred* and *Childe Harold* in
depicting rebelliousness and romantic isolation against a symbolic
landscape: this is Davidson's *Bildungsgedicht*.[21] Here the importance
of the poem's Scottish location is indicated by the repetition of a
refrain at crucial junctures in the narrative:

[21] O'Connor, *John Davidson*, 31.

> For this was in the North, where Time stands still
> And Change holds holiday, where Old and New
> Welter upon the border of the world
> And savage faith works woe.   (139–42)

Davidson's Scotland is remote, inhospitable, and violent; although the poem was written in London, it portrays the urban/rural duality of the Firth of Clyde, its natural beauty despoiled by the shipyards of Greenock. The poem argues that its drama could only take place in Scotland, because of the unique topographical and temperamental characteristics to be found there.

The ballad declaims the young poet's absolute rejection of Christianity, the dogma of his parents standing as representative of the world's slavery to systematized thought, especially religious thought. The poem is a drama of apostasy in which dogmatic belief is replaced by imaginative freedom, a sudden and remarkable intellectual self-discovery providing a sustaining sense of self-confidence and creative potential. The young poet's resolution to obey his instinct and pursue his vocation to self-fulfilment is accompanied by a broadening of his sympathies beyond the parochial limits of his upbringing. He seeks to escape the confines of Scottish small-town life and the intellectual constraints that inhibit him. Although the poem is a fervent and unrestrained declaration of independence, it is yet conscious of the hazards of dogmatism, warning that,

> it were but to found
> A new religion, bringing new offence,
> Setting the child against the father still.
> Some thought imprisons us; we set about
> To bring the world within the woven spell.   (418–22)

The young poet's Promethean assertions are sustained by his sense that 'I am a man apart | A mouthpiece for the creeds of all the world' (426–7). Townsend argues that this 'doctrine of self-realisation . . . is closely allied to the gospel of action and self-reliance preached by Carlyle, Morris, and Ruskin' and that Davidson has simply separated this tradition from Victorian morality and 'welded it to the activism of Henley and Stevenson',[22] but this is to ignore the particular artistic qualities of Davidson's blank verse. The poem's force and vigour are entirely his own, not contrived or literary, and it succeeds precisely because of its

---

[22] Townsend, *John Davidson: Poet of Armageddon*, 270.

convincingly discovered belief in the potential of imagination and
in its hard-won conviction that this is an individual experience.
The blank verse successfully expresses the energy of rebellion
and self-discovery, it exhibits a rhetorical eloquence which is
learned perhaps from his father's evangelist pulpit, and possesses
a linguistic range (scientific and demotic) which is unusual for the
poetry of the 1890s. It is distinguished by its attempt to put new
life into a romantic conception of human personality which had
seemed exhausted: 'No creed for me! I am a man apart, | A
mouthpiece for the creeds of all the world, | A soulless life that
angels may possess | Or demons haunt.' Davidson has something
in common with D. H. Lawrence here, in his use of an evangelist's
rhetorical style as a weapon against Christianity.

'A Ballad in Blank Verse' demonstrates that poetry is capable of
redeeming the apparent poverty of a barren industrial environment and that imagination provides a personal abundance for the
individual who possesses it. The fervour of the young poet's belief
in imagination as a source of illimitable value is sufficient to
supplant Christianity, and to justify heresy and parricide. In
many respects the poem is a calculated assault upon the decorum
and propriety of literary tradition, and in fact upon many of the
other poems in the same volume. It is a contrast that emphasizes
the subversive and original quality of Davidson's sense of Scottish
identity.

'A Woman and Her Son', published in *New Ballads* in 1897, goes
a step further in the formulation of the uniquely Davidsonian hero,
one who abandons even atheism as too dogmatic and argues for
the complete emancipation of belief. All systems of thought are
untenable in the light of modern experience, they are nothing
more than 'the lewd dream of morbid vanity' (139). The protagonist
rails against the tyranny of monism (the philosophical theory that
all being may ultimately be referred to one category, as opposed to
the dualism of matter and spirit). Again the death of a parent is a
central dramatic event (perhaps suggesting a faint sense of guilt),
but although the mother's faith is discredited, the son's sudden
descent into insanity dramatizes the tyranny of any single absolute
philosophy. The poem ends with an expression of severe formal
distancing, the poet moralizing that obstinate devotion to any
creed is outmoded by the variety and confusion of modern life,
'For both were bigots—fateful souls that plague | The gentle
world'.

But there is nothing gentle about Davidson's world; he uses the best of his skill in the compassionate portrayal of dereliction and suffering:

> He set his teeth, and saw his mother die.
> Outside a city-reveller's tipsy tread
> Severed the silence with a jagged rent;
> The tall lamps flickered through the sombre street
> With yellow light hiding the stainless stars:
> In the next house a child awoke and cried;
> Far off a clank and clash of shunting trains
> Broke out and ceased, as if the fettered world
> Started and shook its irons in the night;
> Across the dreary common citywards,
> The moon, among the chimneys sunk again,
> Cast on the clouds a shade of smoky pearl.   (157–68)

The use of perspective here is excellently managed in both its spacial and temporal aspects, giving an impression of both powerlessness and dignity. The elegiac tone conjured from a dilapidated urban interior is matched by Davidson's imagery of spiritual degeneration: 'My heart is eerie, like a rifled grave | Where silent spiders spin among the dust' (221–2). The pathos of the mother's condition is a real achievement, anticipating in a small way the suburban despair of Eliot, whose persona felt 'I should have been a pair of ragged claws | Scuttling across the floors of silent seas' in 'The Love Song of J. Alfred Prufrock' (1917).

'A Woman and Her Son' reveals a technical advance in Davidson's handling of blank verse, his elliptical phrasing and compressed syntax exercising a controlled discipline and tight harnessing of his rhetorical skill. Townsend believes that the metre of this poem is as advanced as 'the early Pound', although he argues that more usually Davidson 'like Hardy, Housman, and the Georgians, preferred to exploit the forgotten resources of traditional English verse patterns'.[23] It is Davidson's manifestly Scottish landscapes and environments which refute this argument; he derives a profound creative energy from the harshness of his location and from the struggles of its inhabitants. W. H. Auden has proposed that the English landscape, in its gentleness, seduced some of the Georgians into writing genteelly;[24] a comparison between their characteristic style and Davidson's is wholly inappropriate here. The Scottish poet's metrical innovations are an integral part of his

[23] Townsend, *John Davidson: Poet of Armageddon*, 230.
[24] *A Choice of de la Mare's Verse*, selected by W. H. Auden (1963), 21.

non-conformist cultural identity and align him with other Modernist outsiders to English culture and its London centre.

In an article on 'English' literature, one writer has described the significance of the impetus which early twentieth-century literature received from poets operating outside its insular confines:

> Modernist language was a collage speech which linked the demotic . . . to the foreign and technical . . . making this energetic startling combination a challenge to standard English usage . . . The geographical correlative of this is that the High Modernists didn't come from the centre of English culture.[25]

The importance of Davidson's innovations are surely of this kind; cultural displacement was a necessary stage in his literary development, but he was a writer, like the eponymous protagonist of his Scottish play *Bruce*, who at no time 'Lost shape and being in an English sea'.

At this point it is worth identifying an influence on Davidson's poetry which had gone underground during the 1890s with his attempts at an English theme but which was strongly revived for the poems of the Edwardian period, and that is the Scottish Spasmodic poets. This school is best represented by P. J. Bailey (*Festus*, 1839), J. W. Marston (*Gerald*, 1842), Alexander Smith (*A Life Drama*, 1853), and Sydney Dobell (*Balder*, 1853), each of whom was immensely popular in the early Victorian period (their mark can be found on Tennyson). J. H. Buckley outlines their style as including,

> the concept of the poet as a divinely inspired creature with an inalienable right to eccentricity, a right to despise the conventions that bound other men and to indulge a brooding genius in studied self-absorption. Inflamed by borrowed passions and their own ranting emotion, the Spasmodics yielded to a titanic egotism.[26]

Davidson's Edwardian testaments can be seen as twentieth-century interpretations of the Spasmodic manner, and it is possible that in his desperate isolation he became conducive to their 'unmitigated individualistic self-absorption'.[27] He might have found a personal significance in the life and writing of Ebenezer Jones, a Spasmodic poet who 'sought release from the rigorous Calvinism of his childhood and the poverty and disease that overshadowed his

---

[25] R. Crawford, 'Larkin's English', *Oxford Magazine*, 23 (fourth week, Trinity Term 1987), 3.

[26] J. H. Buckley, *The Victorian Temper: A Study in Literary Culture* (1952), 42.

[27] *The Poems of John Davidson*, ed. A. Turnbull (1973), vol. i, p. xix.

maturity', who 'was obsessed with a sense of his own failure', and who, because of his employment 'had at no time the leisure or the knowledge to discipline his exuberance'.[28] There are close parallels here with Davidson's situation, and an awareness of them might have intensified his identification with the style of Spasmodic writing. At the turn of the century he embarked on a series of long didactic works, the production of which was to cause increasing alienation, severe financial hardship, personal despair, and finally suicide. The very nature of these poems supports the suggestion that 'it was not fear of cancer, but despair of fulfilling his mission, that forced him "to make an end" '.[29] Again the religious metaphor is appropriate for a poet who mastered its language in order to attack its central tenets.

The Testament of a Vivisector (1901) is the first of Davidson's Edwardian blank verse monologues, and it is worth noting at the outset that a *testament* is 'the solemn declaration in writing of one's will', that in Scottish law it is a decree appointing an executor, and that the word has obvious biblical associations, appropriate to Davidson's apocalyptic message. Henryson's *Testament of Cresseid* might be a Scottish literary ancestor, but except in its austere moral tone it is a remote one. The present poem develops Davidson's attack on contemporary society; beginning in the form of a challenge with the words 'Appraise me', the vivisector demands an audience worthy of judging him. What he calls his 'headstrong passion and austerity' (26) is beaten out in a materialist philosophy which is impenetrably turgid but which represents a sustained hysteria. One critic has valuably noted:

Like Wells's Moreau and Conrad's Kurtz, he is one of a few 'strong minds, delivered and elect' who have isolated themselves from humanity in order to follow pursuits which society abhors. His ostensible motive is scientific curiosity.[30]

The poem is a portrait of a heightened and unnatural state of consciousness, and while Browning may be the model for this form, Davidson's individuality lies in the extremity and radicalism of his thought. The poem is also noteworthy in its use of scientific vocabulary, such as 'usufruct', 'alkahest' and 'solipeds'. This is a feature which Eliot might have learned from, and one which Hugh

---

[28] Buckley, *The Victorian Temper*, 48–9.

[29] P. Turner, 'John Davidson: The Novels of a Poet', *Cambridge Journal*, 5 (Oct. 1951–Sept. 1952), 499.

[30] R. Robertson, 'Science and Myth in John Davidson's Testaments', *Studies in Scottish Literature*, 18 (1983), 97.

McDiarmid has acknowledged as an important Modernist in-
novation.[31] The value of Davidson to modern writers has been
emphasized by Virginia Woolf, who wrote that 'He is always an
interesting poet, and a far better spokesman for his time than
others more mellifluous.'[32]

The Testament of a Man Forbid, also published in 1901, takes its
title from *Macbeth*, Davidson's favourite (Scottish) play. The first
line is 'Mankind has cast me out' and the poem is extreme in its
depiction of an outcast and exile, not simply Byronic but Messianic,
the blank verse forced with great pressure into set pieces of
rhetorical declamation which are brutal and uncompromising in
their violence of action and language. The poem is reminiscent of
Timon of Athens rather than Romantic poetry, crowded with
apocalyptic revelations, and pervaded by an unmitigated cynicism
which espouses a rejection of the cant of modern society. Davidson's poem also recalls the binary structural form of Shakespeare's
play in its dramatization of the abandonment of civilization for a
harsh rural landscape. The nihilism by which the Man Forbid
urges the world to rid itself of all remnant of past culture is severe
but convincingly sustained by the poem's urgency and force.
Occasionally the blank verse touches an elegiac note:

> The rainbow reaches Asgard now no more;
> Olympus stands untenanted; the dead
> Have their serene abode in earth itself,
> Our womb, our nurture, and our sepulchre.
> Expel the sweet imaginings, profound
> Humanities and golden legends, forms
> Heroic, beauties, tripping shades, embalmed
> Through hallowed ages in the fragrant hearts
> And generous blood of men; the climbing thoughts
> Whose roots ethereal grope among the stars,
> Whose passion-flowers perfume eternity,
> Weed out and tear, scatter and tread them down;
> Dismantle and dilapidate high heaven.   (65–77)

Davidson comes upon this tone almost accidentally; it expresses a
powerful disillusionment which is entirely genuine, and although
its subject is Norse mythology the verse retains the pressure of a
personal speaking voice. These changes of tone give a variety of
tempo to the conduct of his longer poems and prevent them from
falling into monotony.

---

[31] *John Davidson: A Selection of his Poems*, ed. M. Lindsay (1961).
[32] V. Woolf, 'John Davidson', *Times Literary Supplement* (16 Aug. 1917), 390.

Contemporary critics were baffled by Davidson's new style, but felt that his next poem was an improvement. *The Testament of an Empire Builder* (1902) was published at a time when anxieties about the British Empire were topical, the Boer War having recently ended in humiliation for the British Army, and imperialists at home. The poem consists of two visions: the first is a fable in which the animal kingdom debates the nature and evolution of man; he is merely a 'quaint abortion' says the snake. As Townsend points out, the poem has a place with Kipling's *Jungle Books* and Orwell's *Animal Farm* 'in the history of the modern satiric animal fable'.[33] The second vision is one of heaven and hell in which the traditional conception of divine justice is reversed; hell, 'An arras-cloth with human eyes embossed', consists of the piled-up bodies of altruists and Christians. It is a vision of eternal pain, the horror of which entirely matches that of Joyce's *A Portrait of the Artist as a Young Man*.

This Testament is distinctly less detached in its manner; it is less a mask adopted for the duration of the poem. Davidson has desisted from declaiming his separateness and as a result the poem is more personal and direct. Yet despite this it can be recognized that the depiction of these fantastical scenes is indicative of the poet's increasing withdrawal into a private imaginary world, a disturbing psychological consequence of Davidson's personal isolation. In an unpublished letter in the Davidson collection of the Harry Ransom Research Center at the University of Texas at Austin (undated but almost certainly 1893), Davidson wrote to Richard Le Gallienne complaining that,

It will, I am afraid, be years before Mrs. Davidson and I can pay and receive visits—and then we will be indifferent, as it is we are so unused to visitors that the thought of it makes us uncomfortable. Some day I may tell you how our lives have been laid waste, and our moods and characters spoiled for society.[34]

The spasmodic quality of the poetry is very distinctive, the perspective shifts from vivid immediate impressions to remote landscapes of the mind; physical violence is counterpointed with abstract mysticism, suggesting perhaps a psychotic split. The blank verse is less compressed, more discursive, yet still capable of displaying the poet's characteristic qualities in impressive bursts:

---

[33] Townsend, *John Davidson: Poet of Armageddon*, 343.
[34] HRHRC MSS Le Gallienne, Richard/Recipient.

> At last, my gaze dynamic grown, I saw
> That this remote environment of Heaven,
> Tier upon tier of flesh from base to crown,
> This human amphitheatre was Hell
> Itself, constructed of its denizens.
> My knitted brows and roofed hand swept the vast
> Eternal cirque of heinous agony
> Still as an icy frontier in the moon.

This poetry is openly didactic and heretical and shows the poet in the process of formulating a faith; it reveals Davidson's need for belief and his search for an appropriate subject. There may be an analogy here with Chesterton's obsession with the subject of faith, and with his desire to teach. Both writers are part of a strong current of Edwardian didacticism which might also include Belloc and Wells.

Davidson's alienation is confessed in the poem's preface, a parable by which he replies to the critics who called for him to return to the theme and style of his earlier lyrics. Davidson consciously and deliberately rejects lyricism as a vehicle for twentieth-century poetry. His Testaments are a working-out of a theme he had first explored in 'The Ballad of a Poet Born' which appeared in *Chapman's Magazine* in May 1895 in which he was already stating the inadequacy of late nineteenth-century poetry to deal with worthy subjects:

> And while the swarthy rafters rang
> With antique praise of wine,
> There rose a conscious youth and sang
> A ditty new and fine.
>
> Of Fate's mills, and the human grist
> They grind at was his song;
> He cursed the canting moralist
> Who measures right and wrong.

These are explicit statements of Davidson's determination to create a new poetry for the twentieth century, and to some extent he can be seen as having turned his back on commercial success to devote his energy to a new art. In this respect he anticipates the shift in Yeats's poetry from Celtic twilight to social themes; the change in Davidson is more radical and dramatic. This is expressly a dissatisfaction with late nineteenth-century romantic lyricism. The change is an Edwardian characteristic which Davidson shares with Wilfred Gibson and Rupert Brooke, who also relinquished romantic lyricism for social realism during the Edwardian years.[35]

The Testament of a Prime Minister (1904) is partly a polemic on the degeneration of mankind as a race, an eschatological poem concerned with death, judgement, and the state after death. It is a strongly didactic and prophetic vision of the end of things, delivered by a politician who speaks from the grave.[36] It is a poem specifically of Edwardian London:

> I reached a loathsome region, foul,
> Malodorous, dark; in every separate pore
> Of noxious atmosphere a separate stench.
> Among the barges, plots of pasturage
> Like old unhealed abrasions opened up
> With sheep like maggots starving in the mud.
> The reaches of the tributary Lea,
> Enamelled filthily in many hues—
> Purple and faded crimson, pallid gold
> And swarthy soot in wrinkled creases—gleamed
> With dusky iridescence, and bewitched
> My wounded fancy like a hellish charm.
> Ashamed I tracked the hideous watercourse
> And lit upon a swamp, a festering swamp,
> An ugly gusset of unholy slime
> Where stunted hemlock fought with tufts of sedge.
> It lay a little lower than the Lea,
> And took a ropy overflow that slunk
> Beneath a ruined bridge: tall chimney-stalks
> On one side belching smoke; the river bank
> Upon another; on the third, relays
> Of jangling trains: a piece of mother earth,
> Most woebegone, most horrible, for years
> Imprisoned, sick with filth and fetid air,
> Irrecognisable.   (317–41)

This portrait of Edwardian London is fuelled by Davidson's disgust at the squalor of urban civilization, and the energy of the language successfully transforms his revulsion into a powerful expression of the defilement, pollution, and corruption of the city, and the misery of its abject inhabitants.

Davidson draws on a tradition of urban poetry represented by fellow Scots, Alexander Smith and James Thomson (who was also

---

[35] See especially Gibson's *Daily Bread* (1910), and Brooke's play *Lithuania* (1911).

[36] The poem was conceived and begun in Scotland and it took Davidson a year to persuade Grant Richards to publish it. See Richards's *Author Hunting*, 218–21.

from Glasgow). Thomson's *The City of Dreadful Night* (1870–4) laments the loss of 'the joy, the peace, the life hope, the abortions | Of all things good which should have been our portions | But have been strangled by that City's curse', and Thomson uses the river as a point of escape from the claustrophobic intensity of inner city life. For Davidson also the river is the last remnant of a natural environment which suburban development has almost completely obliterated,[37] a romantic symbol which still functions as a source of comfort. The central action of Davidson's poem, a Hardyesque jeremiad, takes place on the banks of the Thames:

> Borne on this tide I went
> By the uncouth embankment where the Thames
> In surface eddies coiling and uncoiled
> Entangled by a myriad, myriad keels,
> Propellers, paddles, turbines, dredgers, oars,
> A ravelled skein, a dismal flood winds down
> Its greasy channel.

Despite urban despolation the Thames retains its attraction as a powerful natural element, moving silently through the centre of London, an element capable of bearing desperate citizens away, either by boat or by drowning. Davidson uses a city landscape to depict the spiritual atrophy of the new century ('Soberly I say this twentieth century begins | No other age than the Millennium'), but the river is a recognizably Wordsworthian symbol of natural power. T. S. Eliot's view from Lower Thames Street would seem to owe something to this tradition of urban poetry: 'The river sweats | Oil and tar | The barges drift | With the turning tide | Red sails | Wide | To leeward, swing on the heavy spar' ('The Fire Sermon'). Elsewhere too, Eliot's accumulation of urban detritus and litter is strongly reminiscent of this poem of Davidson's, particularly in his 'Preludes'. Eliot has acknowledged the influence of Davidson's 'Thirty Bob a Week',[38] the Kiplingesque ballad from the *Yellow Book* of 1894,[39] but his debt belongs more naturally to this Testament of 1904. Eliot's interest in the urban poetry of the French Symbolists does not invalidate this claim; his use of scientific language ('Polyphiloprogenitive' and 'piaculative' in

---

[37] The frequency of the word 'suburban' in Davidson's poem is notable. The word also occurs in Thomson's poem: 'Great piers and causeways, many noble bridges, | Connect the town and islet suburbs strewn'.

[38] *John Davidson: A Selection of his Poems*, ed. Lindsay.

[39] Reprinted in *Selected Poems* (1905).

'Mr Eliot's Sunday Morning Service') also finds a strong precedent in Davidson's Edwardian poetry.[40]

In October 1904 Davidson sent Gosse an advance copy of this Testament, saying, 'On one side I am a man with a message. I fought against it because to deliver it may entail the death by starvation of my family and myself.'[41] Davidson uses blank verse for the piling up of effects in a Miltonic or epic manner; he lacked a sympathetic critic to tailor his undoubted gift into something more economical and dramatic, unlike Eliot, whose original drafts of *The Waste Land* contained much lifeless social criticism. Ironically, in the final months before his suicide, Davidson met Ezra Pound at the house of Ernest Rhys, along with Ford Madox Ford, D. H. Lawrence, and W. B. Yeats. It is remarkable that Davidson could be part of this company without his talent being recognized.[42]

The Scottish poet's final work, *The Testament of John Davidson* (1908), was written at Penzance and originally entitled 'The Testament of a Deliverer' and 'The Passionary of John Davidson'; it is his most ambitious poem, and at over 2,000 lines, the longest. It includes a dedicatory preface addressed to the House of Lords, a warning about the condition of England, which might be compared to the 'Epistle Dedicatory' of Shaw's *Man and Superman* (1903). Again Davidson's poem begins with the protagonist's exile and isolation, 'When suddenly the world was closed to me', and it uses a good deal of dramatic exposition to depict the hero's seduction of Diana, here the 'patroness of motherhood', and his wholesale slaughter of the gods in physical combat. By dying, 'John Davidson', Christ-like, purges himself and all the world of belief in super-natural deities: 'And thus I made the world a fit abode | For greatness and the men who yet may be' (2092–3). 'John Davidson' is the martyr who rids the world of slavery to false belief, suffering the agonies of hell to make free thought possible for others: 'Gods and God | Are man's mistake: no brain exists | Behind the galaxies, above them or beneath | No thought inhabiteth eternity | No reason, no intelligence at all | Till conscious life begins' (1316–21). According to this poem, man created God in his inability to comprehend the universe, and in so doing enslaved himself to a fanciful delusion and denied the supreme stature of man; he placed his destiny in

---

[40] The epigraph of Thomson's poem is from Dante, an interesting correspondence with Eliot.

[41] See Townsend, *John Davidson: Poet of Armageddon*, 349.

[42] Ibid. 168.

the governance of a specious supernatural power. The poem is a mythological allegory by which any supernatural faith or worship is exposed and defeated. *The Testament of John Davidson* portrays its eponymous hero dissolving Apollo (literally), 'before the truth | The greatness and the terror of my song' (1337–8).

The poem's use of classical myth gives it a structural coherence lacking in some of the other Testaments, and aligns it with the character of Spenser, with Keats's *Endymion*, Byron's *Manfred*, and Arnold's *Empedocles on Etna*. Keats's poem rhymes, and the blank verse of Byron and Arnold is more carefully regulated than Davidson's; the final Testament returns, more than any of his previous works, to the example of the Spasmodic poets of mid-nineteenth century Scotland.

The bizarre grandeur of *The Testament of John Davidson* comes not only from its exotic mythological action, but from the sustained hysteria of its violent language. The poem gives qualities of movement and action even to the smallest inanimate details; the language's hypersensitivity endows all things with the power of physical life: 'I, following hard behind, shouldered the wind | That like an unseen sighing multitude | Oppressed and swarmed upon me. Turf and stone | With every step the dragon's talons showered' (320–3). The poem's elliptical inversions and costive syntax give it a muscular energy complementing the obsessive attention to physical processes: 'devouring me with eyes | That cracked their sockets' (310–11). The texture is dense and compulsive in its manipulation of vowel and consonantal changes to set up a ranging aural style which is almost pathological in its intensity: 'where the earth exhaled | A spicy redolence of nature's vat | By scaurs of torrent stone, by ivied cliffs, | Thickets and mossy brinks and brakes of fern' (371–4). The poem also exhibits a sexual prurience and voyeurism which contribute to the physicality of the imagery, its intimate associations implying an unnatural intentness upon the body and its functions; 'John Davidson' kills Diana's dragon with his spear: 'upward through his furrowed brisket, rough | With stumps of wiry hair, I dug and wrought | Begetting death devoutly as a groom | Begets a son' (421–4). This style is less well suited to the expression of remote abstract concepts, and parts of this Testament suffer a sense of strain where the rhetoric rings hollow and the language seems merely florid or impotent. But at its best, Davidson's language has a ferocious and uncomfortable concentration disarming moral judgement. The death of Apollo for example:

As he sprang
His clenched teeth mouldered in his jaws, his eyes,
Like gathered leaves that in a kiln curl up,
Shrank in their gloomy sockets, and on my flesh
His withered fingers hung like gossamer
The evening breezes trail . . . I struck
Him down; dismembered him as one might tear
A manikin in pieces; by breech and neck
I seized and kneaded him, and bent and plied
And wrung him like a rag.

Davidson's individuality consists partly in his eagerness to use his poetic skills in the depiction of scenes of horror and repulsion. In an essay on Robert Lowell's early poetry which seems apposite here, Ian Hamilton has written that it 'too often solidifies into a monotonously high-pitched rhetoric of desperation which can be repellent'.[43] Hamilton is probably referring to poems such as Lowell's 'The Exile's Return' in which, like Davidson's poem, dragons make an appearance: 'braced pig-iron dragons grip | The blizzard to their rigor mortis.'

For Townsend, writing of *The Testament of John Davidson*, 'the incoherence is unmistakably Spasmodic and the rhetoric Edwardian',[44] a comment which neatly identifies Davidson's cultural duality, the Scottishness of his creative energy being directed by the professional literary style he learned from his years as a London journalist. The dichotomy is not of course quite as simple as this (the Spasmodics themselves were avowed rhetoricians), but a view of Davidson as part of his contemporary milieu, as feeding off a Scottish cultural inheritance, helps to account for his artistic isolation and to locate his individuality. He is, in a sense, the exception who proves the rule.

Although there is little available criticism of Davidson's verse, there are two unpublished Oxford theses[45] both of which are very well researched but which consider their subject primarily as a lyricist and conclude their discussions of Davidson's career in 1900. Neither work makes a case for Davidson's Scottish individuality because in disregarding the Edwardian context of his later career they overlook the prominence of 'England' as a con-

---

[43] I. Hamilton, *A Poetry Chronicle* (1973), 95.

[44] Townsend, *John Davidson: Poet of Armageddon*, 419.

[45] A. M. Currie, 'A Biographical and Critical Study of John Davidson', B.Litt thesis, University of Oxford (1953), Bodleian MS B.Litt. 186; H. J. Sherman, 'The Lyric and Ballad Poetry of John Davidson, 1890–99', B.Litt thesis, University of Oxford (1970), Bodleian MS B.Litt. d. 1550.

temporary theme. Lacking a sense of the literary context of the
Edwardian period, criticism of Davidson's verse has been largely
unable to come to terms with his difficult later works, and can only
conclude that they are 'at best, merely praiseworthy efforts to
achieve the impossible'.[46] Given the idiosyncracy of these embryonic Modernist epics, it is perhaps only in an Edwardian
context that they can be properly understood.

[46] Currie, 'A Biographical and Critical Study of John Davidson', 213.

7

Rupert Brooke: 'The strife of limbs'

THE legend of Rupert Brooke is inescapable, a romantic myth engendered by numerous accounts of the poet's physical attractiveness, by the sonnets he wrote shortly after the outbreak of the war, and by his death at the age of 27 on the way to Gallipoli by which Brooke became 'a ritual sacrifice offered as evidence of the justice of the cause for which England fought'.[1] The quotation of Brooke's poem 'The Soldier' by the Dean of St Paul's, and the obituary in *The Times* written by Winston Churchill, had the effect of appropriating the poet as a political martyr and have contributed to the decline of his literary reputation. The immolation of Brooke's war sonnets has helped to sustain belief in the excessive romanticism and personal apotheosis which is satirized by Frances Cornford's epigram:

> A Young Apollo, golden haired,
> Stands dreaming on the verge of strife,
> Magnificently unprepared
> For the long littleness of life.

The early twentieth century saw a revolution in poetic taste by which, as Auden expresses it in his 'Letter To Lord Byron', 'For gasworks and dried tubers I forsook | The clock at Grantchester, the English rook'. Yet despite the changes of the post-war years a version of the Brooke myth survives. D. J. Enright believes that 'The Soldier' is still more widely read than Owen's 'Strange Meeting',[2] and at Rugby controversy recently ensued over the design of a memorial statue; some sponsors pressed for a representation of Brooke himself, while others argued that a stylized female figure would be more appropriate to the spirit of his poetry. In 1987 Peter Ackroyd complained that 'The myth is as potent as it ever was'.[3]

[1] B. Bergonzi, *Heroes' Twilight: A Study of the Literature of the Great War* (1965), 36.
[2] D. J. Enright, 'The Literature of the First World War', in *Pelican Guide to English Literature*, ed. B. Ford, vii (Harmondsworth, 1961), 164.
[3] P. Ackroyd, 'Not Honey for Tea *Again*', *The Times* (4 June 1987).

This chapter attempts to demythologize the man and focus serious attention on the poetry, claiming that many of his poems warrant serious critical attention and that they occupy an important position in the early twentieth-century rejection of Victorian romanticism. This chapter refutes the conventional image of Brooke as a poet of pastoral idyll and disputes the value of trying to understand his work in the context of Georgian poetry.

Brooke's *Letters From America* (1916) was written on a tour sponsored by the *Westminster Gazette* in 1913 and it is imbued with a sense of historic discovery, the novelty of which Brooke is imparting to his readers in London: 'I felt the thrill of an explorer before I started' (p. 3). The new continent represents the potential fulfilment of a dream, of that which could only previously be imagined, and it is an excellent vehicle, at the turn of the century, by which to exercise what Anthony Burgess calls the essential 'plasticity' of imagination.[4] Or as another critic expressed the sense of freedom which open spaces promise, 'In America's vast emptiness . . . there are truths to sustain any fiction'.[5] Brooke considers America to be in pursuit of an ideal and it is his role to define and appraise that moral and spiritual goal (a notion of liberty much espoused by the citizens he meets) and to watch for manifestations of it in American society. As he approaches Manhattan from New York harbour he sees the tower-blocks of Wall Street and the financial district and they seem to him 'edifices built to satisfy some faith'. Brooke's depiction of the banks and other money institutions as places of worship anticipates that of W. H. Auden's 'New Year Letter' (1940) whose 'secular cathedrals' determine the direction of cultural life and whose landscape is crowded with 'monasteries where they vow | An economic abstinence'. It is this sense of a perverted spiritual existence which most interests Brooke, and he feels the excitement of discovery and initiation as his boat arrives:

A goddess entering fairyland, I thought; for the huddled beauty of these buildings and the still, silver expanse of the water seemed unreal. Then I looked down at the water immediately beneath me, and knew that New York was a real city. All kinds of refuse went floating by: bits of wood, straw from barges, bottles, boxes, paper, occasionally a dead cat or dog, hideously bladder-like, its four paws stiff and indignant towards heaven. (pp. 8–9)

---

[4] A. Burgess, 'The Wide Plastic Spaces', *Times Literary Supplement* (30 May 1980), 601.

[5] P. Conrad, *Imagining America* (1980), 5.

Brooke's initial euphoria is checked by the details of urban squalor; to his credit, he cannot ignore the reality of an otherwise glamorous city, even if it qualifies his excitement.

This is the characteristic technique of *Letters From America*, tempering the undoubtedly noble aspirations of the New World with pointed visual observations, which suggests that the reality is something less than ideal. Of the Statue of Liberty Brooke says, 'I admired the great gesture of it', but it is beautiful only 'until you get near enough to see its clumsiness' (p. 9). This style enables Brooke to move from the general to the particular in a way which deflates American meliorism while providing the information for a more balanced report. Noticing the graceful gait of the American people he remarks, 'How much of this is due to living in a democracy, and how much to wearing no braces, it is very difficult to determine' (p. 16), and commenting on the smoothness of the American physiognomy he asks, 'Why do American faces hardly ever wrinkle? Is it the absence of a soul? It must be' (p. 19). This rhetorically facetious method satirizes the sometimes obtrusively moral interpretations of Victorian visitors to America such as Trollope and Dickens, and results in an often bizarre comic incongruity:

the stranger finds a divine hand writing slowly across the opposite quarter of the heavens its igneous message of warning to the nations, 'Wear —— Underwear for Youths and Men-Boys' . . . To the right a celestial bottle, stretching from the horizon to the zenith, appears, is uncorked, and scatters the worlds with the foam of what ambrosial liquor may have been within. Beyond, a Spanish goddess, some minor deity in the Dionysian theogony, dances continually, rapt and mysterious, to the music of the spheres, her head in Cassiopeia and her twinkling feet among the Pleiades. And near her, Orion, archer no longer, releases himself from his strained posture to drive a sidereal golf-ball out of sight through the meadows of Paradise. (pp. 31–2)

The humour is composed of two distinct elements, the epic stature of mythological gods, and the utter banality of underwear advertisements. In the descent from the sublime to the ridiculous the thematic opposition compromises the other-worldly and successfully makes artistic use of the ugliness of modern society. In New York the stars are replaced by 'two vast fiery tooth-brushes' (p. 30), and the queen of the night, 'an archaic Greek or early Egyptian figure', provides the answer to the riddle of American life with the magic words 'buy pepsin chewing-gum' (p. 33). These illuminated hoardings declaim that spiritual atrophy which is the presiding spectre over a people for whom money represents the height of human aspirations. Brooke's icons prefigure those of Scott Fitzgerald's *The Great Gatsby* (published ten years later in 1926) in which the eyes of Dr T. J. Eckleburg, 'their retinas one yard high', gaze out blankly over a waste land of suburban ash dumps.

The ugliness which Brooke perceives is to some extent redeemed however, for his characteristic double-view works both ways:

He was big, well-made, and strong, and he drove the car, not wildly, but a little too fast, leaning back rather insolently conscious of power. In private life, no doubt, a very ordinary youth, interested only in baseball scores; but in this brief passage he seemed like a Greek god, in a fantastically modern, yet not unworthy way emblemed and incarnate. (p. 22)

This kind of dual perspective is the chief stylistic method of the early chapters of *Letters From America*, a strategy (not always comic) which suggests there is for Brooke a genuine attraction in the frenetically superficial pointlessness of much that he sees. He is at once horrified and fascinated by the variety of commercial activity. Brooke's travel-writing systematically degrades all forms of abstract beauty and idealism by bringing it into direct confrontation with contemporary evils such as pollution, corruption, and depravity. He tests virtuous ambitions against the quality of everyday life. The Swinburnean young man becomes an image for America in Brooke's search for metaphors which do not provide an interpretative thesis but which simply exist for their own sake, self-referential, intellectually static. This is one of the unique pleasures of *Letters From America*; it is seldom doctrinaire or moralistic and has no argument other than the difficulty of reducing its subject to any single comprehensive interpretation. Brooke reiterates the impossibility of fathoming the workings of this society with a regularity suggestive of an epistemological crisis, except for the evident pleasure he takes in his own careless detachment. Brooke declares himself an Edwardian, freed of the dictates of Carlylean inquiry and unburdened of the prescriptive evaluative requirement which characterized the nineteenth century, a time he describes as 'an unfortunate period' (p. 56).

The best travel-writing recounts both the physical progress across country and the unobtrusive psychological journey of its author. Brooke's portrayal of most Americans as possessing the charm, simplicity, and unaffectedness of primitive beings (as having all the endearing qualities of children) implies a degree of naïvety or regression in his point of view. He watches a contortionist demonstrating the mobility afforded by a certain brand of under-pants, 'Not daring to imagine his state of mind' (p. 21), and observing commercial travellers he finds that 'It is impossible to guess what, or if, anything is in their minds' (p. 26). The impression that he is delighted by people's unsophisticated attractiveness is compounded by his tendency (in refraining from analysing the American personality) to be obsessive about their physical ap-pearance. Brooke's attention is fixed on bodies rather than the complex relations beneath the surface; he hopes that the Indians will not be engulfed by 'that ugliness of shops and trousers with which we enchain the earth' (p. 143). His treatment might be distinguished from that of D. H. Lawrence who, in New Mexico, sought a primitive mythological ancestry with greater seriousness and purpose.

Yet *Letters From America* gradually abandons the quick and easy rhetorical manner of its first impressions and gives way to the slightly Paterian aesthetic creed that 'A man's life is of many flashing moments, and yet one stream' (p. 95), a notion in fact of the stream of consciousness or 'dark flood' which is illumined by transcendent moments of epiphany. One such incident occurs by the railway in Toronto, by trains which toll 'an immense melan-choly bell, intent, apparently, on some private and incommunicable grief'(p. 81). Such moments hint at the emotional neurosis which prompts the desire for travel, as if a new environment promised therapy or release:

The lake was a terrible dead-silver colour, the gleam of its surface shot with flecks of blue and a vapoury enamel-green. It was like a gigantic silver shield. Its glint was inexplicably sinister and dead, like the glint on glasses worn by a blind man . . . Our boat appeared to leave no wake; those strange waters closed up foamlessly behind her. But our black smoke hung, away back on the trail, in a thick, clearly-bounded cloud, becalmed in the hot, windless air, very close over the water, like an evil soul after death that cannot win dissolution. (p. 78)

These dark and disturbing images (suggesting the symbolism of Philip Larkin's boat in 'Next, Please', 'In her wake | No waters breed or break'), are as close as Brooke comes in *Letters From America* to identifying the anxiety of which his travels were designed to relieve him. Elsewhere he describes 'that kind of ill-health which afflicts men who are cases of "double personality"—debility and spiritual paralysis' (p. 53) with the degree of understanding which comes only from personal knowledge. The progress of Brooke's narrative reaches a climax when thoughts of home become most urgent: he sees a steamer 'bound to England perhaps', he watches driftwood logs and wonders 'if they could have floated across from England, or if they could be from the Titanic', and standing under a sky 'like an English sky', suddenly,

> I stripped, hovered a while on the brink, and plunged. The current was unexpectedly strong. I seemed to feel that two-mile-deep body of black water moving against me. And it was cold as death. (p. 71)

Here the emotional drama takes over, and prompted by memories of England the writer's psychological progress reaches climactic absolution. The emotional crisis is a kind of purge by which Brooke, flirting with self-extinction, tries to discharge himself of the guilt or other anxiety (primarily sexual) which characterizes his writing. It prefigures the desire for spiritual health by which he was soon to imagine recruits 'as swimmers into cleanness leaping' ('Peace'), and provides the dominant motif for all his poetry.

    Letters From America is an important text for the study of Brooke and a consistently interesting and lively piece of travel-writing. One critic has written that 'Brooke's is the first modern imaginative appreciation of the country because it joyfully discerns in America not social accoutrement or complication of detail but irrelevance, irresponsibility, absence.'[6] Commenting on its social criticism John Carey has written that *Letters From America* expresses a 'remarkably modern angst',[7] and in this respect Brooke's work might be favourably compared to Martin Amis's American travel journalism *The Moronic Inferno and Other Visits to America* (1986).

    The idealism which Brooke searches for, both in America and in himself, finds expression in his poetry especially in its presentation of the theme of love. A sonnet such as 'I said I splendidly loved you' is inspired by a high-minded conception of the transcendent power of intense emotion: 'Love soars from earth to ecstasies unwist. | Love is flung Lucifer-like from Heaven to Hell.' The love of this poem is granted a mythological status and is accompanied by a notion of spiritual redemption; it is airily abstract and lacks visual realization. Simultaneously love is seen in terms of entertainment or art, 'An old song's lady, a fool in fancy dress', where music and costume become metaphors for love itself. This is

---

[6] P. Conrad, *Imagining America* (1980), 89.
[7] J. Carey, 'Simplify Me When I'm Dead', *Sunday Times* (7 June 1987).

appropriate because the lover consciously adopts a pose and participates in affected role-play not unlike that of Shakespeare's Orsino. For them, love is gestural and dramatic, but their artifice is designed to disguise the absence of experience and maturity. The result is a narcissism by which the players come to love 'their own face' and ultimately express only 'love of Love' and, thereby, a mannered adolescent self-absorption. The poem dramatizes a moment of pre-adult recognition and is therefore necessarily unresolved and incomplete.

This sonnet is typical of one aspect of Brooke's poetry in combining an inflated imaginative conception of love with fanciful poetic artifice and contrived dramatic situations. Another love sonnet, 'Oh! Death will find me long before I tire | Of watching you', conceives a dead lover who waits for his mistress to join him 'across the Stygian tide'. The meeting of lovers after death reduces the relationship to a purely spiritual or imaginative dimension; the loss of the physical body banishes the uncomfortable tensions of a genuine union. The poem is correspondingly inert, the lover can only watch and wait, passive and immobile in his imaginary world. The classical location contributes to the sense of formalized remoteness, and the final effect is vaguely macabre and unhealthy, suggestive of a love-tryst or suicide pact.

'Day and Night' externalizes the lover's affections with the metaphor 'my heart's palace' and employs suitably courtly imagery to describe the way in which all his thoughts are attendant upon his lady:

> High-throned you sit, and gracious. All day long
> Great Hopes gold-armoured, jester Fantasies,
> And pilgrim Dreams, and little beggar Sighs,
> Bow to your benediction, go their way.
> And the grave jewelled courtier Memories
> Worship and love and tend you, all the day.

The technique serves to stylize love and remove it from any sense of real relationship. The poem is self-reflexive, another version of imaginative narcissism by which the poet, Orsino-like, becomes infatuated with the idea of being in love. The extended metaphor with its elaborate personifications is a highly involved mirror-image, and the poem concerns little beyond the internalized deliberations of the poet himself.

There are many poems such as these, 'Victory' for example, in which the lovers are cast as a post-Romantic Adam and Eve, exiled from heaven by knowledge but 'silent and all-knowing'. This couple leave paradise and its claustrophobic piety doomed to suffer forever the unforgiving 'black battalions of the Gods'. The poem 'Failure' also rehearses the Brookeian love theme in a quasi-religious context; here the lover's aspirations are thwarted by his consciousness of sin, a complication which is rendered by the poem's dramatic opposition: 'Earth shuddered at my crown of blasphemy, | But love was a flame about my feet.' The petulant young hero defies his authoritarian master and bursts in upon the palace of his desire:

> All the great courts were quiet in the sun,
> And full of vacant echoes: moss had grown
> Over the glassy pavement, and begun
> To creep within the dusty council-halls.
> An idle wind blew round an empty throne
> And stirred the heavy curtains on the walls.

Ending in this way, free of the allegorical implications of the poem's octet, the sestet is an intelligent and restrained piece of writing which uses visual perceptions to create a sense of emptiness and dereliction, what Philip Larkin has called 'fulfilment's desolate attic' ('Deceptions'). Within the context of the whole poem this is still ponderously self-reflexive, but it uses an exactness of observation in a way which is quietly effective.

The separate experiences of falling in love and expressing a feeling of love through art become synonymous in 'My Song' where the lover's initial 'sad whining moods' are transformed into poetry for the amusement of his lady. At the time of her death his embrace will be replaced by that of another world, 'And God's own hand will lay, as aureole, | My song, a flame of scarlet, on your brows.' By these curiously displaced relations the processes of artistic conception act as a substitute for physical union and the lady retains her 'white and perfect soul'; she is revered and celebrated by poetry but personally untouched. In 'My Song' the lover takes only imaginative possession of his mistress.

These love sonnets are indebted to Renaissance models, employing the imagery of courtly love, personifications and dramatic scenes from which the poet is significantly detached. Some of Brooke's poems lack visual detail and physical immediacy because their theme is not love but the abstract idea of love. These are the poems of spectacle: the spectacle of love witnessed from a distance, and the spectacle of art with its rhetorical conventions, gestures, and flourishes. They register the poet's remoteness from the object of his desire in a manner reminiscent of the early poetry of Yeats, except that Brooke more usually introduces death as a means to dramatic separation from his imagined lover.

The passivity or inertia of the speaker in these dramatic scenes is taken to a logical conclusion by the poem 'Paralysis' in which the poet attempts to obviate problems of physical contact by removing the body altogether. The platonic relationship thus conceived has a special purity:

> With our hearts we love, immutable,
> You without pity, I without shame.

Such sentiments and language represent the virtuous ideal, which the poet tests against experience. Here the lover finds that physical removal extinguishes mutual affection, and so the environment in which the lady moves takes over the role of lover: 'the woods that love you | Close lovely and conquering arms above you'. As with 'My Song' above, the poet imagines his mistress possessed by another, inanimate presence. The poem acknowledges that a physical dimension is necessary for a complete relationship to flourish and uses this understanding to challenge the assumption that 'With our hearts we love'. In the process of verifying man's noble aspirations, the lover's impotence acts as a severe qualification.

'Paralysis', despite its title, is cryptic in the way it finds a metaphor for physical contact: the poet is impotent because his lover can move away into another environment, not because he has lost all sensory functions. Such coyness takes a different form in 'The Life Beyond', another imaginative world in which the poet is reduced to insignificance by the loss of corporeality, where he becomes 'An unmeaning point upon the mud; a speck | Of moveless horror'. Notions of spiritual purity and religious grace are systematically eroded by a vigorous depiction of bodily sickness and disease which culminates with the image of 'a fly | Fast-stuck in grey sweat on a corpse's neck'.

These are poems of adolescence in the sense that they are primarily concerned with various states of inexperience or ir-resolution; their speaker does not actually participate in the process of becoming adult which they tentatively approach. These poems articulate an impression of coming of age in a way which puts a strain on the poet's linguistic resources, because he seeks a language of inexperience, of not knowing, which must nevertheless convey his youthful consciousness accurately and effectively. This

is a difficult technical problem, suggesting a precocious talent
coming to terms with a relationship between personality and
poetry which is for the moment inaccessible. 'The Hill' is a poem
which expresses dissatisfaction with that exuberant idealism often
associated with adolescence in a form which is dramatic and
somewhat painful. The lovers attain the physical and metaphorical
perspective of the hill they ascend, and the poet exclaims, ' "Heart
of my heart, our heaven is now, is won" '. But his 'heaven' is sadly
qualified:

> Proud we were,
> And laughed, that had such brave true things to say.
> —And then you suddenly cried, and turned away.

The poem ends with a dramatic compromise of the confidence
it formerly expressed, and the incursion of doubt in Brooke's
imaginative world marks a point of departure from his earlier
attitudinizing. With 'The Hill' the poet still lacks the knowledge
which debars him from adulthood, but in 'Success' the lover's
desire 'To have seen and known you' is confronted directly. The
poet's passion is described as 'my wild sick blasphemous prayer',
and the same feverish desperation characterizes his vision of his
partner's 'white godhead in new fear | Intolerably so struggling,
and so shamed'. The poem is impelled by the tension it dramatizes
between the interpretative ideas of pity and wisdom by which the
lady is 'Most holy and far', and the difficult physical contact of
'wild limbs tamed, | Shaken, and trapped, and shivering, for my
touch'. The poem returns finally to the immediate dramatic
context with 'One last shame's spared me, one black word's
unspoken; | And I'm alone; and you have not awoken', but although
this argues that nothing has happened, a genuine confrontation
has occurred and the corrupting potential of the poet's thought is
enacted in the poem's diction.

There is a strong feeling of violence and disgust in the epithets
used to describe sex in this poem; the 'success' of the title is the
poet's very precarious physical restraint. The suggestion that sex
is difficult and dangerous is developed by 'Lust', the title of which
Brooke refused to change to 'Libido' probably because it concerns
precisely that type of love relationship which is not redeemed by
emotional or spiritual benefit. 'Lust' evinces increased pressure of
physical awareness in its use of numerous and disparate parts of
the body: feet, arms, throat, eyes, mouth, wrist, head, heart,
blood, hand. This physical fragmentation is accompanied by the

sensory deprivation of phrases such as 'cold-eyed', 'void arms', and 'I starved for you'. This aspect of the poem contrasts sharply with the imprecision of the expressions 'The enormous wheels of will' and 'your far light', the tired diction of which signals the unsuccessful formulation of interpretative ideas. In 'Lust' the conflict of mind and body emerges in the stylistic contrast between two different realms of language. Ultimately the poem exhibits an epistemological breakdown, 'How should I know?', because the type of emotional response which concludes with the poet imagining himself 'Quieter than a dead man on a bed' is necessarily unsatisfactory.

The physical disintegration of 'Lust' is appropriate to describe that kind of love which is incomplete. The poem's depiction of a disturbing confusion is matched by that of 'Jealousy' in which the poet's prurience is given full vent:

> And you, that loved young life and clean, must tend
> A foul sick fumbling dribbling body and old,
> When his rare lips hang flabby and can't hold
> Slobber, and you're enduring that worst thing,
> Senility's queasy furtive love-making,
> And searching those dear eyes for human meaning,
> Propping the bald and helpless head, and cleaning
> A scrap that life's flung by, and love's forgotten,—
> Then you'll be tired; and passion dead and rotten;
> And he'll be dirty, dirty!

This extraordinary outburst should be seen in the context of a clash with both an elevated conception of love and the refined language which commonly expresses it. The poem directs its physical disgust at descriptions of the lady as 'you who were so wise and cool' and it is a concerted attempt to violate the nobility of her 'holiest dreams'. The awe and reverence of the traditional Petrarchan love sonneteer is exposed to the full force of voyeuristic hysteria: 'grace' is confronted by 'strong arms and legs'; 'rosy' by 'Wrinkle'; 'flame of love' by 'thickening nose | And sweaty neck'.

Brooke's 'Dead Men's Love' has some of the spite and vituperation of 'Jealousy'. Here the couple are possessed of bodies only, they are lustful, self-satisfying, and narcissistic, and they desire not emotional exchange but self-confirmation: 'in the other's eyes, to see | Each his own tiny face'. As a consequence of this selfishness they are fragmented into physical components, 'breast and lip and arm', and their only contact takes place 'knee to knee'. Because they lack the physical and emotional integration which is the theme of all these poems, they are led to discover the truth of their own vacuous nature 'with a sick surprise, | The emptiness of eyes', and are finally reduced to complete physical disintegration, 'Dust, and a filthy smell'.

These poems constitute a consistently developed thematic and stylistic struggle in which Brooke's love theme is qualified by grotesque physical circumstances and noble humanistic aspirations are confronted by a disgusted fascination with man's basic animal nature. 'Thoughts on the Shape of the Human Body' addresses these problems directly and explicitly, asking 'how can | We, being gods, win joy, or peace, being man?' The highly Romantic conception of man as the ultimate source of all transcendent endeavour, 'gods', is made human and individual by the characterization of men as those 'Who want, and know not what we want, and cry | With crooked mouths for Heaven, and throw it by'. The disparity between the spirit and the flesh is the central predicament of man's nature, and his physical fragmentation reduces him to a collection of incongruous anatomical components; contact through these parts, 'finger with finger' and 'knee toward knee', is the only union he can achieve. To become 'disentangled from humanity' is to be released from the physical prison-house which confines and degrades him, a fantasy which many of Brooke's poems enact. The geometrical contrast between 'some perfect sphere' and the irregularity of the human body is highly metaphysical, and in Brooke's poem it is symbolic of man's tragic departure from simplicity and unity: Brooke's physical existence is perpetually dissected, detached, and alien. 'Thoughts on the Shape of the Human Body' is not a successful poem because its rhetorical structure, by which the initial questions are answered only by the final apostrophizing construction 'Could we but . . .', is once again necessarily incomplete. Also, unlike some of the poems above, these lines are sometimes prosaic in their exposition of an argument. The poem can express but not resolve the dilemma it poses.

A measure of satisfaction seems to be achieved by two further poems which lack the violence of struggle, 'The Busy Heart' and 'The Great Lover'. These are both poems which replace human contact with the contemplation of inanimate objects: 'I would think of a thousand things | Lovely and durable, and taste them slowly | One by one.' Thus the poet of 'The Busy Heart' sustains himself with forms of aesthetic pleasure which lack a human element to disturb him: 'I'll think of love in books.' The poem represents a moment of calm, cured of the apoplexy of earlier verse on this theme. Similarly 'The Great Lover' fixes his attention on the inanimate in order to 'fill my mind with thoughts that will not rend', and so implicitly distinguishes the unreliable nature of personal relations. The poem eulogizes the pleasures of immediate sensory experience:

> White plates and cups, clean gleaming,
> Ringed with blue lines; and feathery, faery dust;
> Wet roofs, beneath the lamp-light; the strong crust
> Of friendly bread; and many-tasting food;
> Rainbows; and the blue bitter smoke of wood;
> And radiant raindrops couching in cool flowers.

This curious mixture cannot conceal a conspicuous absence of human life, and is accompanied by the disintegration of the body into 'fingers', 'hair', 'voices', and 'footprints'. The 'Great Lover' of the title does not extend his affection to people, a point which is perhaps made deliberately obvious. In this respect 'The Busy Heart' and 'The Great Lover' represent a breakdown of faith in human relationships. Although this is not Brooke's final statement on the matter, these poems should be seen in the context of his disaffection with the Bloomsbury group with whom he had a casual acquaintance. While the details are still unclear (important letters remain unpublished) it seems that both Brooke and his beloved Ka Cox were casualties of Bloomsbury's sexual bohemianism. It is possible that Cox (while in love with Henry Lamb) had Brooke's illegitimate child aborted in Germany, and it is certain that Brooke suffered a nervous breakdown at this time (1911–12) as a result of various sexual problems. Brooke's residual conservatism is demonstrated by the fact that 'He hated and feared Bloomsbury because it took a positive relish in bringing together impulses that Rupert believed should never be allowed to meet.'[8] The above poems distinguish Brooke from the cult of personal relationships which was given philosophical credence by G. E. Moore's *Principia Ethica* (1902), an important text for Bloomsbury intellectuals.

If these poems attain only a partial success it is because they are concerned with states of emotional incompleteness. But Brooke's collected poems include those in which the introduction of a human physical dimension creates a specific and original effect. 'A Channel Passage', for example, confronts the Renaissance

---

[8] P. Delany, *The Neo-pagans: Friendship and Love in the Rupert Brooke Circle* (1987), 181.

sentiment of lovesickness with the vivid portrayal of seasickness, an intention made explicit in the poem's original title 'A Shakespearean Love Sonnet'. The poem is possibly a satire on a poem by Swinburne also entitled 'A Channel Passage' (1899), which expresses delight at the exhilaration of a storm at sea: 'And an end was made of it: only remembrance endures of the glad loud strife | And the sense that a rapture so royal may come not again in the passage of life.' Similarly, the Edwardian Poet Laureate Alfred Austin had published in 1898 his *Songs of England* which included 'Three Sonnets Written in Mid-Channel', which Brooke might have regarded as a suitable subject for parodic adaptation. Brooke's turmoil is not entirely emotional:

> Retchings twist and tie me,
> Old meat, good meals, brown gobbets, up I throw.
> Do I remember? Acrid return and slimy,
> The sobs and slobber of last year's woe.
> And still the sick ship rolls.

Brooke's characteristic depiction of physical frailty becomes comic; the poem's strategy is blatant and is probably the kind of effect which leads one critic to remark that 'his mind remained to the end that of a clever public schoolboy'.[9] Yet the use of alliterative and assonantal techniques to portray nauseous vomiting suggests a subversion of poetic tradition which is more than just cleverness, especially when viewed in the context of Brooke's increasing antipathy to romantic and idealistic aspirations. Similarly any conventional expectations aroused by the title of the poem 'Dawn' are entirely refuted, for the poet uses the sonnet form to describe the boredom and restlessness of a railway journey at night. The poetic vision of sunrise observed 'From the train between Bologna and Milan, second class' is largely obscured by the poet's travelling companions: 'Opposite me two Germans sweat and snore.' As with *Letters From America*, the romance of foreign travel is qualified by discomforts which intrude and disturb. That the sonnet should be used in what might be termed an anti-lyrical manner (what Hynes describes as 'aggressively anti-Apollonian'[10]), that is to say upon an occasion which is entirely parochial, is a new development in the form's history.

The same tactic is at work in the poem 'Wagner' which expresses a

---

[9] V. de S. Pinto, *Crisis in English Poetry 1880–1940* (1951), 132.

[10] S. Hynes, *Edwardian Occasions: Essays on English Writing in the Early Twentieth Century* (1972), 147.

tasteless fascination with the composer's corpulent bulk. Brooke's poem completely disregards Wagner's artistic accomplishments and reduces him to a man who 'likes love-music that is cheap'. Wagner's disgusting obesity is in tune, however, with the harmonies he creates, 'And all the while, in perfect time, | His pendulous stomach hangs a-shaking'. For Brooke, the man's artistic achievements are incompatible with his physical corruption. This debasement takes a different form in 'Menelaus and Helen', a diptych offering opposing views of classical legend. The first sonnet is weak because it presents a highly selective view of the subject, characteristic of early Brooke: 'High sat white Helen, lonely and serene'. The remoteness of this art is vigorously countered by Brooke's later style, full of the energy of physical disgust and personal antagonism:

> He does not tell you how white Helen bears
> Child on legitimate child, becomes a scold,
> Haggard with virtue. Menelaus bold
>   Waxed garrulous, and sacked a hundred Troys
> 'Twixt noon and supper. And her golden voice
> Got shrill as he grew deafer. And both were old.

This is severe in its attack both on art and on the smug insularity of idealized love which art conventionally upholds. 'Menelaus and Helen' is reminiscent of Tennyson's 'Ulysses' in depicting the quotidian pressures which reduce heroism to domesticity, and George Meredith's *Modern Love* (1862) certainly anticipates Brooke here, although the reductive process is conducted with different degrees of mockery. Brooke may well have been familiar with 'The strange low sobs that shook their common bed . . . strangled mute like gaping little snakes' (Sonnet I), and his sustained use of the sonnet suggests that a formal influence may also have been at work.

The culmination of this artistic venture is 'Sonnet Reversed'. This poem, contrary to the sonnet's usual progression, begins with a climactic couplet and then descends into suburban monotony:

> Ah, the delirious weeks of honeymoon!
> Soon they returned, and, after strange adventures,
> Settled at Balham by the end of June.
> Their money was in Can. Pacs. B. Debentures.

As John Fuller has pointed out, Brooke is the only poet to use the inverted form as an essential element in the meaning of the poem as 'the sonnet works its way through to an octave expository of the long anti-climax of a petit-bourgeois existence'.[11] 'Sonnet Reversed' is an intelligent and creative subversion of poetic tradition which also disturbs traditionally romantic conceptions of love and marriage. Brooke persists with the sonnet form because it enables him to make attacks on both love and art at the same time. Peter Conrad has described 'the vacant poetic images he venerated'[12] and compared Brooke's style to advertising, a 'mystifying species of image worship'.[13] These poems show Brooke manipulating his early style by using it in a new context to disturb contemporary preconceptions about poetic subjects and poetic treatment. The family of 'Sonnet Reversed' are comically reduced by suburbanization; they are social units performing social functions. This is a very Edwardian process, one which John Betjeman has exploited in poems such as 'Westminster Abbey': 'And now, dear Lord, I cannot wait | Because I have a luncheon date.'

In his development of pre-war realism, Brooke anticipates Owen more than other Edwardians, especially in his presentation of the human body in states of physical disintegration. Brooke's obsession with inert and grotesque physical circumstances might have acted as a model for Owen's presentation of the body as a collection of anatomical components. Brooke's use of the word 'slobber' in 'Jealousy' and 'A Channel Passage' might conceivably be the source of Owen's use of it in 'Mental Cases': 'Drooping tongues from jaws that slob their relish'. These points constitute a contradiction of Silkin's argument that Owen's 'use of physical detail marks him off in the main from Brooke'.[14] Brooke's poetry demonstrates the line of continuation between the more innovative Edwardians and the war poet who contributed most successfully to the development of tradition.

The conventional image of Brooke as an indulgently romantic young socialite hopelessly ill-equipped to cope with the ugly realities of Edwardian social and political issues (women's suffrage, the new left, Irish home rule, the end of Empire) cannot be entirely refuted by the evidence of these poems. But they do suggest the way in which his work looks forward to the later twentieth century in its use of apparently unpromising material for lyrical occasions. A perusal of contemporary responses to poems such as 'A Channel Passage' reveals the intensity of the controversy to which he was prepared to commit himself in order to escape the 'unimportant

---

[11] J. Fuller, *The Sonnet* (1972), 29–30.
[12] Conrad, *Imagining America*, 76.   [13] Ibid. 78.
[14] J. Silkin, *Out of Battle: The Poetry of the Great War* (Oxford, 1972), 212.

prettiness [and] that sort of wash'[15] which he felt characterized his earlier poetry. Brooke was thought to be in the vanguard of 'the new renaissance' which included some of his Georgian friends. Brooke's interest in Renaissance drama and the poetry of John Donne also testifies to his value as a figure in early twentieth-century attempts to bring to poetry a stronger intellectual flavour. Brooke was a considerable Renaissance scholar; the thesis by which in 1913 he was elected to a Fellowship at King's College Cambridge was later published as *John Webster and the Elizabethan Drama* (1916). This survey gravitates towards the energy of Renaissance writing where it is most violent and disturbing, and Brooke applauds his subject on the basis of what he feels is its truth to life:

Marston's chief passion was for truth. He preferred it if it hurt; but he loved it anyhow. It comes out in the snarling speculations and harangues of those satirical malcontents he was so fond of. He bequeathed the type to Tourneur and Webster. For Marston, who was a wit and a scholar and a great poet, was pre-eminently a satirist. It was because he loved truth in that queer, violent way that some men do love, desirous to hurt. It fits in with his whole temperament—vivid, snarling, itching, dirty. He loved dirt for truth's sake; also for its own. Filth, horror and wit were his legacy; it was a splendid one. (pp. 68–9)

Brooke's thesis could hardly be said to evince a selfless attention to the text; his imaginative sympathy is more in the nature of a highly personal celebration. His sense of affinity prompts him to coin metaphors to match those of the writers he studies: of the developments of Kyd and Marlowe he remarks, 'It was rather as if a man should dash two dead babies together into one strident and living being' (p. 54).

Brooke's critical interest in Renaissance drama anticipates that of T. S. Eliot whose essays on nine individual writers were published later between 1919 ('Marlowe') and 1934 ('Marston'). Brooke prefigures Eliot in a further significant respect:

Some of Brooke's critical essays strikingly suggest those of Eliot in their sensitive insight, style, and treatment of similar ideas. In his 'John Donne' and 'John Donne the Elizabethan', both inspired by the Grierson edition, he gave a preliminary formulation to ideas which Eliot was to treat more definitively in the 1920s.[16]

---

[15] C. Hassall, *Rupert Brooke: A Biography* (1964), 287.

[16] J. E. Duncan, *The Revival of Metaphysical Poetry* (Minneapolis, 1959), 120.

Also like Eliot, Brooke was alert to the potential re-interpretation of the metaphysical style in the early twentieth century. In fact it is possible to argue that Brooke's contradictions and incongruities went unresolved not simply because he died young, but because he had a genuine and profound affinity with the Renaissance mind. Brooke lived during a critical historical period, and it might be proposed that he represents the quintessential illustration of the tensions of Edwardian thought, tensions which it was not within his purpose or ability to resolve. In the course of his discussion of Webster, Brooke considers the dramatic denouement and comments that 'A well-known modern play called *Waste* ends, "The waste! The waste of it all!" The Elizabethans were very fond of doing this' (p. 139). Brooke is acutely conscious of a parallel between the Renaissance and his own turbulent period and his awareness of it deeply colours much of his creative writing. It is not a superficial stylistic imitation but the re-enactment of a similarly transitional intellectual crisis.

. Brooke belongs exclusively to the Edwardian period, and, curiously, it is a time which critics have tended to divide into radically opposed camps and to interpret in terms of a single major antithesis or polarization. Pinto develops an idea from C. F. G. Masterman's *The Condition of England* (1909) of the 'journey within' and the 'journey without', suggesting that the Edwardian period might be seen in terms of 'introverts' and 'extroverts'.[17] Stephen Spender distinguishes 'Recognisers' from 'Non-recognisers' and even 'Over-recognisers',[18] and G. S. Fraser delineates those poets with an unscrupulous greed for a public audience from those whose verse smacks of scholarly withdrawal, 'a flavour of Fleet Street at Midnight' in contrast to 'the atmosphere of the British Museum'.[19] These divisions are both aesthetic and political and they affect Brooke crucially: they are nowhere more strongly apparent than in responses to the First World War. Brooke is traditionally presented as the poet of adolescence, a charge which is difficult to refute because much of the verse which comprises the Brooke canon is undoubtedly juvenilia. But it is noticeable how often this criticism is brought against poets of the Edwardian period; A. E. Housman lived until he was 77, but it has been argued that 'all his themes are adolescent',[20] and he has been

---

[17] Pinto, *Crisis in English Poetry 1880–1940*, 13.
[18] S. Spender, *The Struggle of the Modern* (1963), 159.
[19] G. S. Fraser, *The Modern Writer and His World* (1953), 253.
[20] G. Orwell, *Inside the Whale and Other Essays* (1940), 149.

described as 'a desperately solemn purveyor of a single adolescent emotion'.[21] Similarly John Davidson's major work, *The Testament of John Davidson*, has been described by his biographer as being pervaded by 'something schoolboyish'.[22] It is possible that Brooke and the Edwardians appear diminutive because they come at the end of a romantic lyrical tradition and because they are often disparaged by unfavourable comparison with the stature of the Modernists (as in C. K. Stead's *The New Poetic*) whose achievements are of quite a different kind.

The metaphysical conceit enables a poet to express a romantic notion in anti-romantic terms; its excessive or facetious quality formally distances personal involvement. Such is the effect of 'a fly | Fast-stuck in grey sweat on a corpse's neck' ('The Life Beyond'), which allows the writer to express ideas without necessarily being committed to them. This artistic expedient can be seen operating in a wider sense in 'The Old Vicarage, Grantchester', the original title of which, 'The Sentimental Exile', casts the poem in quite a different light, and makes its elaborate attitudinizing an integral part of the total effect of the poem. For the nostalgic indulgence of the speaker is held up for both sympathetic recognition and gentle ridicule; 'Grantchester' is a satire on the sincerity and earnestness of Browning's 'Home Thoughts from Abroad'. The speaker of Brooke's poem makes no attempt to disguise his inconsistency in feeling a strong sense of English pride while berating the people of all but a tiny hamlet. Brooke's original title alerts the reader to that excessively local self-esteem by which the speaker satirizes his neighbours with such verve:

> And Ditton girls are mean and dirty,
> And there's none in Harston under thirty,
> And folks in Shelford and those parts
> Have twisted lips and twisted hearts,
> And Barton men make Cockney rhymes,
> And Coton's full of nameless crimes,
> And things are done you'd not believe
> At Madingley, on Christmas Eve.
> Strong men have run for miles and miles,
> When one from Cherry Hinton smiles;

The tone of parochial gossip is nicely caught in these emphatic couplets, but the final effect is ludicrously partisan. This speaker's

[21] R. P. Blackmur, *The Expense of Greatness* (New York, 1940), 202.
[22] J. B. Townsend, *John Davidson: Poet of Armageddon* (New Haven, Conn., 1961), 422.

characteristic ambivalence is such that he can dismiss those who see the country in terms of classical literature with a peremptory 'But these are things I do not know', and then immediately people his landscape with the Chaucer and Tennyson of his own literary education and speak of 'Hellespont' and 'Styx'. Brooke's persona draws attention to the contradictions of exile while the energy and humour of the poem invite the reader to excuse them. The note of self-parody is strongly felt at 'God! I will pack, and take a train, | And get me to England once again', which prompts the finest comic section of the poem. Here, the speaker's foreign travel does not broaden the mind but commits him to a perspective which becomes progressively narrow, until it ends in a comic *reductio ad absurdum*. Of course 'Grantchester' is not all humour; there are occasions such as the evocation of pastoral idyll which probably encouraged Marsh to take the poem entirely seriously and change its title.

'Grantchester' is a more self-conscious piece of art than it has been given credit for, a dramatic monologue in which the reader is allowed to see round the poem's equivocal persona. Recognition of the poem's irony is crucial to its proper understanding and should influence the reception of the last lines, 'Stands the Church clock at ten to three?' The place where time is perpetually suspended in a summer afternoon is obviously utopian, it is a distortion of the memory which encourages all manner of romantic delusions. As Paul Fussell observes, 'Grantchester' is 'a poem whose one hundred and forty lines manage to encompass four separate dawns and three sunsets'.[23] It is perhaps a mistake then to take entirely seriously the final question, 'And is there honey still for tea?' Brooke was not so unself-conscious that he could dramatize homesickness, like the lovesickness and seasickness of 'A Channel Passage', without being tongue-in-cheek, and he should be credited with the ingenious ambivalence which 'Grantchester' sustains. It is with the same self-conscious irony that Brooke proposed his first book of poetry should be entitled 'Dead Pansy Leaves and Other Flowerets'.[24]

The importance of 'Grantchester' in Brooke's work is that its comic exaggeration shows the poet both celebrating and satirizing the traditional first-person speaker. Brooke began by attempting a lyric intensity of personal utterance but his collected poems show signs that as he matured he developed artistic expedients which

---

[23] P. Fussell, *The Great War and Modern Memory* (Oxford, 1975), 60.

[24] Hassall, *Rupert Brooke: A Biography*, 214.

convey emotion by less direct means. The poem 'Heaven', for example, uses the flippancy of 'Grantchester' in a parodic trans-ference of human anxieties to the world of the fish. In this way the poem tries to escape the problems of the human personality altogether. A similarly anthropomorphic strategy is at work in 'The Fish', which concentrates its attention on animal life with an intensity suggestive of fulfilment:

> Those silent waters weave for him
> A fluctuant mutable world and dim,
> Where wavering masses bulge and gape
> Mysterious, and shape to shape
> Dies momently through whorl and hollow,
> And form and line and solid follow
> Solid and line and form to dream
> Fantastic down the eternal stream.

With 'The Fish' Brooke's metrical control and the characteristic tendency of his diction to slip between the general and the particular are especially suited to his theme. The creative realization of this submarine world is strong enough to displace any human intrusion; human life is glimpsed only momentarily, across an insurmountable divide, and here the emotional life is discovered to be profoundly disturbed:

> You know the hands, the eyes of love!
> The strife of limbs, the sightless clinging,
> The infinite distance, and the singing
> Blown by the wind.

Again the portrayal of a love relationship is characterized by physical fragmentation, struggle, and deprivation, and by a sense of futility and pain. The form of classical apostrophe is used in its technical sense, to address something which remains off-stage, viewed only from the relative safety of an ascetic aquatic isolation. Here life is not only submerged, it is different in nature. The poet of 'The Fish' is not concerned to establish an analogue with the human world; for him it is too remote and problematical to be properly comprehended. The success with which the poem creatively sustains the world below the surface is achieved at the expense of human relations, and the final impression is suggestive of Philip Larkin's conviction that 'Beneath it all, desire of oblivion runs' ('Wants'). For Brooke the attraction of the fish is that 'the clinging stream | Closes his memory'.

'The Fish' dramatizes what might be expressed as the self of the poem, the human subject, in the process of being displaced into something other than the self; the poem systematically marginalizes human emotional life through the depiction of its subject, and the fish 'Unconscious and directly driven, | Fades to some dank sufficient heaven'. Further evidence that Brooke was making deliberate attempts to develop a style which located its central emotional event outside human personality is provided by his South Seas poems. This group contains much of Brooke's best poetry, including the sestet of 'Waikiki':

> And I recall, lose, grasp, forget again,
> And still remember, a tale I have heard or known,
> An empty tale of idleness and pain,
> Of two that loved—or did not love—and one
> Whose perplexed heart did evil, foolishly,
> A long while since, and by some other sea.

For Brooke the technical advance of these poems lies in the studied obliquity with which they end. The emotional development of the poem is attached to another subject, the tale, and is so externalized. This method of lyrical marginalization is enhanced by the sestet's depiction of removal to the margin, 'by some other sea'. This is a dramatic shift which extends the immediate context without losing the pathos of the individual voice in which it originates. The effect of this method is that in attributing the moment of personal integration to something beyond the poet, it is given over to the public realm, it is no longer simply a private satisfaction:

> So a poor ghost, beside his misty streams,
> Is haunted by strange doubts, evasive dreams,
> Hints of a pre-Lethean life, of men,
> Stars, rocks, and flesh, things unintelligible,
> And light on waving grass, he knows not when,
> And feet that ran, but where, he cannot tell.

As with the previous poem, the sestet of 'Hauntings' ends by crediting a metaphor with a special value, and the technique creates a unity of personal voice and external phenomena. At this level these subjects become symbolic, they are detached from the 'I' of the poem but imbued with the life of his voice. These poems move beyond human personality in concluding with that which is unknown, 'by some other sea', and 'but where, he cannot tell'; they might be instructively compared with Philip Larkin's 'High Windows', which dramatizes the failure of communicative language, 'rather than words', and ends in a similarly oblique fashion by speaking of 'The sun-comprehending glass | And beyond it, the deep blue air, that shows | Nothing, and is nowhere, and is endless'. Larkin's poem achieves a final liberation from the mortal personality and so discovers and expresses a moment of experience which is not simply personal. Brooke's South Seas poems attain a similarly mature resolution. A comparable moment of epiphany is conveyed by 'In Freiburg Station' where the poet sings 'for that hour's sake': 'In Freiburg station, waiting for a train | I saw a bishop in puce gloves go by.' This poem, or at least its refrain, bears a striking resemblance to Ezra Pound's famous two-line poem 'In a Station of the Metro' (1915) which has been credited as an important Modernist landmark. These observations help to refute Hynes's argument that Brooke's poems are 'uniformly and conventionally dull'.[25]

While this style suits reflective love poems, it is not perhaps appropriate to the sonnets of 1914, of which it might be said that Brooke did not have the technical resources equal to the occasion. It is not true that Brooke had had no experience of war when he wrote these poems, he was present at the evacuation of Antwerp in October 1914, which made a deep impression upon him: 'The eye grows clearer, and the heart. But it's a bloody thing, half the youth of Europe, blown through pain to nothingness, in the incessant mechanical slaughter of these modern battles.'[26] That Brooke had shown himself willing to use anti-lyrical material for his poetry makes the literary posturing of these sonnets more unfortunate. However, his original title for the most famous of them, 'The Recruit', casts the poem as a pre-war artefact (recounting perhaps the discovery of moral purpose) rather than as a work directly about the war as implied by 'The Soldier'. The first line of this poem 'If I should die, think only this of me' (which bears a striking resemblance to the iambic pentameter of Keats's sonnet 'When I have fears that I may cease to be') signals the imaginary projection of his reputation to future generations. John Carey has written of 'The Soldier' that 'critics seem to miss that his make-believe is quite conscious. It tells how the poet would like to be remembered, a different thing from how he really was.'[27] Viewed in this way the proper comparison is not with any poem by Wilfred Owen but with 'Afterwards' by Thomas Hardy with its variations on the refrain ' "He was a man who used to notice such things" '

[25] Hynes, *Edwardian Occasions*, 145.
[26] Hassall, *Rupert Brooke: A Biography*, 466.
[27] Carey, 'Simplify Me When I'm Dead', 56.

and its contemplation of how the poet might survive in the minds of others. In this sense Brooke can be seen as trying to escape the confines of his personality by imagining himself dead and creating himself again in the mind of his potential audience. When interpreted in the context of Brooke's development 'The Soldier' can be recognized as another artistic expedient by which the tensions and contradictions of the human personality are evaded.

The preponderance of the word 'England' in this poem is remarkable: 'for ever England', 'A dust whom England bore', 'A body of England's, breathing English air', 'thoughts by England given', 'under an English heaven'. In such a short poem these moments have the value of a totemic incantation reminiscent of Henry Newbolt. As the first chapter of this book showed, the repetition of the word 'England' was the means by which Newbolt held on to a conception of England which was undergoing rapid change. Brooke's use of the word has a similarly therapeutic function; 'England' acts as the repository for those ideas of stability and security which are needed in times of crisis. 'The Soldier' is a distinctively post-Edwardian response to the war, part of the spirit of romantic adventure shared by contemporaries such as Owen, who wrote that 'There is a fine heroic feeling about being in France'.[28] Clearly it is a mistake to divide responses to the war into two simple and diametrically opposed camps without reference to the Edwardian period of which it is a product.

'The Soldier' should be considered alongside Brooke's war poem 'Fragment', a further poem in which the poet imagines himself dead, and ghost-like he returns to watch his friends who will also soon perish:

> I would have thought of them
> —Heedless, within a week of battle—in pity,
> Pride in their strength and in the weight and firmness
> And link'd beauty of bodies, and pity that
> This gay machine of splendour'ld soon be broken,
> Thought little of, pashed, scattered . . .

The dramatic situation recalls Hardy's numerous spectre poems, while the depiction of the soldiers' bodies as 'pashed, scattered' is especially anticipatory of Owen. The tone of 'Fragment' suggests also the threatened sensitivity of Edward Thomas, as does Brooke's concluding use of the first person: 'Perishing things and strange

---

[28] W. Owen, *Collected Letters*, ed. H. Owen and J. Bell (1967), 421.

ghosts—soon to die | To other ghosts—this one, or that, or I'. This technique is particularly characteristic of Thomas, who uses it in 'Melancholy': 'And, softer, and remote as if in history, | Rumours of what had touched my friends, my foes, or me'. But perhaps the best parallel is with Thomas's 'Lights Out':

> The tall forest towers:
> Its cloudy foliage lowers
> Ahead, shelf above shelf;
> Its silence I hear and obey
> That I may lose my way
> And myself.

The features which Brooke and Thomas share are a heightened, even morbid self-consciousness, and a preoccupation with the possible extinguishing of human personality. Here their anxiety takes the form of a death-wish. This is the final stage of that Edwardian crisis of creative authority which is implied by the absence of a clear authorial voice in Hardy's *The Dynasts* (1903–8) and by Housman's adoption of an ostentatiously fictitious rural persona. In their persistently determined efforts not to speak, the Edwardian poets articulate a desire not to expose themselves in verse and by analogy not to accept the onerous responsibilities of poet. The scene from *Letters From America* in which Brooke dives into the St Lawrence River, 'And it was cold as death', acts as a coda to his poetry and to his life.

It may seem excessive to devote such space to a poet who wrote little, whose best work is much less, and who died at the age of 27; but the incompleteness of Brooke's struggle with what might be called the inheritance of late-Victorian romanticism is more explicitly developed than that of other Edwardians. In his final failure in the war sonnets Brooke marks the admission of poetic defeat which decisively separates Edwardians from Modernists. It was a failure which he did not live to redeem. Brooke is typical of the period in making some innovative advances, which contribute to the individuality of the turn of the century, but he is also characteristically Edwardian in his final inability to relinquish the propriety and decorum (the rhetoric) which the Modernists set out to eliminate. A final comparison might be with Thomas Hardy's Angel Clare:

With all his attempted independence of judgement this advanced and well-meaning young man, a sample product of the last five and twenty years, was yet the slave to custom and conventionality when surprised back into his early teachings.[29]

The analogy with Hardy's fictional character (including its sexual aspect) is a reminder that Brooke's contradictions were in part those of his historical period. What is distinctive about his contribution to the Edwardian period is that he recognized the transitional nature of his time and made concerted efforts to liberate the thematic range of poetry. Brooke's formal experiments are more modest, but in their eagerness to escape the vicissitudes of personality, no less important. It was for the Modernists however to open up the ground at which he had tentatively scratched, and the death of Brooke's generation heralds their advent.

[29] T. Hardy, *Tess of the D'Urbervilles*, New Wessex Edition (1974), 290.

Conclusion

ALTHOUGH nearly fifty years separate the births of Hardy and Brooke they nevertheless share characteristics that are common to the Edwardian period. Each of the poets included here is imbued with a sense of nostalgia for an earlier, if fictional or mythical, time which they seek to revivify in their poetry. Yet there remains a pervasive impression of loss rather than recovery; much of this poetry is muted and elegiac. The poets of this book are engaged in attempts to offer an expression of the definitive or quintessential England. There are various historical reasons for this, the Boer War perhaps, the death of Victoria, or it may be simply that the lost past they try to recapture is given easy focus by notions of national identity. Edwardian poetry is characterized in part by its annihilation of the traditional romantic self of poetry, and it expresses a corresponding loss of faith in writing, and occasionally in the faculty of imagination in whatever form it takes. The utterances of these poets seem to have been reduced to a whisper, their faith in the value of poetry as a worthwhile medium of expression severely depleted and at times completely exhausted. With the exception of John Davidson, Edwardian poets are almost exclusively concerned with rural rather than urban subjects and landscapes. Again this may be part of their nostalgia, or it may be an unresponsiveness to urban experience as a potential source of material for poetry. The reluctance of Brooke and Masefield to use their experiences of war in a positive artistic way is indicative of their nostalgia; they looked back, and finding no precedent for poetry about war, they wrote none. But, it is argued, the absence of motor cars and aeroplanes does not necessarily debar their poetry from the term 'modern'.

These characteristics outlined above distinguish the Edwardians from the Victorians. Browning, Arnold, and Tennyson had a far greater belief in the value of their discourse than any of the poets included here. In this sense Oscar Wilde is still a Victorian in evincing a high moral purpose which by 1900 seems to have been defunct. Some of the poetry here is specifically about a lack of self-confidence in its own value, and yet it perseveres to make poetry from that lack. In some ways Edwardian poetry might be said to anticipate Modernism but that is not a central contention of this book. Edwardian poetry is modern in its anxieties about literary form, if not always in its solutions to those anxieties. In particular there is a prevalent distrust of the correlation between words and things, signifier and signified, that undermines the Edwardian poet's capacity to say what he means. This links turn-of-the-century poets with their novelist contemporaries, who have been characterized as expressing a sense of epistemological crisis. But the value of the poetry included here is not dependent on its anticipation of modernism. *Edwardian Poetry* suggests the outline of a kind of modern British poetry which can be distinguished from the more radical advances of modernism. It is argued that the poets of the Edwardian period would certainly benefit from being set in a broader context of English poetry, from Wordsworth to Larkin. This is the kind of poetry which makes use of English provinces and certain 'traditional' or accessible formal methods, such as regular metre, rhyme, and ordered syntax. It is difficult to make sound critical generalizations about such a 'line' of poetry, but it has been the subject of some interest recently, in the writing of Lucas, Longley, Harvey, and others. Each of these critics finds a good deal of material to support their arguments in the poetry of the Edwardians. *Edwardian Poetry* is historically based, it is partly a work of literary history, but further elucidation of what constitutes such a line of poetry would be of great help to the Edwardians since they stand in important relation to it. The clarification of this broader context may lead to the discovery of other Edwardians such as Gibson, Abercrombie, and Binyon.

This book has used the poetry of Philip Larkin as a shorthand way of demonstrating the continuing value of pre-war methods exemplified by the Edwardians. The references to Larkin also help to identify those characteristics which constitute the line of British poetry that the Edwardians are a part of. More work needs to be done on Larkin's position in relation to 'modern' and 'modernist' poetry; there are certainly tentative experiments at liberty in Larkin's verse that belie its sometimes pawky suburban subject-matter. Similarly, what is the place of Auden in such a tradition? Does the tradition originate with Wordsworth? Pope? Chaucer? Such a tradition must include extensive reference to Wilfred Owen and other poets who are the immediate successors of Hardy, Masefield and Brooke. Who are the contemporary writers that might be seen as living exponents of the same tradition? Any argument about the history of English poetry that can answer these questions would inevitably discover the importance of the Edwardians and help to resuscitate them.

The poets included here are usually allowed to slip between the canonical literary periods; they are rarely assigned a prominent place in a history of Victorian or twentieth-century poetry, and this perpetuates their neglect. It is hoped that *Edwardian Poetry*, in providing its subjects with a literary and historical context, allows them to be seen as a coherent group rather than as a collection of isolated individuals.

Select Bibliography

The bibliography is divided into two parts, the seven major poets discussed (subdivided into manuscripts, primary works, secondary works), and all general secondary works. The place of publication is London unless otherwise specified.

HRHRC is an abbreviation for the Harry Ransom Humanities Research Center at the University of Texas at Austin.

Henry Newbolt

Corpus Christi College, Oxford, MS 468.

Taken From The Enemy (1892).
Mordred: A Tragedy (1895).
Admirals All, and Other Verses (1897).
The Island Race (1898).
The Sailing of the Long-ships, and Other Poems (1902).
The Year of Trafalgar (1905).
The Old Country (1906).
Clifton Chapel, and Other School Poems (1908).
Songs of Memory and Hope (1909).
The New June (Edinburgh, 1909).
Collected Poems, 1897–1907 (1910).
The Twymans (Edinburgh, 1911).
Poems: New and Old (1912).
Drake's Drum, and Other Songs of the Sea (1914).
Aladore (Edinburgh, 1914).
A New Study of English Poetry, Essays (1917).
St. George's Day, and Other Poems (1918).
My World as in My Time: Memoirs (1932).
The Later Life and Letters of Sir Henry Newbolt, ed. M. Newbolt (1942).

BETJEMAN, J., *Selected Poems of Henry Newbolt* (1940).
DICKINSON, P., *Selected Poems of Henry Newbolt* (1981).
HOWARTH, P., *Play Up and Play the Game: The Heroes of Popular Fiction* (1973).
WEBB, P., 'Newbolt For Poets' Corner', *Spectator* (19/26 Dec. 1987).

John Masefield

HRHRC MSS Masefield, John/Works.
Bodleian MS d. 1967.
Bodleian MSS Sidgwick and Jackson.
Bodleian MS Eng. lett. c.376 f 1.105.
Bodleian MS Eng. misc. g. 77.

Salt-Water Ballads (1902).
Ballads (1903).
A Mainsail Haul (1905).
Sea Life in Nelson's Time (1905).
A Tarpaulin Muster (1907).
Captain Margaret (1908).
Multitude and Solitude (1909).
Ballads and Poems (1910).
Lost Endeavour (1910).
The Everlasting Mercy (1911).
William Shakespeare (1911).
The Widow in the Bye Street (1912).
The Daffodil Fields (1913).
Dauber (1913).
Lollingdon Downs, and Other Poems (1917).
Letters to Florence Lamont, ed. C. and M. Lamont (1979).
Letters to Reyna, ed. W. Buchan (1983).
Letters from the Front, 1915–1917, ed. P. Vansittart (1984).
John Masefield's Letters to Margaret Bridges (1915–1919), ed. D. Stanford (Manchester, 1984).

BABINGTON-SMITH, C., *John Masefield: A Life* (1978).
BIGGANE, C., *John Masefield* (1924).
CORCORAN, N., 'Too Much of Green', *Times Literary Supplement* (26 Apr. 1985).
DODSWORTH, M., 'The Editorial Miscellany', *English* (summer 1986).
GRAVES, R., 'Robert Graves on John Masefield', *Times Literary Supplement* (22 June 1967).
HAMILTON, W. H., *John Masefield: A Critical Study* (1922).
SPARK, M., *John Masefield* (1953).
STRONG, L. A. G., *John Masefield* (1952).

Thomas Hardy

The Dynasts: A Drama of the Napoleonic Wars (1910).
Collected Poems of Thomas Hardy (1919).
The Dynasts: An Epic-Drama, ed. H. Orel (1978).

ABERCROMBIE, L., *Thomas Hardy: A Critical Study* (1912).

BAILEY, J. C., *The Continuity of Letters* (Oxford, 1923).

BAILEY, J. O., *Thomas Hardy and the Cosmic Mind: A New Reading of* The Dynasts (Chapel Hill, NC, 1956).

BAYLEY, J., *An Essay on Hardy* (Cambridge, 1978).

BUCKLER, W. E., *The Poetry of Thomas Hardy: A Study in Art and Ideas* (1983).

CHAKRAVARTY, A., The Dynasts *and the Post-War Age in Poetry: A Study in Modern Ideas* (1938).

DEAN, S., *Hardy's Poetic Vision in* The Dynasts: *The Diorama of a Dream* (Princeton, NJ, 1977).

DUFFIN, H. C., *Thomas Hardy: A Study of the Wessex Novels, the Poems, and* The Dynasts (3rd edn. rev., Manchester, 1937).

GARRISON, C. A., *The Vast Venture: Hardy's Epic-Drama* The Dynasts (Saltzburg, 1973).

GERBER, H. E., AND DAVIS, W. E., *Thomas Hardy: An Annotated Bibliography of Writings about him* (1973).

GITTINGS, R., *Young Thomas Hardy* (1975).

—— *The Older Hardy* (1978).

HYNES, S., *The Pattern of Hardy's Poetry* (Chapel Hill, NC, 1961).

MILLER, J. H., *Thomas Hardy: Distance and Desire* (1970).

MILLGATE, M., *Thomas Hardy: A Biography* (Oxford, 1982).

MORRELL, R., *Thomas Hardy: The Will and the Way* (Singapore, 1965).

OREL, H., *Thomas Hardy's Epic-Drama: A Study of* The Dynasts (Lawrence, Kan., 1963).

PAULIN, T., *Thomas Hardy: The Poetry of Perception* (1975).

RUTLAND, W. R., *Thomas Hardy: A Study of his Writings and their Background* (1938).

SCOTT-JAMES, R. A., *Thomas Hardy* (1951).

WRIGHT, W. F., *The Shaping of* The Dynasts: *A Study in Thomas Hardy* (Lincoln, Nebr., 1967).

A. E. Housman

A Shropshire Lad (1896).
Last Poems (1922).
More Poems (1936).
The Letters of A. E. Housman, ed. H. Maas (1971).

ALLISON, A. F., 'The Poetry of Housman', *Review of English Studies*, 19 (1943).

CARTER, J., (ed.), *A. E. Housman: Selected Prose* (Cambridge, 1961).

EMPSON, W., 'Rhythm and Imagery in English Poetry', *British Journal of Aesthetics*, 2 (1962).

FRIEDMAN, E., 'The Divided Self in the Poems of A. E. Housman', *English Literature in Transition*, 20/1 (1977).

GARROD, H. W., 'A. E. Housman, 1939', *Essays and Studies*, 25 (1939).

GOW, A. S. F., *A. E. Housman: A Sketch* (Cambridge, 1936).

GRAVES, R. P., *A. E. Housman: The Scholar-Poet* (1979).

HABER, T. B., *The Making of A Shropshire Lad: A Manuscript Variorium* (Seattle, Wash., 1966).

HOUSMAN, L., *A.E.H.: A Memoir* (1937).

JARRELL, R., 'Texts from Housman', *Kenyon Review*, 1 (1939).

LARKIN, P., 'Palgrave's Last Anthology: A. E. Housman's Copy', *Review of English Studies*, NS 22 (1971).

—— 'Lost Content', *Observer* (29 Jan. 1984).

LEGGETT, B. J., *The Poetic Art of A. E. Housman: Theory and Practice* (Lincoln, Nebr., 1978).

MARLOW, N., *A. E. Housman: Scholar and Poet* (1958).

NOSWORTHY, J. M., 'A. E. Housman and the Woolwich Cadet', *Notes and Queries*, 17/9 (Sept. 1970).

PAGE, N., *A. E. Housman: A Critical Biography* (1983).

POUND, E., 'Mr. Housman at Little Bethel', *Criterion*, 13/51 (Jan. 1934).

RANSOM, J. C., 'Honey and Gall', *Southern Review*, 6 (1940).

RICKS, C. (ed.), *A. E. Housman: A Collection of Critical Essays* (Princeton, NJ, 1968).

SCOTT-KILVERT, I., *A. E. Housman*, 'Writers and their Work', 69 (1955).

SPENDER, S., 'The Essential Housman', *Horizon*, 1 (1940).

STEVENSON, J. W., 'The Martyr as Innocent: Housman's Lonely Lad', *South Atlantic Quarterly*, 57 (winter 1958).

WITHERS, P., *A. E. Housman: A Buried Life* (1940).

Edward Thomas

Edward Thomas notebook MSS, Poetry/Rare Books Collection, State University of New York at Buffalo.

HRHRC MSS Thomas, Edward/Works.

HRHRC MSS Thomas, Edward/Letters.

Bodleian MS Don. e. 10.

Bodleian MS Don. d. 28.

Bodleian MS Eng. poet. d. 214.

The Heart of England (1906).

The South Country (1909).

The Country (1913).

The Happy-Go-Lucky Morgans (1913).

Cloud Castle and Other Papers (1922).

The Last Sheaf (1928).

A Language not to be Betrayed: Selected Prose of Edward Thomas, ed. E. Longley (Manchester, 1981).

Letters from Edward Thomas to Gordon Bottomley, ed. R. G. Thomas (1968).

Poems and Last Poems, ed. E. Longley (1973).
The Collected Poems of Edward Thomas, ed. R. G. Thomas (Oxford, 1978).

BARKER, J. (ed.), *The Art of Edward Thomas* (Cardiff, 1986).
BURROW, J., 'Keats and Edward Thomas', *Essays in Criticism* (Oct. 1957).
COOKE, W., *Edward Thomas: A Critical Biography* (1970).
COOMBES, H., *Edward Thomas: A Critical Study* (1956).
DANBY, J., 'Edward Thomas', *Critical Quarterly* (winter 1959).
ECKERT, R. P., *Edward Thomas: A Biography and a Bibliography* (1937).
ELLIOTT, C., 'Dunwich and Edward Thomas', *East Anglian Magazine* (Aug. 1967).
FARJEON, E., *Edward Thomas: The Last Four Years* (1958).
HARDING, D. W., 'A Note on Nostalgia', *Scrutiny*, 1/1 (May 1932).
KIRKHAM, M., *The Imagination of Edward Thomas* (Cambridge, 1986).
MARSH, J., *Edward Thomas: A Poet for his Country* (1978).
MITCHELL, P. E., 'Edward Thomas', *English Literature in Transition 1880–1920*, 32/1 (1989), 80–4.
MOORE, J., *The Life and Letters of Edward Thomas* (1939).
MOTION, A., *The Poetry of Edward Thomas* (1980).
ROBSON, W. W., 'Edward Thomas's "Roads"', *Times Literary Supplement* (23 Mar., 1962).
SCANNELL, V., *Edward Thomas* (1963).
SMITH, S., *Edward Thomas* (1986).
THOMAS, H., *As It Was* (1956).
—— *World Without End* (1956).
THOMAS, M., *One of These Fine Days: Memoirs* (Manchester, 1982).
THOMAS, R. G., *Edward Thomas: A Portrait* (Oxford, 1985).
—— 'Edward Thomas, Poet and Critic', *Essays and Studies*, 21 (1968).
—— *Edward Thomas* (Cardiff, 1972).
—— (ed.), 'Six Letters From Robert Frost to Edward Thomas', *Poetry Wales*, 22/4 (1987).
WALKER, D. C., 'The Poetry of Edward Thomas', thesis, University of Oxford, Bodleian MS B.Litt d. 1207 (1966).
WARD, J. P., 'The Solitary Note: Edward Thomas and Modernism', *Poetry Wales*, 13/4 (spring 1978).

John Davidson

HRHRC MSS Davidson, John/Works.
HRHRC MSS Davidson, John/Letters.

The North Wall (Glasgow, 1885).
Bruce: A Drama in Five Acts (Glasgow, 1886).
Smith: A Tragedy (Glasgow, 1888).
Scaramouch in Naxos: A Pantomime; and Other Plays (1890).
Perfervid: The Career of Ninian Jamieson (1890).

Sentences and Paragraphs (1893).
A Full and True Account of the Wonderful Mission of Earl Lavender (1895).
The Poems of John Davidson, ed. A. R. Turnbull, 2 vols. (1973).

CURRIE, A. M., 'A Biographical and Critical Study of John Davidson', thesis, University of Oxford, Bodleian MS B.Litt 186 (1953).

FINEMAN, H., *John Davidson: A Study of the Relation of his Ideas to his Poetry* (Philadelphia, 1916).

LESTER, J. A., 'Friedrick Nietzsche and John Davidson: A Study in Influence', *Journal of the History of Ideas*, 18 (1957).

—— 'Prose–Poetry Transmutation in the Poetry of John Davidson', *Modern Philology*, 56 (1958).

LINDSAY, M. (ed.), *John Davidson: A Selection of his Poems* (1961).

O'CONNOR, M., 'John Davidson: An Annotated Bibliography of Writings about Him', *English Literature in Transition*, 20 (1977).

—— 'Did Bernard Shaw Kill John Davidson? The "Tragi-comedy" of a Commissioned Play', *Shaw Review* 21/3 (Sept. 1978).

—— *John Davidson* (Edinburgh, 1987).

ROBERTSON, R., 'Science and Myth in John Davidson's Testaments', *Studies in Scottish Literature*, 18 (1983).

SHERMAN, H. J., 'The Lyric and Ballad Poetry of John Davidson, 1890–9', thesis, University of Oxford, Bodleian MS B.Litt d. 1550 (1970).

TOWNSEND, J. B., *John Davidson: Poet of Armageddon* (New Haven, Conn., 1961).

TURNER, P., 'John Davidson: The Novels of a Poet', *Cambridge Journal*, 5 (Oct. 1951–Sept. 1952).

WOOLF, V., 'John Davidson', *Times Literary Supplement* (16 Aug. 1917).

Rupert Brooke

Bodleian MS Don. d. 1.

Lithuania (1911).
Letters From America (1916).
John Webster and the Elizabethan Drama (1916).
The Collected Poems of Rupert Brooke, with a Memoir by Edward Marsh (1918).
The Poetical Works of Rupert Brooke, ed. G. Keynes (1960).
The Letters of Rupert Brooke, ed. G. Keynes (1968).

ACKROYD, P., 'Not Honey for Tea *Again*', *The Times* (4 June 1987).

CAREY, J., 'Simplify Me When I'm Dead', *Sunday Times* (7 June 1987).

DELANY, P., *The Neo-pagans: Friendship and Love in the Rupert Brooke Circle* (1987).

HASSALL, C., *Rupert Brooke: A Biography* (1964).

HASTINGS, M., *The Handsomest Young Man in England: Rupert Brooke* (1967).

LEHMANN, J., *Rupert Brooke: His Life and his Legend* (1980).

GENERAL

ANON., 'The Edwardian Novel', *Times Literary Supplement* (28 June 1947).
ANON., 'Edwardian Poets', *Times Literary Supplement* (20 Mar. 1953).
ARCHER, W., *Poets of the Younger Generation* (1902).
BALDICK, C., *The Social Mission of English Criticism 1848–1932* (Oxford, 1983).
BATCHELOR, J., *The Edwardian Novelists* (1982).
BAYLEY, J., *The Romantic Survival: A Study in Poetic Evolution* (1957).
—— 'Too Good for This World', *Times Literary Supplement* (21 June 1974).
—— *Selected Essays* (Cambridge, 1984).
—— 'The Undercover Poet: W. H. Davies', *Times Literary Supplement* (25 Jan. 1985).
—— 'English Equivocation', *Poetry Review*, 76 (June 1986).
BEACH, J. W., *The Concept of Nature in Nineteenth Century Poetry* (New York, 1936).
BENSON, A. C., *Edwardian Excursions: The Diaries of A. C. Benson 1898–1904*, ed. D. Newsome (1981).
BERGONZI, B., *Heroes' Twilight: A Study of the Literature of the Great War* (1965).
—— *The Turn of a Century: Essays on Victorian and Modern English Literature* (1973).
—— (ed.), *A History of Literature in the English Language*, 7 (1970).
BIRKENHEAD, L., *Rudyard Kipling* (1978).
BLACKMUR, R. P., *The Expense of Greatness* (New York, 1940).
BLAMIRES, H., *Twentieth Century English Literature* (1982).
BOTTOMLEY, G., *Poems and Plays* (1953), ed. C. C. Abbott.
BRIDGE, U. (ed.), *W. B. Yeats and T. Sturge Moore: Their Correspondence 1901–37* (1953).
BROADUS, E. K., *The Laureateship: A Study of the Office of Poet Laureate in England with Some Account of the Poets* (Oxford, 1921).
BUCKLEY, J. H., *The Victorian Temper: A Study in Literary Culture* (1952).
—— *William Ernest Henley: A Study in the 'Counter-Decadence' of the 'Nineties* (Princeton, NJ, 1945).
BURGESS, A., 'The Wide Plastic Spaces', *Times Literary Supplement* (30 May 1980).
BUSH, D., *Mythology and the Romantic Tradition in English Poetry* (Cambridge, Mass., 1937).
CAVALIERO, G., *The Rural Tradition in the English Novel, 1900–1939* (1977).
CHAPPLE, J. A. V., *Documentary and Imaginative Literature 1880–1920* (1970).
COATES, J. D., *Chesterton and the Edwardian Cultural Crisis* (Hull, 1984).
COCKBURN, F. C., *Bestsellers: The Books that Everyone Read, 1900–1939* (1972).
CONQUEST, R., 'But What Good Came of It at Last? An Inquest on Modernism', *Essays by Divers Hands*, 42 (1982).

CONRAD, P., 'The Victim of Inheritance', *Times Literary Supplement* (15 May 1982).

—— *Imagining America* (1980).

CRAWFORD, R., 'Larkin's English', *Oxford Magazine*, 23 (fourth week, Trinity Term 1987).

CRUSE, A., *After The Victorians* (1938).

DAICHES, D., *Some Late Victorian Attitudes* (1969).

DANGERFIELD, G., *The Strange Death of Liberal England* (1936).

DAVIE, D., *Thomas Hardy and British Poetry* (1973).

DONOGHUE, D., *Yeats* (1971).

—— *Ferocious Alphabets* (1981).

DOWLING, L., *Language and Decadence in the Victorian Fin de Siècle* (Princeton, NJ, 1986).

DUNCAN, J. E., *The Revival of Metaphysical Poetry* (Minneapolis, 1959).

DURRELL, L., *Key to Modern Poetry* (1952).

EAGLETON, T., *Exiles and Émigrés: Studies in Modern Literature* (1970).

ELIOT, T. S., *The Letters of T. S. Eliot*, i. *1898–1922*, ed. Valerie Eliot (1988).

ELLMANN, R., *Edwardians and Late Victorians* (New York, 1959).

—— 'Romantic Pantomime in Oscar Wilde', *Partisan Review*, 30 (1963).

—— *Golden Codgers: Biographical Speculations* (Oxford, 1973).

—— *Oscar Wilde* (1987).

EMPSON, W., 'Rhythm and Imagery in English Poetry', *British Journal of Aesthetics* (1962).

ENRIGHT, D. J. (ed.), *Poets of the 1950s: An Anthology of New English Verse* (1955).

—— 'The Literature of the First World War', in *Pelican Guide to English Literature*, ed. B. Ford, vii (Harmondsworth, 1961).

EVANS, B. I., *English Poetry in the Later Nineteenth Century* (1933).

EVERETT, B., 'Philip Larkin: After Symbolism', *Essays in Criticism*, 30 (1980).

FAULKNER, P., *Modernism* (1977).

FRASER, G. S., *The Modern Writer and His World* (1953).

FUSSELL, P., *The Great War and Modern Memory* (Oxford, 1975).

GARROD, H. W., *The Profession of Poetry and Other Lectures* (Oxford, 1929).

Georgian Poetry 1911–1912, ed. E. Marsh (1912).

Georgian Poetry 1913–1915, ed. E. Marsh (1915).

Georgian Poetry 1916–1917, ed. E. Marsh (1917).

Georgian Poetry 1918–1919, ed. E. Marsh (1919).

Georgian Poetry 1920–1922, ed. E. Marsh (1922).

Georgian Poetry (1962), selected and introduced J. Reeves.

GIBBONS, T., *Rooms in the Darwin Hotel: Studies in English Literary Criticism and Ideas 1880–1920* (Univ. of Western Australia, 1973).

GRAY, H. B., *The Public Schools and the Empire* (1913).

GREEN, M., *Children of the Sun: A Narrative of 'Decadence' in England after 1918* (1977).

—— *Dreams of Adventure, Deeds of Empire* (1980).

GROSS, J., *The Rise and Fall of the Man of Letters: Aspects of English Literary Life Since 1800* (1969).

GWYNN, F. L., *Sturge Moore and the Life of Art* (1952).

HAMILTON, I., *A Poetry Chronicle* (1973).

HARRIS, F., *Contemporary Portraits* (1915).

HARVEY, G., *The Romantic Tradition in Modern English Poetry: Rhetoric and Experience* (1986).

HASSALL, C., *Edward Marsh: Patron of the Arts* (1959).

HEARNSHAW, F. J. C. (ed.), *Edwardian England 1901–1910* (1933).

HOBSBAUM, P., *Tradition and Experiment in English Poetry* (1979).

HOUGH, G., *The Last Romantics* (1948).

—— *Image and Experience: Studies in a Literary Revolution* (1960).

HUNTER, J., *Edwardian Fiction* (Cambridge, Mass., 1982).

HYNES, S., *The Edwardian Turn of Mind* (Princeton, NJ, 1968).

—— *Edwardian Occasions: Essays on English Writing in the Early Twentieth Century* (1972).

JACKSON, H., *The Eighteen Nineties* (1913).

JENKYNS, R., 'Jumping the Q', *Times Literary Supplement* (26 June 1987).

JEPSON, E., *Memories of an Edwardian and Neo-Georgian* (1937).

JOHNSTON, J. H., *English Poetry of the First World War* (Princeton, NJ, 1964).

KEATING, P. (ed.), *Into Unknown England 1866–1913* (Manchester, 1976).

KENNEDY, J. M., *English Literature 1880–1905* (1912).

KENNER, H., 'Modernism and What Happened to It', *Essays in Criticism*, 37/2 (Apr. 1987).

KERMODE, F., *Continuities* (1968).

—— *The Sense of an Ending* (Oxford, 1967).

—— *Essays on Fiction 1971–82* (1983).

KIPLING, R., *Early Verse by Rudyard Kipling 1879–1889* (Oxford, 1986), ed. A. Rutherford.

KNIGHT, G. W., *Neglected Powers* (1971).

LANGBAUM, R., *The Poetry of Experience: The Dramatic Monologue in Modern Literary Tradition* (1957).

LARKIN, P., 'A Conversation with Philip Larkin', *Tracks*, 1 (summer 1967).

—— 'A Great Parade of Single Poems: Interview with Anthony Thwaite', *Listener* (12 Apr. 1973).

—— *Required Writing: Miscellaneous Pieces 1955–1982* (1983).

—— *All What Jazz: A Record Diary 1961–1971* (2nd edn., rev., 1985).

LEAVIS, F. R., *New Bearings in English Poetry* (1932).

LE GALLIENNE, R., *The Romantic '90s* (1926).

LESTER, J. A., *Journey Through Despair 1880–1914: Transformations in British Literary Culture* (Princeton, NJ, 1968).

LEVENSON, M. H., *A Genealogy of Modernism: A Study of English Literary Doctrine 1908–1922* (Cambridge, 1984).

LEVIN, H., *Refractions: Essays in Comparative Literature* (New York, 1966).

LONGLEY, E., 'Larkin, Edward Thomas and the Tradition', *Phoenix* (autumn and winter 1973–4).
—— *Poetry in the Wars* (Newcastle, 1986).
LUCAS, F. L., *The Decline and Fall of the Romantic Ideal* (Cambridge, 1936).
—— *The Greatest Problem and Other Essays* (1960).
LUCAS, W. J., *Modern English Poetry From Hardy to Hughes* (1986).
MARTIN, W., *'The New Age' Under Orage: Chapters in English Cultural History* (1967).
MASTERMAN, C. F. G., *The Condition of England* (1909, repr. 1968).
MASUR, G., *Prophets of Yesterday: Studies in European Culture 1840–1914* (1963).
MAYNARD, T., *Our Best Poets: English and American* (1924).
MEGROZ, R. L., *Modern English Poetry 1882–1932* (1933).
MEYERS, J., *Fiction and the Colonial Experience* (1973).
MILLER, J. H., *The Disappearance of God* (Harvard, 1963).
—— *Poets of Reality: Six Twentieth Century Writers* (Cambridge, Mass., 1966).
MINNEY, R. J., *The Edwardian Age* (1964).
MORRISON, B., *The Movement: English Poetry and Fiction of the 1950s* (Oxford, 1980).
MOTION, A., *Philip Larkin* (1982).
MUDDIMAN, B., *The Men of the Nineties* (1920).
MURRY, J. M., *Aspects of Literature* (1920).
—— *Between Two Worlds* (1935).
NEILL, E., 'Modernism and Englishness: Reflections on Auden and Larkin', *Essays and Studies*, 36 (1983).
NELSON, J. G., *Sir William Watson* (New York, 1966).
NOWELL-SMITH, S. (ed.), *Edwardian England 1901–14* (Oxford, 1964).
ORWELL, G., *Inside the Whale and Other Essays* (1940).
OWEN, W., *Collected Letters*, ed. H. Owen and J. Bell (1967).
PALMER, H., *Post Victorian Poetry* (1938).
PINTO, V. DE S., *Crisis in English Poetry 1880–1940* (1951).
PRESS, J., *A Map of Modern English Verse* (Oxford, 1969).
—— 'The Poetry of Philip Larkin', *Essays by Divers Hands*, 39 (1977).
—— *Poets of World War One* (1983).
PRIESTLEY, J. B., *The Edwardians* (1970).
READ, D., *Documents from Edwardian England* (1973).
—— *Edwardian England 1901–1915: Society and Politics* (1972).
REIBETANZ, J., 'Lyric Poetry as Self-Possession: Philip Larkin', *University of Toronto Quarterly*, 54/3 (spring, 1985).
RICHARDS, G., *Author Hunting . . . Publishing, 1897–1925* (1934).
RICKS, C., *The Force of Poetry* (Oxford, 1984).
RITZ, J., *Robert Bridges and Gerard Hopkins 1863–1889: A Literary Friendship* (1960).
ROBERTS, S., *Edwardian Retrospect* (Oxford, 1963).
ROBSON, W. W., *Modern English Literature* (1970).

ROSE, J., *The Edwardian Temperament 1895–1919* (1986).

ROSS, R. H., *The Georgian Revolt: Rise and Fall of a Poetic Ideal 1910–1922* (1967).

ROUTH, H. V., *Towards the Twentieth Century: Essays in the Spiritual History of the Nineteenth Century* (Cambridge, 1937).

SANDISON, A., *The Wheel of Empire: A Study of the Imperial Idea in Some Late Nineteenth and Early Twentieth Century Literature* (1967).

SCOTT-JAMES, R. A., *Fifty Years of English Literature 1900–1950* (1951).

SHARROCK, R., 'Private Faces in Public Places: The Poetry of Larkin and Lowell', *English*, 36/155 (summer 1987).

SHERMAN, S. P., *On Contemporary Literature* (1923).

SILKIN, J., *Out of Battle: The Poetry of the Great War* (Oxford, 1972).

SISSON, C. H., *English Poetry 1900–1950: An Assessment* (1971).

SMITH, S., *Inviolable Voice: History and Twentieth Century Poetry* (Dublin, 1982).

SNITOW, A. B., *Ford Madox Ford and the Voice of Uncertainty* (Baton Rouge, La., 1984).

SPENDER, S., *The Struggle of the Modern* (1963).

STALLWORTHY, J., *Poets of the First World War* (Oxford, 1974).

STEAD, C. K., *The New Poetic: Yeats to Eliot* (1964).

STEVENSON, A. L., *Darwin Among the Poets* (Chicago, 1932).

SWINNERTON, F., *The Georgian Literary Scene* (1935).

TEMPLE, R. Z., *The Critic's Alchemy: A Study of the Introduction of French Symbolism into England* (New Haven, Conn., 1953).

THOMPSON, P., *The Edwardians: The Remaking of British Society* (1975).

THORNTON, R. K. R., *The Decadent Dilemma* (1983).

THOULESS, P., *Modern Poetic Drama* (Oxford, 1934).

THURLEY, G., *The Ironic Harvest: English Poetry in the Twentieth Century* (1974).

THWAITE, A., *Twentieth Century English Poetry: An Introduction* (1978).

TREWIN, J. C., *The Edwardian Theatre* (Oxford, 1976).

WARD, A. C., *Twentieth Century Literature 1901–1950* (1956).

WHALEN, T., *Philip Larkin and English Poetry* (1986).

WILLIAMS, H. H., *Outlines in Modern English Literature 1890–1914* (1920).

WILSON, E., *The Triple Thinkers* (1938).

WINTERS, Y., *Forms of Discovery* (1967).

—— *Uncollected Essays and Reviews*, ed. F. Murphy (1973).

WYK SMITH, M. VAN, *Drummer Hodge: The Poetry of the Anglo-Boer War (1899–1902)* (1978).

YEATS, W. B., *Autobiographies* (1926).

—— (ed.), *The Oxford Book of Modern Verse* (1936).

YOUNGHUSBAND, F. E., *England's Mission* (1920).

Index